# VOICES
# FROM ISRAEL

# VOICES FROM ISRAEL

## Understanding the Israeli Mind

Edited by ETAN LEVINE

Herzl Press

Cornwall Books
New York • London • Toronto

Cornwall Books
440 Forsgate Drive
Cranbury, NJ 08512

Cornwall Books
25 Sicilian Avenue
London WC1A 2QH, England

Cornwall Books
2133 Royal Windsor Drive
Unit 1
Mississauga, Ontario
Canada L5J 1K5

Herzl Press
515 Park Avenue
New York, NY 10022

The paper used in this publication meets the minimum requirements of the American National Standard for Permanence of Paper for Printed Library Materials Z39.48-1984.

**Library of Congress Cataloging-in-Publication Data**

Main entry under title:

Voices from Israel.

1. Israel—Addresses, essays, lectures.
2. National characteristics, Israeli—Addresses, essays, lectures.   3. Jews—Israel—Identity—Addresses, essays, lectures.   4. Israel and the Diaspora—Addresses, essays, lectures.   I. Levine, Etan.
DS102.95.V65   1986        956.94        85-47911
ISBN 0-8453-4825-6 (alk. paper)

Printed in the United States of America

A faithful witness will not lie;
A false witness breathes untruth.

(Proverbs XIV, 5)


As cool waters to a faint soul,
So is good news from a far country.

(Proverbs XXIV, 25)

# Contents

# Notes on Contributors

Hanoch Bartov is a prominent Israeli journalist and author of essays on contemporary affairs.

David Ben-Gurion served as the first prime minister and minister of defense of the State of Israel.

Martin Buber was professor of social philosophy at the Hebrew University.

Abba Eban is a member of Knesset who has served as Israel's foreign minister and ambassador to the United Nations.

Eli Eyal is an author and activist in Israeli Zionist institutions.

William Freedman is a professor of English literature at the University of Haifa, and a prominent spokesman of counterculture movements in Israel.

Nahum Goldmann was for many years president of the World Zionist Organization and the World Jewish Congress.

Isaiah Leibowitz is editor of the *Hebrew Encyclopedia* and professor of biochemistry at the Hebrew University.

Etan Levine serves as professor of biblical studies at the University of Haifa.

Stanley Maron is an American who has opted for kibbutz life.

Golda Meir was a prime minister of Israel, and first ambassador to the USSR.

Bernard Och serves as Hillel director at the University of Haifa and at the Haifa Technion, Israel's Institute of Technology.

Abba Oren is a veteran kibbutz educator who teaches at Oranim Teachers' Seminary.

Yitzhak Rabin now Israel's defense minister; has served as prime minister, and as the Israeli ambassador to the United States, and Chief-of-staff of the IDF.

Michael Rosenak lectures in philosophy of Jewish education at the Hebrew University's Center for Jewish Education in the Diaspora.

Chaim Schatzker is a prominent Israeli educator and theoretician of sociology.

GERSHON SHAKED is Israel's leading literary cirtic, and teaches at the Hebrew University.

MOSHE SHARETT served as prime minister and foreign minister of the State of Israel.

B. Z. SOBEL is professor of sociology at the University of Haifa.

EUGENE C. WEINER teaches sociology at the University of Haifa.

A. B. YEHOSHUA is a distinguished Israeli essayist and novelist.

# Preface

The purpose of this anthology is to present insights into the Israeli mind: What he thinks and what he feels, what guides his actions and determines his behavior. For to genuinely know Israel means to fathom the internal spiritual, intellectual, and ideological forces that shape the distinguishing characteristics of that land: a land that is not only a young state assuming the mantle of history from an old diaspora, and not only a focus of international scrutiny, but an entity that is as heatedly debated as it is misunderstood, by both friend and foe.

I have included a wide diversity of materials, all of which seemed both significant in their own right and representative of some aspect of Israeli thought. Given the scope of the subject and the dimensions it embraces, only a partial overview was possible, for nothing less than the *entirety* of the Israeli reality is involved, in its overwhelming diversity and multiplicity, moving through the present into the future with dizzying speed. Every moment appears to be an absolute pivot-point in Israeli life, with irreconcilable conflicts, insoluble problems, and improbable challenges threatening the existence and essence of the fledgling Jewish state.

Two principles guided the selection of these essays as authentic voices from Israel. First, was the realization that the truth about Israel cannot be conveyed by anyone indifferent or hostile to its fate. Truth is not the exclusive possession of the disengaged mind: Whenever an ultimate statement is made, it is made not as a proposition but as a commitment. Thus, understanding Israel intellectually and spiritually requires listening to Israeli voices that do not conceal their loyalties.

Similarly, the realities of Israel cannot be exposed by anyone to whom Israel is an unqualified success. Thus, all of these Israelis, despite their diversity, share this: They intend to convey a message, not a massage, even if this should afflict the comfortable rather than comfort the afflicted. For it is in the honest avowal of values and the openly articulated espousal of patriotic mission that tunnel vison, self-aggrandisement and chauvinism may be avoided.

I have chosen three basic categories. First, some of these essays are deliberately provocative and purposely controversial. For they intend to involve the reader in the real issues that are now confronting the feeling and thinking Israeli. These essays endeavor to create dialogue and debate, not mere assent; they assume the reader's willingness to become engaged. Out of the agony of their own integrity, these writers highlight the issues: Israel's problems of existence, purpose, and direction.

No anthology can ignore the essentially informational message, for truth is always found in details, and ideas invariably exist within the context of history. Therefore, several of these essays describe the objective realities of Israel, given the subjectivity inherently involved in all such descriptions.

Finally, some of these essays are best described as dreams, revealing the author's own concept of felicitous Israeli life. For a dream may in some ways be less than a reality, but in other ways it is more. It provides the feel of things, endowing the future with some semblance of reality that may be seen. And however flawed the cause-effect relationship the dreamer affirms between ideal and reality, the author is a true witness to his own dream. And dream is very much part of the Israeli reality: It was virtually created out of nothing more—not less—than a dream.

These essays are intended to provide a journey, however hurried, along the trails of Israeli thought: an intellectual-spiritual map. No map is identical to that which it intends to describe, of course, and this map is no exception. Yet what better guides are there than those who have thought, those who have experienced, those who have felt, and those who have dreamed?

This anthology would itself have remained a dream were it not for the assistance of several colleagues and institutions. The University of Haifa granted me generous research assistance, and Columbia University granted me visiting scholar status during the period in which this anthology was composed. The libraries of Yale University and of the Jewish Theological Seminary of America were most helpful in providing the manuscripts, typescripts, and mimeographed texts that were required. Amnon Hadary, the distinguished editor of *Forum* (Jerusalem) graciously allowed me to publish the Hebrew addresses and English papers of prominent Israelis of yesteryear that originally appeared in the Zionist journal. And Mordecai S. Chertoff, editor of the Herzl Press (New York) transformed a rough manuscript into a completed anthology. His guidance and skill were as indispensable as they are appreciated. I sincerely acknowledge my indebtedness.

E. L.

# Acknowledgments

The articles by David Ben-Gurion, Martin Buber, Abba Eban, Nahum Goldmann, Isaiah Leibowitz, and Moshe Sharett have been extracted from papers delivered to the World Zionist Organization Congress in Jerusalem, 1954, and the Proceedings published in *Forum on the Jewish People, Zionism and Israel.* I am grateful to the distinguished editor of *Forum*, Mr. Amnon Hadary, for permission to publish these materials, as well as the essays by Eli Eyal, Hanoch Bar-Tov, Michael Rosenak, Gershon Shaked, Chaim Schatzker, and A. B. Yehoshua, which appeared in the pages of that dauntless Zionist house organ over the years. Parts of my essay appeared in Etan Levine, *Diaspora; Exile and the Jewish People* (New York: Jason Aronson, 1983), and are reprinted by permission of the publisher.

# VOICES
# FROM ISRAEL

# Introduction

A nation's thought cannot be defined, but it can be described. Its distinguishing characteristics may be identified and analyzed, just as one may meaningfully discuss the original Zionist idea: the radical concept that galvanized a people, altered its history, and forged a nation. In the case of Israel, however, several factors conspire to complicate the task, and perforce to render its completion partial.

First, it is difficult to speak of Israeli thought, and refrain from mystique. The very existence of a Jewish state constitutes the fulfillment of the longest-kept promise in human history: the vow of Jewish exiles twenty-five centuries ago by the waters of Babylon: "If I forget thee, Oh Jerusalem. . . ." To this very day, Israel remains a focus of the world's fascination: an admixture of reality and myth, fact and fiction. And even the relationship of Israelis to Israel—like all genuine relationships—is grounded in mystery: a synthesis of fact and fiction, a union of truth and wish, a wedding of the logical to the poetic.

Second, there is the sui generis diversity of Israeli culture, in which authentic creativity, cultural pluralism, and intellectual dynamism cohabit with ossified Orthodoxy, debased ethnicity, unrooted secularism, and the latest flotsam and jetsam of Western civilization that wash up on the country's shores.

Third, Israeli thought reflects Israeli life with all of its inner contradictions. There is the ongoing tension between being and becoming: Our national life is not identical to the vision we carry. And to the extent that it is not, and that it remains mere potential, we cannot adequately accept our own self-image, let alone convey an authentic self-portrait to our own youth, to diaspora Jewry, and to the world at large. For these reasons, it is small wonder that it is often more comfortable to speak of Israel by definition than of Israel in fact.

### In The Beginning . . .

The creation of the modern State of Israel in 1948 was virtually without precedent. In the past, nations had grown up organically from the life-giving soil of shared language, shared geography, shared culture, and shared economics, or by the separation or conquest of one such nation by another. Never had a people—or the disparate fragments of a people—decided deliberately and freely to transplant itself, and to forge itself into a nation on the basis of nothing more in common than an ancient past, present necessity, and future ideal: to create its own national identity, rather than to maintain the status that history had long dictated.

The Israeli Declaration of Independence, and ensuing laws such as the Law of Return, defined that national identity, but only in theoretical, abstract terms, as law invariably must: like a mold waiting to be filled. The actual content of the national mold would be supplied by the variegated interactions of the diverse people with one another and with their environment. And given the rapidly changing demographic, economic, military, and cultural realities of Israel, its realities would not remain fixed: It would be in a state of continual flux, evolving almost from day to day, with an intensity atypical of national entities.

One overwhelming force for change was released by independence itself: The Jews in Israel (and, to a lesser but significant degree, the Jews in the diaspora) would never be the same. The derivative factors are both varied and familiar: the constant state of siege, periodic wars, waves of diverse immigration, an expanding economy, the rise of divisive subcultures, etc. The list is a long one indeed, for the young state changed in many less dramatic ways. Founded by a population of approximately one-half million, the population rapidly expanded to four million. This number represented not only many Moslem and Christian sects but a host of diverse Jewish cultures: groups that came from the most primitive and the most modern lands on earth, with exceedingly different cultures and value systems. From its inception, government in Israel became the art of balancing the interests and neutralizing the pressures of citizens with conflicting religious, economic, cultural, political, and ethnic postures, some of which were so intense that loyalty to the State of Israel itself was secondary.

On the individual level, living in Israel perforce involved ongoing adaptation of the citizen to compatriots reflecting different mentalities, values, and cultures, and to institutions that reflected this diversity. For the State of Israel began with little more than the shared conviction that there must be an autonomous Jewish homeland to which Jews the world over could come as a matter of right. Beyond this prerogative, however, there was no general consensus as to specifics on which to base political, institutional, legal, and cultural forms. There was no unanimity to the basic concepts of *which* society should exist, to protect, express, and enhance *which* cherished values. Faced by ideological complexities unparalleled in history, the founders of the state chose to leave unresolved some of the most fundamental issues: issues that were soon to prove as basic as they were inescapable. There *were* sustained attempts at clarifying and unifying the vision, at infusing the emerging potpourri of society with the perspectives and methods of humanism, Zionism, democratic government, egalitarianism, etc. And major efforts were invested in trying to impart a temporal dimension to the usually abstract models of the various Israeli subcultures, from kibbutz to yeshivah. But people are shaped not in orderly, chronological sequence, but in relation to innumerable forces and events: the tangled skeins of interdependence, necessity, and chance that produce living reality.

In Israel today the most diverse subcultures are related dialectically, each focusing on one aspect or level of national life, with each dimension seen as both underpinning yet at odds with the other. The dominant foci shift as the equilibrium changes, with displacements and replacements the only constants. In a country that has but recently absorbed (and that continues to absorb) immigrants from more than 120 lands, with the most diverse intellectual, valuational, political, religious, technological, economic, and cultural predilictions, postures, and passions, the minuscule State of Israel finds itself a stage on which one of the most dramatic social experiments in the history of mankind is being enacted. Often it seems insoluble, save through the intervention of miracle. The traditional Israeli response reflected the bon mot of Israel's first prime minister, who declared, "Any man who does not believe in miracles is not a realist."

### The Legacy of Classical Zionism

In even conceiving of a Jewish state, the early Zionist pioneers crossed intellectual and emotional borders that had been foreign to Jews. For the Zionist idea then, and the Israeli mind now, differ from Jewish tradition fundamentally: Whereas Jewish thought, ritual, and sentiment was primarily past-oriented, Israeli culture *ab initio* faced the future. Thinkers may have differed as to goals as well as means, but they shared the conviction that a people is alive only when it believes that its future is, in large measure, the work of its own hands. Zionist historiography required that the Jew cease being a passive spectator and become a responsible actor on the stage of history. It proclaimed a dynamic, heroic mission, with an arduous present subordinated as an investment in a glorious future.

Unlike Jewish scholars during the long night of exile, Israeli thinkers do not analyze the specifics of hoary antiquity, but of the future yet to be born. For as the Jewish people (or part of it) acquired the courage to act, they also acquired the courage to trust their own strength and their ability to shape their own destiny. It is in *this* sense that Israeli society, for all its diversity, may legitimately be described as a "community of faith." Some critics have dismissed it as hubris or chutzpah or worse, but emerging from the shadows of exile and the darkness of its theology, the Zionist idea heralded the dawn of autonomy; instead of being subjected to the terrors of history, power was now transferred from without (or above) to within (or below).

Self-evident differences notwithstanding, one cannot resist the limited analogy found in biblical antiquity, when part of Israel opted to forgo servitude, and to risk both the promises and problems of self-determination, even if the Promised Land (like every promised land!) should require traversing a wilderness. Zionism was the rejection of the ingrained Jewish concept of sin, which had regarded diaspora status as divine retribution, and which had dismissed Jewish will, reason, virtue, and power as faculties too feeble to alter reality. It was a frontal assault on the doctrine, "And because of our sins we are exiled from our land. . . ." It asserted that Israel is not the prisoner of antiquity but the architect of its future.

Both Israel's ardent advocates and antagonistic critics agree about this basic feature: that it is a future-oriented society determined to mold its own destiny. There is energy in the land, and elemental hunger for challenge, achievement, and experience that has not been predigested by earlier generations. Nobody can approach the Israeli scene or the Israeli psyche without sensing the Zionist futurism, sometimes bordering on naïveté and arrogance, that pervades Israeli thought and action.

Unlike the disparaging professional agronomists, the early Zionists recognized that the soil of the Land of Israel was teeming with life-sustaining properties of energy, meaning, and value. The small Jewish colonies and settlements produced a voluminous literature of fact, fiction, and special pleading, again demonstrating how compulsively attractive adventure, challenge, creativity, bravery, and even violent death can be. For the first time, these men and women saw life in terms of noble principles and how far they could go to achieve them, rather than as a matter of personal success. It was an ideological life in the fullest sense of the term, and no matter how bleak the daily reality, it was infused by a kind of exhiliration at the prospect of what was going to be created. The "Old-New Land," as it was perceived there and abroad, was the creation of heroic vision: the product of speculative historical thinking linked to daring personal commitment.

These early Zionists negated the diaspora: They regarded it as a ship with no sail, adrift at sea, and manned by people who were convinced that by subjecting life aboard to the traditions and regulations of elaborate protocol, they could keep from thinking either of their home port or their ultimate destination. The world of the Jewish diaspora was perceived as an illusion. To say that the universe is an illusion is not to say that it is unreal; it is to say, instead, that it is not what it appears to be. Further, that it is something constantly being made. Yet fantasy may well be the last redoubt of freedom, and Zionism substituted its own dream.

To understand how it is possible to create a universe by dreaming, one must refer to contemporary sociology of knowledge and philosophy of science, which show how social conventions established by members of a group predetermine how individuals relate to reality. What appear to be self-evident facts of the external world are actually complex social fabrications. The interplay of subjectivity and objectivity is consistent with much of modern science, as, to a great extent, faith in a fact makes it so. The Zionist movement was a sterling example of this phenomenon.

The ideology inherent in the Zionist revolution and in its view of man is that there is no deterministic connectedness from era to era in social development. The past need not limit the possibilities of the present, for man has the capacity to make himself anew. And as it permeated the farms, shops, factories, and homes of the fledgling Zionist presence in the land of Israel, the message was clear: We do not have to lead great lives, but we do have to understand, survive, and ennoble the lives we have. We are writing a new page in Jewish history, amid hard labor, fear, poverty, and pain. But it is pain that provokes a poem, not tranquility. Stress, change, anxiety, and crisis are difficult, but they are also exhilirating. The poles of despair and ecstasy are alike in that each propels us above the petty world. Each looks to an ultimate.

Some observers point to disturbing phenomena within Iraeli society—consumerism, alienation, apathy, emigration, etc.—and question to what extent there remains a Zionist society galvanized by confident idealism: a society that genuinely and faithfully pursues a dream, absorbing, guiding, and enhancing the lives of its varied constituencies. Israelis themselves are no longer moved by the familiar incantation of political clichés that have little to do with contemporary experience. And however tempting it may be to oversimplify, tired slogans are ultimately self-defeating, for polemics that describe Zionism as either thriving or fossilized distort the realities and mask the complexities.

Paradoxically, to the extent that the daringly original Zionist idea—that a dynamic Jewish state could be forged—has, in fact, lost some of its grandeur, it is not because of its failure, but because of its success. It is now simply taken for granted. The Zionist vision was nothing short of magnificent, yet what happens to a dream when it comes true? In today's Israel most of the populace was born in a sovereign Jewish state, speaks Hebrew as a mother tongue, serves in a Jewish army, and grows up thinking that all this is quite normal. The earth is firm under their feet: They live it, and therefore it is no dream.

The more cogent of the Israeli thinkers take as axiomatic the truism that maintaining the country's Zionist momentum will always be a challenge; it would be naive to expect otherwise, particularly in a country such as Israel, which is a veritable crucible that tempers human resiliency and idealism. Success will never appear as a finished product, nor will victory be assured or permanent. Just as responses are inseparable from challenges, social values cannot be uprooted from the ground out of which they grow, for then they wilt into lifeless slogans, formal espousals, and inorganic abstraction.

Given this caveat, however, we can retrospectively examine Zionist futurism in the light of the Israeli present—the kibbutzim, moshavim, armed forces, development towns, academic institutions, cultural creations, etc.—and say that if it is to be judged solely by the criteria of prediction and truth, it is doubtful whether the early Zionists misread the Israeli future more than non-Zionists distorted the Jewish past. And lucid Israeli educators, writers, and social activists continue to declare that Israel's mission is not fulfilled when it has taken a step, albeit a giant step: The heroic age lies not in the past but in the present, with Israel as the model and the measure of what the Jewish people can, and must, attain.

### *Forging Spiritual Autonomy*

Political independence was only the most obvious means by which the new nation sought to define itself. Quite naturally, at the outset of the movement for Jewish statehood, independence was essentially negative, in that it sought to limit and then destroy the juridical-political-military power of the enemy occupying the Land of Israel. But as statehood was achieved, independence took on a positive meaning: the creation of a genuine nationality united not only by governmental institutions and resistance to external threat, but by a broad system of shared ideas and values, a civilization. The terms civilization, people, and nationality had been much used; now, under the pressure of historical processes, they expressed new realities. Prior to statehood, the *yishuv* had been subjected to a colonial culture and had been in political servitude to British policy. But furthermore, it had, in its literary, religious, financial, and institutional facets, relied upon the world Jewish community, particularly (though not exclusively) that of Europe. But political autonomy, the decimation of East European Jewry, and the uprooting of the entire

Jewish population of the Arab world emptied the reservoirs. Now there was no kindred hinterland sharing a common past; there was no alternative but to attempt cultural autonomy and establish a separate identity. So, much of the art and literature indigenous to Israel was self-consciously that, in effect: declarations of independence from the Jewish diaspora. Quite naturally, Israeli intellectuals furthered the process by giving literary definition to the immense reality of the *Israeli* experience.

Other Israeli thinkers expressed their spirituality in other ways. In particular, they turned their attention to the Jewish past—removed in time and thus both simplified and intelligible, a source of meaning for a confused and often painful present. They looked with romantic longing to the past for material for literature, for ideas, and for content—for meaning.

For many perceptive Israelis, the period of the nation's greatest achievements was also a time of ruinous spiritual costs: The exuberant national idea of almost limitless development, of wild successes, of possibilities for fulfillment both personal and national, unchecked by internal restraint, created a dilemma. The original settlers, despite occasionally flamboyant rhetoric, were rational, balanced, and essentially moderate. They were limited in their goals and in their means by their actual situation: small in number, compact in size, relatively homogeneous in their communal villages and towns. And then the force of will and of historic necessity converted their land into the actual homeland of the Jewish people. A flood of immigrants and a frenzy of activity created a historical reality. The very successes of Israel infused a furious momentum in which the possibility of creating an organic culture waned. What confusion, as a new romanticism took root in Israel, prizing whatever was unrestrained, remote, limitless—almost turning inside out the rationalist mood of early Zionist thinkers.

To many it was clear that the Zionist revolution had significantly failed to alter some of the most negative aspects of diaspora life, which had returned to plague Israeli society. And yet this was but part of the problem, because Zionism had, in fact, uprooted some of the most positive, cohesive, promising aspects of diaspora life. The baby had been thrown out *instead* of the bath water. The society Zionism had created, marked by increasing avoidance of physical labor, decreased loyalty to state institutions, and exaggerated pursuit of personal goals, was a sort of Middle East shtetl bereft of the traditional Jewish values and strengths that could enable the fledgling state to elicit the sacrifices its existence would require.

The manifold defects in the collective personality ultimately derive from a single phenomenon: the absence of an authentic Israeli culture in the broadest sense. There simply is no all-embracing, compelling framework to direct and shape the individual's relationship to society and to self, and to locate his place in the collective past, present, and future.

## Cohesion and Culture

A deeply felt need of contemporary Israeli thinkers is some program of dual restoration: to restore to Israel the cultural vitality of the diaspora and the social idealism of early Zionism. Ideally, such a program would include a fusion of historical Judaism and revolutionary Zionism, producing a cohesive, mutually supported, purposeful society. Some are committed to the early Zionist method of personal example, asserting that mere declarations and slogans are inadequate to alleviate the poisons that are infecting the body politic. Others engage in intellectual-aesthetic pursuits, asserting that it is precisely the function of literature and art to create patterns, to select fragments out of the welter of human experience and shape them into coherent and desirable forms.

Of course, the creative artist's process of selecting and shaping depends on his own value system, his sense of self, his connectedness with others, his perceptions of society and of the universe. And the creativity that results from this process, in turn, will be meaningful to Israeli society only to the extent that it shares the basic values from which the creativity arises. In the absence of such shared values, the Israeli thinker, writer, composer, and artist is thrown back upon his own resources, talking to himself before he can communicate his beliefs, hoping that eventually his creations will be perceived by his society as having meaning.

Many of today's Israeli thinkers share a fundamental concern for the lack of cultural and valuational cohesion in a land marked by ongoing national tensions, interethnic conflict, and an intense individualism raised to the level of a moral system. In art, as in life, when anything is possible, everything is possible, perhaps even a catalyst to a new kind of pioneering that will challenge the prevailing cynicism, initiate social experiment, and vindicate the hope that it is still possible to be creative in Israel. To do so will mean to breathe a renewed spirit into a tiny land that has been satiated by its successes, exhausted by its sacrifices, perplexed by the alienation of its young, and shamed by its fall from the symbol of national rejuvenation and idealism to that of an international pariah and near-outcast.

## The Populist Posture

To the extent that it constitutes an organic society in a meaningful sense of the term, one of the distinguishing characteristics of the Israeli mentality is its populism. Despite the proliferation of high culture institutions, populism remains a hallmark of Israeli culture. Thus, for example, physical fitness in the populace is encouraged through innumerable popular athletic events and institutions, with little concern over the fact that Israel has yet to produce even one Olympic bronze medalist. Despite the elitism of Israeli concert halls, the authentic Israeli music is heard around campfires, in living rooms, and in community dining halls. And Israeli political, economic, cultural, and military policies are not created anew in the rarified atmosphere of aristocratic institutions: they gestate in the exhaustive (and often exhausting) deliberations of popular meetings, discussion groups, and other exchanges in which the farm laborer is as involved as the faculty lecturer. It is from this broad demographic base that—for better or for worse—a series of related ideas begins to coalesce and a national attitude and policy emerges.

What accounts for the emphasis upon the demos in Israeli culture? In measure it is a continuation of traditional Jewish culture. Throughout the centuries, when kings and church princes could not even sign their names, the humblest Jewish village child could read the classics of his civilization. The Greeks and their cultural descendants produced drama, fiction, plastic arts, and symposia primarily for the edification and stimulation of the elite, whereas the major Jewish creations were not analogous, but rather homilies *(aggadah)* for the masses, law *(halakhah)* for the masses, liturgical poetry and music for the masses, etc. In brief, Jewish civilization was traditionally oriented to the people qua people.

The Zionist movement not only inherited traditional Jewish populism but enhanced it by infusion of socialist egalitarianism. For the Zionist vision concerned the life of an entire people: a small corner of the world in which Jewish life would be happier than it was in the past. Despite the ambiguity in the term, the lives of ordinary men and women, boys and girls, would be rendered happier in some significant way than they had been in the diaspora. Small wonder that Israeli culture echoes vox populi! If Israel has devoted much of its divided energies to the quality of human life, it is precisely because it originally shunned elitism and chose to relate to the masses. And if Israeli aesthetics is sometimes abrasive, its thinking simplistic, and its language debased, in measure this is due to its culture being an authentic involvement with life as experienced by ordinary men and women. This emphasis upon community, people, and nation embraced Israeli threater, art, literature, and music. There is no need to demarcate with precision the distinctions between these forms, because it is not the form that defines the Israeli universe of discourse, but rather the attempt to relate it to the Israeli reality.

Israel is also a world center of high culture, of course: An impressive, growing array of scholars, authors, artists, musicians, and scientists have achieved deserved international prominence despite the myriad difficulties that attach to such creativity in Israel. In the physical and social sciences there are more-or-less objective criteria for evaluation, whereas in literary or artistic creativity there is no slide rule for measuring the magnitude of achievement. Since aesthetic judgment cannot be proved, evaluation is inherently subjective. In many countries, reputations are significantly enhanced or diminished on the basis of academic judgments; in Israel the ultimate verdict is largely determined by the popular heart and the popular mind. It would be presumptuous to hazard a guess as to the future insofar as Israeli culture is concerned, for a time lag invariably separates creativity from recognition. Who can confidently predict what the contours and content of Israeli culture will be, how it will react to its near-inundation by American and European influences, and which of its creations will emerge as classics? In the final analysis, it depends on the soul and the shape of emerging Israeli society.

### The Tradition of Critical Loyalty

A striking characteristic of the Israeli mentality is its familiar self-criticism. Not only in their newspapers, literature, television, theater, and public forums, but in private living rooms, coffeehouses and wherever they may gather, Israelis openly and ardently criticize their government, societal norms, policies, and whatever happens to be the subject of the day. There is no immunity: economic policies, bureaucracy, social inequities, erosion of values, abandonment of traditions, procedures in Judea and Samaria, disparities between Western and Eastern Jews, aesthetics, Hebrew usage, driving habits—the list is exhaustive and exhausting. No holds are barred, and no quarter is granted: If the army is unprepared for all-out war, it is because apathy has eroded resolve; if ethnic tensions threaten the cohesion of the state, it is because Jewish mutual support has been abandoned; if religious polarity creates divisiveness, it is because we utilize coercion rather than convince; if Arab labor has flooded sectors of the economy, it is because we have abandoned the Zionist tradition of physical labor; if we receive huge support from the Jews of diaspora and the American government, it is because we have divorced ourselves from our early self-reliance; if mutual mistrust marks our interpersonal relations, it is because the ideal that united Israel in a collective struggle has now been distorted into an individual rat race.

Many observers, understandably, ask, "How is it that in a country that is itself the target of sustained, malignant criticism on the part of so many hostile blocs of nations and that is so viciously castigated even by elements within the 'friendly' nations, the favorite indoor sport seems to be self-criticism?" Although the observation is itself valid, whether it is to be lamented or celebrated is less certain. What can be ascertained, however, is the genealogy of the phenomenon.

Israeli culture is the legitimate child of a powerful critical tradition, as was its immediate forebear, the Zionist movement, in which all thinkers were uncompromisingly critical of the major ideas and institutions of their own time and place. From its very origins, Jewish civilization was typified by a dialectic between criticism and creativity. It was the cohabitation of skepticism and faith, rejection and affirmation, question and response that gave birth to Jewish civilization. Abraham said no to Mesopotamian culture, Moses said no to Canaanite culture, their descendants said no to much of Greco-Roman civilization, Christian and Moslem dogma. In this way, the Jews escaped intellectual and spiritual servitude, the facile identification of the voguish and the apparent with the noble and the true. And the crowning achievement of that tradition was its ability to be inner-directed: to say no to aspects of Jewish civilization itself. By selecting, modifying, rejecting, and enhancing itself through critical judgment, Jewish life transcended the ravages of fossilization and sclerosis. Through self-criticism it conquered parochialism, and through creativity it assured its self-determination. It is not atypical that the major diaspora document, the Talmud, both begins with and largely consists of questions rather than answers. For, long before the establishment of the State of Israel, the Jewish mind had intuited that wisdom and well-being could be achieved only by criticism, and not by the uncritical acceptance of dogmas, authorities, or prevailing norms.

Today many articulate Israelis feel that this tradition has been muted, that the Zionist revolution has abdicated its mission to criticize and to alter the defective aspects of Israeli life. They charge that the tradition of self-criticism has been abandoned because, whereas past generations were willing to pay the price for their commitments and values, today those who are in favor of widespread social change are content to issue statements, participate in demonstrations, and engage in symbolic protest.

Other Israelis consider much of Israeli self-criticism to be exaggerated, reflecting pathology rather than ideology in the forms of internalized anti-Semitism and Jewish self-hate. Yet they, too, admit that it is a loyal criticism. In recent years those who besieged government offices demanding the resignation of ministers involved in military blunders were themselves combat soldiers; those demonstrators massed to protest a broad spectrum of national policies were themselves the spiritual, ethical elite of the land; those who cried out that personal responsibility had been obliterated by individual expedience were themselves, to an overwhelming extent, the living models of what an Israeli should be. Their credentials were very much in order.

In recent decades Israel, like Western civilization generally, has become increasingly disenchanted with idealism: Intellectual trends have moved away from utopianisms, due to their presumably malevolent effects wherever people en masse have become captivated by extravagant visions. And although Israelis are not immune to this fear, they rightly sense that to attack Zionism or to attack Israel per se is about as intelligent or desirable as to attack dreaming. They know that no great civilization has ever lived without a dream, and they do not reject that of Israel. Rather, they insist that it not be paralyzed by a nondialectical polarity of empty assent or equally empty rejection (such as "America: Love it or leave it").

Israelis know that they are living in an emerging civilization that is pressed to the point where it must act critically toward its own powers and its own ideas. Loyalty must acquire criticism, and criticism must maintain responsibility. No Israeli, of any shade of opinion, should or can be absolved of his birthright: the exhilirating obligation of participation, even if he is gripped by a sense of helplessness; even if he has a fundamental opposition to Israeli policies; even if he is stunned by a realization of Israel's vulnerability and mortality; and even if he must constantly resist personal alienation and disengagement.

### The Countercultures

There was a period in prestatehood days, and even thereafter, when in certain quarters criticism was regarded as disloyal and seditious. This was an era when political parties and ideologies were highly authoritarian and dogmatic, attempting to determine people's attitudes as well as behavior. But the Israelis soon reverted to type, refusing to abdicate their critical faculties and jeopardize their valuational independence. Today one hears a multitude of voices insisting that we confront ourselves honestly, that there is no rebirth without pain. For were we to accept our present realities and forego our prophetic passions, we would lose our capacity to judge ourselves by our own magnificent vision of what Israel must be.

The highest form of criticism is self-criticism, and whereas diaspora Jewish criticism was characteristically, and continues to be, directed outward at the non-Jewish world (and at Israel, as well), in Israel itself criticism is concentrated almost exclusively within. What distinguishes most Israeli critics and counterculturists from the fanatical elements are their characteristic rationality, gentility, aesthetics, and appeal to higher sentiments.

It is not only in the political-social-economic arena, but in the areas of culture, aesthetics, education, and related spheres that this phenomenon is pronounced. As part of a genuinely free, democratic, pluralistic society, Israeli culture includes individuals and trends that are avowedly experimental, controversial, and even subversive. The creators of Israeli expressionism, surrealism, and absurdism are openly committed to rocking the boat. They challenge the various establishments by asking, "What great virtue is there in merely copying and acclaiming that which is already achieved and applauded?" Or, "Can the Israeli educational and cultural establishments justify their claims to be the authentic media of Jewish idealism? Ought they not be challenged to do so?" Again, "Must we not justify ourselves by criteria more noble than those of expediency and self-interest?" In sum, "Do we have nothing more to offer than merely consecrating that which is, instead of groping toward that which might yet be?"

Yet the Israeli personality is not one-dimensional, and along with the self-critical tradition there coexists a powerful conservatism in most spheres of life (to the exclusion of the military, agriculture, high-technology industry, and related areas). Jewish history itself is replete with examples of thinkers, writers, leaders, and visionaries who were ignored by their fellow Jews—and who *deserved* to be ignored! Yet, in general, in recent decades a new concept of criticism has taken hold, wherein loyalty is not viewed as an exercise disengaged from reality; skepticism and criticism are not dismissed as purely negative roles. This relative openness has allowed the flourishing of a genuine counterculture, individuals and groups vastly different from the norms in aesthetics, life-style, political posture, and cultural expression. What they face today, by and large, is not repression, but resounding public indifference. The spectrum of Israeli malcontent ranges from vague reformism to actual belief that government is merely the agent of the owners of capital and power who seek the economic, political, and cultural subjugation of the masses. The state qua state is nothing less than an organized conspiracy to deprive the common Israeli of his natural right. Power is centralized, and virtually absolute.

These extreme postures have received a measure of support from the Israeli "culture of narcissism": a vague, amorphous cultural trend addressing the issue of psychic survival in trying times. In eminently provocative terms, they address psychic survival, the wide-ranging dangers that assault Israelis today, and that threaten their psychic as well as physical survival—economic chaos, environmental decline, violence, unemployment, terrorism, fear of the future, etc. Trenchant social critics offer new and convincing diagnostic perspectives on the interrelations of Israel's culture, politics, economy, and religious bent. And frequently they are meticulous, suggestive, and lucid. Further, they challenge the sources of Israeli thought, a crucial element in both the writing and the making of history.

In general terms, what these political counterculturists are seeking is a political soul, for without a soul, politics can only immortalize the practical and the banal. Classical Zionist political philosophy had demanded subtle statesmanship, but had held out the promise of nobility. Contemporary political philosophy demands less of leaders. It actually insists on modest, even trivial goals, yet it promises clarity and certainty in its limited goals. The two virtues of modern political philosophy, in its own estimation, are the related virtues of simplicity and egalitarianism. Thus, the relevant personal traits of today's leader are self-interestedness and tolerance, and these are within reach of the most mediocre of men. For if we define excellence recklessly enough, there is no shortage of leaders, just as there is no shortage of scholars in academe, or artists in the creative world.

Patently, what is needed in Israel today is a cadre of men of science and the humanities who have also mastered the art of communication. These would be people who, like the early Zionists, have a breadth of vision, elegantly blending intellectual history, anthropology, history, religion, and philosophy with psychological insight. But today such wider perspectives are on the decline in the behavioral sciences, where more and more people with parochial minds define their portion of the human condition in ever-decreasing, professionally guarded, narrow turfs. Further, it is difficult for man to look at himself without bias: Ideology guides science, particularly the human sciences. How, then, can the Israeli counterculturist take heart? For if destiny is defined as a tyrant's warrant for repression, or a fool's excuse for failure, there is little reason for optimism, let alone loyalty.

### Judaism in the Jewish State

One of the most charged and divisive of all issues within Israeli society is one that has defied solution: the relationship between Judaism and the Jewish state. Even prior to independence there was a marked division between the religious and the secular communities: separate schools, social-welfare institutions, political organizations, neighborhoods, newspapers, etc. They largely constitute two distinct entities, even today, each with its own priorities, agenda, and life-style, living side by side with little mutual understanding and less mutual acceptance.

The religious community is far from monolithic, of course: One need only compare the life-style and values of the sallow, anti-Zionist groups, huddled in urban yeshivas and rabbinic courts, to the suntanned young men in knitted *kipot*, surrounded by wives and children in their little villages on both sides of the Green Line, attempting to live Zionist lives, marked by a concern for military security as well as spirituality. However, the common denominator is openly articulated by religious leaders and their followers: that Jewish law *(halakhah) only as interpreted by them* must prevail over the law of the land, since divine law takes precedence over human law. The issue is whether the Jewish state will be conducted according to the mandates (or at least not against the mandates) of Jewish religious law. Ever since 1948, uneasy compromises and alliances of necessity have satisfied neither community, and the conflict has grown even more intense as the religious community has increased the scope of its concerns and developed more political acumen and aggressiveness.

The impassioned articles and addresses of Israel's religious leaders betray the intensity of feeling involved. As they see it, the purpose of the State of Israel is not simply to be another country on the world map, even if that country does provide a haven for homeless Jews who opt to immigrate. For these religious intellectuals, Israel is preeminently a state of mind and a spiritual attitude, as well as a sociopolitical entity. Further, they assert that were there to be a diminution of reality-transcending religious idealism, Israel itself would succumb to a deadening matter-of-factness, and would become not a force for Jewish renaissance, but an institution presiding over the demise of the Jewish people. Without living its religious tradition, the Israeli would be unable to understand Jewish civilization, let alone shape it.

To the Orthodox Israeli mind, Judaism is of ultimate significance or it is of no significance, and having a Jewish state requires putting Jewish law into practice, whether it be observing the Sabbath, enforcing marriage restrictions, formulating foreign policy, or whatever. Religion consists of bonding the ultimate to the ordinary, wedding the sacred to the secular, and although diaspora intellectualism may have stressed tedious and often irrelevant commentaries on Jewish classics, in the Jewish state one can and must fulfill God's mandates. The alternative, to their mind, would be a travesty: a Jewish state conducted in opposition to Jewish religion. The challenge is to take a populace lethargic in its observance and antithetical in its beliefs, and infuse it with a *halakhic*, vibrant Israeli-Jewish life-style.

### The Secular Stance

Israeli secularists quite naturally accuse the religious community of coercion, of attempting to force observance. Israelis bitterly resent any attempts to limit personal or societal freedoms, a fortiori when such attempts originate from a sector of the community that in the diaspora was traditionally hostile to the Zionist movement itself. Further, they charge, in a democratic state the Orthodox must accept the pluralistic intellectual and spiritual realities, which they would never have dared challenge in a non-Jewish country. They must reconcile themselves to the fact that the disintegration of traditional Judaism in past decades has made it impossible for most Israelis to return to classical sources as authorities. And despite whatever nostalgic appreciation Israelis may have for Jewish lore and folkways, they will not allow their lives to be dictated by *halakhah*. To the average Israeli, the very idea constitutes a repugnant throwback to medievalism.

Although asserting the indispensability of a strong empiric foundation for Israel, many secularists admit that it is inadequate. If it were to become the exclusive mode, they concede, Israel would lose its most valuable possession, its spiritual and intellectual diversity. Were empiricism, technology, and science to overpower and confine the soul, less and less could it soar to the heights of spiritualty. And should the rainbow of the Israeli intellect be reduced to *any* monochrome, intellectual dullness would prevail. Thus, one does not hear the strident cry of spiritual-intellectual totalitarianism from the secularist camp. What one does hear are calls for a coherent program that will allow for harmonious coexistence between the two extremes. All recognize that the issue will not be resolved easily: The indications are that the intensity of the conflict will even increase. Nobody can approach the Israeli scene without feeling the earnest passions and high seriousness aroused by the issue. What all affirm is that Israel's physical survival and her "messianic" potential both depend upon a moral rehabilitation of society. Any other priority is a counterproductive diversion.

### Secular Religion?

Due to the fervor of its adherents, Zionism from its inception was represented by some analysts as a type of religiosity. They maintained that the Zionist idea itself and the Israeli ethos it created are forms of messianism or of a transplanted eschatological consciousness. And when one considers that many Israelis are either hostile or indifferent to traditional Judaism, both in form and in content, one may well ask whether the appropriate designation it deserves is that of a religious heresy.

For many who participated, and who continue to participate, in the creation of the Jewish state, Zionist ideology satisfied spiritual needs that could not be met by Orthodox Judaism, and so in this sense we may regard Israeli culture as an unconventional Jewish religion. However, beyond this, obvious distinctions destroy the analogy. For religious messianism invariably involves an element of external salvation, and it was precisely this traditional concept of divine intervention that Zionism rejected. The byword was autoemancipation, a new self-discipline and a new responsibility that is not theocentric but homocentric.

If religion is defined as the use of a God-hypothesis to explain nature and history, then there is less religion in Israel than many intimates realize. Israeli culture *is* full of religious vocabulary, folkways, and texts, but for the majority of its populace, Israel itself—past, present and future—is a matter of social policy, not of supernatural truth. The very existence of a state is not the attempt to fulfill a messianic prerogative. Israel is an end in itself. *Ipsu pretium est:* It is its own reward.

Even if one should conclude that Israeli idealism may be regarded as a heresy of sorts, surely it is not an entirely new heresy but a daring response to a significantly changed world. Zionism was never interested in replacing all of inherited Jewish tradition. Witness the rationalism and social idealism that it shares with much of the Talmud and rabbinic thought. To the secularist it is, in many ways, not a matter of a tradition rejected, but a tradition rejuvenated. "However," he would add, "Let's leave eschatology for the future!"

### Religious Zealotry

Many Israelis today—including religious Israelis—are profoundly affected by the shock waves caused by fanatical elements that are avowedly contemptuous of Israeli law, democratic procedure, and normative ethics. These religio-nationalist elements advocate and resort to violence and the most outrageous treatment of "the enemy" within Israel, as they define the term. Whether stoning these they regard as violators of Shabbat, beating secular-leftists, or terrorizing Arab civilians, these fringe elements, though hardly representative of Israeli society, are nevertheless a version of Judaism, of Zionism, and of Israeli thought. Many Israelis prefer to discount them as lunatic fringes, statistically negligible aberrations. Yet they do have authentic roots, archaic traditions that raise discrimination, intolerance, and animosity to the level of religious imperatives. By reference to traditional texts within Judaism that advocate discriminatory procedures to those considered heretical as well as toward the non-Jew, and by the invocation of supposed political and cultural expediency, chauvinistic behavior is legitimized. Consequently, there is a broader sympathy for the attitudes articulated by such extremist groups than their actual numbers would indicate.

The average Israeli cannot help but lend credence to what the zealots say and do, for even the personal example of many prominent leaders corroborates these attitudes. And in an age of renewed religious fanaticism in various parts of the world, an indigenous Israeli version seems quite natural, understandable, and even excusable. Of course, to most Israelis the phenomenon is as frightening as it is impervious to rational discourse and felicitous resolution.

### Living Under Siege

Ever since, and even prior to, its birth, the people of Israel have lived in a state of siege. Whether it be terrorism and sabotage, infiltration and static attrition, or full-sale war, Israel has been exposed to military attack, political hostility, psychological warfare, and economic embargo. The openly articulated threat of total destruction is sometimes veiled in language more amenable to Western ears, but the intention of applying a "final solution" is clear, as Arab actions eloquently testify. And there is no dimension of Israeli thought, and no aspect of Israeli life, that is not profoundly affected by this overarching reality.

Israel is a very military country; it is equally unmilitaristic. And therefore every casualty, every military action, every war, elicits widespread questioning: Perhaps it was unnecessary; perhaps there was an alternative. Must this endless round of pain and death continue? Thus, for example, the Peace Now movement may be politically simplistic, functionally irrelevant, and even counterproductive for achieving peace, but it does honestly reflect a deep emotion, the Jewish revulsion and abhorrence of violence. Stated clearly, the Israeli desires neither to kill nor be killed, to wound nor be wounded, to cause suffering nor to bear suffering. Yet paradoxically, this quintessentially peace-loving people has been condemned by historical necessity to live by the sword. And the scars it bears have lacerated Jewish hearts as well as Jewish bodies.

It is not only at official ceremonies, by freshly dug graves, or on national days of mourning that the clouds of grief and anguish hang heavy. For there is no home in Israel that is whole, in which some relative or dear one has not been offered on the altar of the Jewish state. As the poet Nathan Alterman put it, those young boys and girls (as well as older men and women) who lie in Israel's dust before their time are the "silver platter" upon which a Jewish state was granted to the Jewish people. In poem, song, drama, story, and picture, the message is repeated, for the Israeli cannot forget, even if he would. How gratuitous it is for Israelis to be treated to various admonitions about peace from various quarters of the world, as though peace were not the most passionately desired of all goods, and as though for 2,000 years the Jews had not suffered the most unspeakable horrors at the hands of the followers of these very preachers themselves!

The Zionist dream was that normalizing the Jews' national status in the world would create a corresponding normalcy in the world's relations to the Jewish people. Yet anti-Israelism has largely replaced anti-Semitism. Israel has been forced to forge a powerful military force, divert its energies to military use, and develop strategies, tactics, and arms to assure its survival. At the same time, it has had to deal with the human aspects and the Jewish implications of living in a garrison state. One cannot overestimate the impact of this reality on Israeli thought on all levels, in all dimensions.

To cite one specific case in point, we may take the Israeli army's concept of "purity of arms" *(taharat ha-neshek),* in which the traditional Jewish reverence for life must be considered along with the military necessity to destroy human life. This idea that a weapon, too, must be used in a "kosher" way is not a homiletic slogan to those whose lives are jeopardized in its execution. It affects tactics, battle plans, technology, and strategy: how to avoid the unnecessary taking of enemy lives, and how to inflict the minimal amount of casualties necessary to achieve a particular military objective.

These are not theoretical questions, nor are they attempts to win the approval of the nations of the world: Israel has been the victim of almost universal vilification rather than appreciation, and vicious distortion rather than praise. The issue is a function of our most prized possession: our soul. The enemy may, in fact, be able to destroy our bodies, but never our Jewish soul. We will never become a nation of haters, a people of killers or a country of the bloodthirsty—despite the overwhelming pressures to respond in kind to our would-be murderers. Israel's military prowess has met with universal respect, but what Israelis have most to be proud of is something quite different: What other people the world over would have behaved as Israel continues to behave to the Arabs in its midst, the Arabs in the liberated areas, and the Arabs across its borders who have sworn to destroy it? Again, the issue is not whether the world appreciates our having removed the threat of nuclear war in the Middle East by destroying the Iraqi reactor; our strike against international terrorism by Operation Peace in Galilee; our lifesaving raid into Entebbe; or our benign occupation of the Gaza, Samaria, and Judea areas. The point is that *we* know.

Dissension on all levels concerning military activity exists in Israel, again proving that military strength does not require totalitarianism any more than it requires dehumanization. Every military action, beginning with the War of Independence in 1948, has seen some Israelis objecting to some specific, either the action itself, or part of its execution. The complexity of a military action makes this unavoidable in a society in which people are capable of feeling and of thinking. This will, it is to be hoped, continue as long as Israel is forced to wield the sword. For however much Peace Now may not be a feasible program, it is the universal Jewish prayer.

Few of Israel's founders imagined that after forty years of statehood there would still be armed conflict. And peace is still far from sight, no matter how much wishful thinking may becloud vision. Israelis, apparently, will have to live with the ongoing tension between two value systems, with the constant juxtaposition of military necessity and pacific sensitivity. They will continue to gather in their wounded and mourn their dead; they will continue to be in inner turmoil over the cruel role that the people of shalom must adopt; they will continue to yearn and struggle for that day when shalom will be not only a greeting and a blessing, but a reality.

### Hawks, Doves, and the Israel Aviary

After decades of Arab-Israel conflict, many Israelis are in despair of a solution, and have adopted a sympathy for extremist positions. Regarding those who oppose them as lacking in mettle, they assert that their own tough-minded stance is based on a realistic view of reality. The doves declare that Israel's policies since 1967 were in error, that they have failed, and that they derive from an arrogant ideology that has misperceived and distorted reality. They affirm that the Palestinian Arabs cannot be neutralized or expelled, annexation of the "occupied territories" is a disaster, and the settlement policy is a wasteful blunder. And since political events will force Israel to recognize the degree to which its policies have been self-defeating and unrealistic, the sooner this reality is learned the better. The doves call for a sober reassessment of national thought, a reexamination of Zionism as now understood (and misunderstood) in Israel, for to be overly attentive is less dangerous than to be neglectful.

Ever since the new realities brought by the Six Day War of 1967, these people have lamented what to them is the entirely erroneous view that has gained widespread currency in Israel: That Israeli will can suffice to mold the future, regardless of the constraints imposed by external realities. To their mind, there is a malaise in the Israeli soul: The hawkish extremism of recent Israeli political elections is a spiritual, as well as a political event. Not only has it elicited a wave of disavowal in Israel, but it has alienated world Jewry (which knows that it is judged by what is articulated and done in the Jewish state), and provided hostile propaganda for enemies of Israel the world over.

The dovish position admits that the inner realities of will and resolve are components of reality, but holds that Israel has no monopoly on determination: Its enemies, too, have a will, as is evidenced by Israel's contemporary quagmire. To dovish minds we have only begun to suffer the consequences of our unrealistic assessment of our strategic and economic situation. We think, they say, that we can now act with impunity, because the hand of Israel now prevails over the gentiles. But only disaster can result if we adopt the archaic formulas that were so wisely ignored by diaspora Jewry.

The Israeli hawks decry what to them is squeamishness and a lack of realism. To their mind, if Israel is to prevent suicide, annexation of the "occupied territories" is a necessity. Political expediency may require population transfer of indigenous Arabs, and it may require fulfillment of the biblical injunction "Drive out all the inhabitants of the land before you" (Num. 33:52), not as a relic of antiquity, but as a standing order for modern Israel.

Almost all Israelis sense that accommodation is a necessity. And the middle-of-the-road Israeli is unreservedly convinced of the desperate need for coexistence with Arabs, both in Israel itself and in the Middle East. He intuits that if there is no coexistence, it is the Jews, whose numbers are so limited, who will disappear; it is in Israel's interest to resolve the conflict.

The religious circles in Israel have largely relied on the messianic dictum that ultimately Jewish force will triumph. Others have declared that this is merely wishful thinking and a misuse of classical sources, which encourage bellicose chauvinism.

Few Israelis in 1948 could have predicted that for four decades their country would be a victim of terrorist attacks, boycott, and open warfare—the most brutal and flagrant violations of the elementary standards of justice and humanity, as well as an open challenge to international law and the world community—with the democracies of the world doing next to nothing to end these threats. Israel is not linked to the West by ethnic, religious, or cultural origins, but it does share a commitment to some of the most basic issues: democracy, tolerance, freedom before the law, etc. In fact, Israel continues to face tremendous internal challenges precisely because it upholds these principles. Despite that sharing, Israel finds that most of the world's democracies are not allies but antagonists who make common cause with its sworn enemies. These democracies themselves serve to hamper Israel's freedom of action, and even in Israel there is ongoing concern for the need to balance power with diplomacy.

As a moral people, Israelis want their foreign policy to reflect the values that they espouse as a nation. But they also want their foreign policy to be as effective as possible. Consequently, they are faced with the ongoing problem of how to reconcile their morality with their practical sense, how to relate their strength to their purpose, how to combine military power and diplomatic skill intelligently.

Some Israelis tend to regard military power and diplomacy as distinct alternatives; the more cosmopolitan among them recognize that power and politics are inseparable. Diplomacy not backed by strength will be ineffectual at best, and suicidal at worst. The ongoing challenge is to determine how and when one of these means is appropriate. And there is no such thing, in Israel, as an advance guarantee of public support for either approach. Further, Israel has in the past made errors of judgment, as all nations invariably must. However, in keeping with their critical tradition, the people of Israel have engaged in open and enlightened debate on this issue, and they continue to do so. In so doing they maintain the moral responsibility inherent in a country deeply devoted to justice, even when the democracies of the world appear willing to tolerate the regimes and organizations actively intent upon its destruction.

The diplomatic and political challenge to Israel is for it to forge policies that keep faith with its principles: using power with discretion, yet not shrinking from military action when necessary. And responsible leadership means pursuing a course of action, be it military or diplomatic, even in the absence of public support. For not every decision can be submitted to referendum without the very concept of leadership being rendered meaningless.

### Israel and the Diaspora

Although Zionism is a free alternative to, rather than a moral plea against, the diaspora, Israeli thinkers betray profound feelings about the diaspora. Virtually all thinking people see the frayed, tenuous, and inadequate bonds between Israel and world Jewry. Many ask, "How can we create an honest, productive, consequential tension with the diaspora? What is legitimate to expect of world Jewry? How can we increase immigration to Israel, and other forms of involvement and participation?"

From its very inception, the Zionist movement was dedicated to bringing the Jewish people home—not a fragment of it, not just the displaced persons, not just refugees, not just those with no options—but the Jewish people qua people. And in previous decades Israeli spokesmen may have been blunt and offensive, but they were honestly authentic when they turned to diaspora Jewry and said, in effect, "Come and be part of Jewish history in the making. Join us in the resurrection of our people in its homeland, instead of merely sitting on the sidelines and basking in the vicarious warmth of our passions and our achievements." Those Jews who did come to Israel came from more than 120 countries. From the affluent Western countries very few answered the call; less than .001 percent of American Jewry immigrates to Israel annually. The challenge of being a part of the Israeli adventure is rejected almost unanimously by American Jewry.

Not only is the Israeli faced by a rejection of his invitation, but he is also faced by the phenomenon of diaspora Jewry claiming legitimacy. We Are One, the slogan proclaims. And the slogan is backed up by impressive fund-raising, extensive political action, and educational and cultural activities centering about Israel. However much they may welcome this support, Israelis universally consider it an inadequate response, a proxy participation. The Israeli response to world Jewry is, "We are *not* one, by any meaningful criterion. You do not share our realities, our triumphs and our disasters. You do not bear our military burdens, our societal problems, our economic liabilities, our cultural challenges, or any of the crises. You live in a totally different environment that is affluent, secure, and almost irresistible, witness the Russian Jews, Israelis, and others who flock to your shores. You opt to live a life almost totally divorced from Israel. Whether exercising that option brings you personal fulfillment or meaningful Jewish life is your affair. But the reality is that no matter how heatedly you may attempt to deny it, you are *not* part of the Israeli adventure."

Israelis view this phenomenon as a loss for diaspora Jewry as well as for the Jewish state. For it is not simply that Western Jewry did not join in 1948, when the Jewish people, or part of it, reconstituted itself in its ancestral home. Nor is it only that in the subsequent decades they did not come, sharing their massive talents in technology, science, social work, the democratic process, government, public relations, the humanities, and virtually every area of human endeavor. Rather, or further, it is because many Israelis, even from afar, can see the crisis in American Jewry. The existential reality is that of assimilation, acculturation, alienation, and a dissolving, increasingly amorphous mass, without an authentic community, without genuine roots, and without a meaningful direction. The Israeli turns to his American counterpart and says, whether caringly or accusingly, "Look at *your* situation. You have no faith by which you live, no sense of mission, and no compelling vision. We may have little else to offer, but we do offer that!"

Transcending recrimination and polemics, many Israelis, in the humanities and in the social sciences, are endeavoring to grapple with the problem of establishing stronger bilateral relations with diaspora Jewry, while at the same time trying to create in Israel a more compelling social reality to attract Jews from abroad. Many are asking, "Where did *we* go wrong?" For Israel, like all ideological programs and creative ideas, can flourish only if it has the courage to confront itself. If it prefers not to risk communication it isolates itself and becomes defensive, it perforce becomes the captive of its own security system. And before Israel ventures into a productive ideological battle with the diaspora it must leave its protected battlements and sally forth. We must be willing to expose ourselves: our comforting clichés, our norms, and our familiar lifestyles. Otherwise, insofar as world Jewry is concerned, Israel will become a monument rather than a liberating challenge.

Israel is not only a philosophical issue, but a sociological reality. The basis of Zionist thought is political theory: the kind of polis they wish to create. And they must accept the diaspora's pluralistic intellectual, social, and religious complexities. As Israelis witness the ongoing disintegration of diaspora institutions and allegiances, they also look inward, wondering how Israel can offer an existential, social, cultural haven to those Jews abroad who share a Zionist world view and self-identity. The Israeli knows that success will only be partial: The Israeli rallying cry will always be a frightening as well as exciting invitation and challenge. Some diaspora Jews will respond; others will not want to see their private universe explode. And they will avoid the Zionist challenge in the most obvious way: by dismissing the vision and the mission. But Israelis are increasingly declaring, "We must get *our* house in order for *our* sake. For it is *our* house!"

## The Demographic Time Bombs

Israeli thinkers have always endeavored to provide societal blueprints. They describe a society capable of both controlling and transforming history in the interests of Jewish culture, freedom, democracy, and self-fulfillment—as they envision these various desiderata. But in the background of their messages there are the ominous and disturbing sounds of demographic time bombs ticking away.

Compared with the situation today, Israel of yesterday was relatively homogeneous. The early settlers were largely European in background, secular in orientation, Western in outlook, and committed to Zionist values and those norms that typify the Jewish middle class on the European and American continents. Thus, for all the differences that may have existed among Jews from various Polish, Russian, and neighboring areas, the commonality on all levels greatly exceeded the differences. Therefore, it was not difficult to conceive of an eventual blending, a melting pot or even a pressure cooker in which the differences would be leveled and a harmonious mixture attained.

Today a new demographic picture has become apparent: The early settlers are increasingly becoming a minority, not only numerically but culturally as well. The Arab birthrate vastly exceeds the Jewish. Were the Arabs' rate of increase to prove linear, in time they would outnumber the Jewish population of the Jewish state. And this would occur wherever the eventual border of Israel was drawn. The religious-secular proportion is also changing significantly, due to the fact that Orthodox Jews produce more offspring than do secular Jews. The Ashkenzic-Sephardic balance has already shifted, and since Sephardim have a higher birthrate, this increase will continue. More and more will the "average" Israeli be of Moroccan, Ethiopian, or Algerian background. Finally, as in most countries, it is the poor and the culturally deprived who multiply with greatest rapidity. In sum, therefore, Israel is faced with a population that is increasingly Arab, religious, Sephardic, or culturally deprived, often in combination.

Some social thinkers attempt to assuage fears by pointing out that the birthrates will not remain linear, as affluence, acculturation, and other factors come into play. Further, they maintain, each of these groups has *something* positive to contribute to society. But finally, they admit, there is little that can be done to alter the situation without violating our own moral code and the canons of a free society.

The problems all center on the nature of the individual Israeli and his commitment to a culture in the making. Numerous subcultures in Israel share differing, and even conflicting, values: How can an Arab accept "Hatikvah" as his national anthem, the Star of David as his national emblem, and Herzl as his spiritual father, let alone a Jewish state as his authentic homeland? Can an Orthodox Jew accept a secular Jewish society, or a North African or Asian Jew live authentically in a Western society? Further, why should he want to, particularly when he sees demographic factors working in his favor, with his political leverage, economic resources, and population strength increasing?

Israel is an obviously problematic entity: What it is by definition and what it is in fact are separated by a wide gulf. The country is composed of subcultures, some of which are unsympathetic to the Zionist vision, unmoved by the experiences and untutored in the values of a Jewish state. Definitions do not confer reality, and beyond definition lies the necessity for implementation. Israelis know that they must address the growing number of the unaffiliated, their fears, frustrations, expectations, and needs, if Israel is to be adequately welded into an organic, purposeful, harmonious society. The cost of neglect would be horrendous.

## The Sephardic Sector

In order actually to integrate its Sephardic majority, Israeli leaders have, of late, begun to rectify the disastrous concept of an exclusively Western-oriented culture. They know that Israel must deliberately adopt a cultural pluralism that reflects Jewish culture derived from all parts of the diaspora. Thus, no more can Israeli schoolchildren memorize the waves of immigration (aliyah) to Israel, in which the Sephardic immigrants are not mentioned, as though they never arrived in the country. It must be a serious cultural renewal, not the debased ethnicity that one often finds, and that doubles the evil rather than redresses the wrong.

Israel's Sephardim from Arab lands originated in cohesive, mutually dependent, tradition-bound societies. They suddenly found themselves in a largely secular, Western atomized culture, in which their indigenous traditions were functionally inappropriate, hence neglected or ridiculed as primitive. To this day, many live in slums that are plagued by overcrowding, unemployment, petty crime, and the inevitable erosion of personal initiative, responsibility, and mutual trust. With inadequate living space, schools, day-care centers, kindergartens, youth clubs, and cultural programs, it is small wonder that Moroccans account for 90 percent of Israel's prison population. And this a community that in its native land was far from a criminal element. Crime was learned in Israel itself—a land that largely forgot its Sephardim in the exuberance of its rebirth.

There is real hostility in the Sephardic community today. The Ashkenazim are identified as responsible for every injustice—real or imagined—that the Sephardim suffered since arriving in Israel. This resentment has been expressed in Sephardic voting patterns, in violent demonstrations, and in a host of other less bellicose ways. Today there are new political alliances and experiments in cultural, social, and economic synthesis, changing boundaries that in the past were inviolate. For many

Israelis are openly acknowledging that the inferior status of many Sephardim is a symptom and a manifestation of Israel's abandonment of the sublime humanistic values that were so characteristically Jewish.

New attitudes and new constellations are affecting the Sephardim today, reflecting the effect of ongoing economic, social, and cultural transformation. There is a greater receptivity on the part of Israeli society, and this has somewhat affected the limitations of the past, in work opportunities, religio-cultural activity, political affiliation, marriage patterns, etc. The limits of the possible have been expanded, as Sephardic individuals and Sephardic institutions have discovered new opportunities, new skills, and new powers. This progress has been essential for the country as a whole; however, all Israeli analysts agree that while it was indispensable, it is also inadequate, and the situation is still highly explosive.

Many spokesmen in Israel declare that the Sephardic situation is a thundering indictment of Zionism, proof that by and large it has failed. Its aim had been not only to separate all Jews—Sephardim and Ashkenazim—from the diaspora, and not only to establish them in a new and independent nation, but also to provide better lives than those they had lived. Yet immigrating to Israel caused social upheavals in ways that were neither foreseen nor intended. Neither the Sephardim nor the state would ever be the same again.

Today Sephardim *are* involved in defining the national character. They constitute a subculture that is growing side by side, and interacting, with the established culture. Along with the myriad military and economic fronts, Israelis are faced with Jewish bifurcation, a problem that demands resolution on obvious functional as well as moral grounds.

### The Israeli Arabs

Israel began in contradiction. Although its fundamental law grants equality of rights to all, and its form of government is democratic, its self-definition is that of a Jewish state: Its anthem is "Hatikvah," and its symbol is the Star of David. Yet the populace includes a large Arab element, growing in numbers, in wealth, and in political sophistication, with the expected ideologies and institutions, given the Arab-Israeli conflict. These people are not fully accepted by their Arab brethren across the borders, nor are they fully accepted by Jewish Israelis, and their own self-image is confused, albeit unabashedly Arab or Palestinian. Obviously their loyalties are divided; in some cases they openly espouse the dismantling of the Jewish state.

Nature does not tolerate such contradiction: Just as a person cannot fight against himself and remain alive, neither can a nation. Thus, Israelis know that they must resolve this conflict before it becomes unmanageable. In earlier days various kinds of compromise seemed possible, and did, in fact, quiet the waters. The country was small and compact, the Arab economy was rising rapidly, and most Israeli Arabs did benefit from citizenship. Yet no progress has been made at ideological fusion, because Jews and Arabs differ fundamentally in their expectations. Ideological conflict, particularly when the frame of reference is immediate political advantage, is likely to produce propaganda, not literature. An intellectual's first necessity is to see other people directly and fairly, as they are in themselves, and not through the prism of abstract categories, of ideologies, that dictate to him what he should see and feel. With the Arab sector, decades of increasingly shrill and bellicose declarations have produced much propaganda and very little genuine thought. Words and ideas are used as weapons, separating the soul of the Arab community even further from the Jewish majority, and disenfranchising those Arab leaders and intellectuals who were of a less bellicose bent.

The Jewish response has been widely varied, of course, ranging from genuine brotherhood to outright hostility. In past centuries the Jewish position had been the opposite: They lived as a minority group, virtually powerless, unable to react freely to anti-Semitism, whether governmental, ethnic, or individual. Physical violence was not an option, nor was antagonistic behavior of any kind. In Israel, however, even though the state provides security for all, and advocates respect for all groups, some Jewish elements advocate repression of the Arabs, whether for reasons of national defense, religiosity, or cultural viability. To this end, some feel free to disobey the state laws, for, to their mind, they are nothing but an inadvertent formula for the dissolution of the Jewish state.

The issue of Jewish-Arab relations is a life-and-death matter for Israel, and there are no guidelines. The issue has largely been avoided and neglected, with the notable exception of the far left and far right on the political spectrum. The future of Israeli politics and of Israeli society will be determined, in large measure, by the relationship between these vastly disparate communities, these two peoples dwelling in one home. Israeli public figures and intellectuals are profoundly disturbed, lest the past dictate the future. Israel cannot continue to be increasingly divided along ethnic lines, with each sector more committed to its own interests than to the nation as as whole, lest inevitable civil war ensue, with catastrophic results. There *are* positive contacts between Jewish and Arab intellectuals, social activists, students, and others, but these are minimal and patently inadequate to shape the thought and behavior of the two communities. Predictions of civil war may yet prove to be self-fulfilling prophecies.

## The Posture of Social Science

Starting from the most meager of beginnings, Israeli thought is increasingly becoming enriched through the contributions of men and women working in the social sciences, from the theoretical to the practical. Significant energies are being devoted to sociology, social psychology, social work, urban planning, community-center education, rehabilitation, and related areas. Since its very inception, Israeli society has endeavored to better the life of its constituents, but only recently has there been a sustained attempt to provide an intellectual underpinning to these efforts. In the past, rhetoric was often substituted for specificity and programming. And this has inevitably produced confusion and frustration.

For many decades, the intellectual marketplace of Israel served as a purveyor of abstract formulations. As cases in point one may consider Jewish state, ingathering of the exiles, absorption, narrowing the ethnic gap, coexistence of communities, healing the economy, etc. And although intellectuals may best be addressed in abstractions, only concrete descriptions actually provide the two essential checks needed for thought and action: whether the outcome of an abstraction is likely and whether it is likable. The author or speaker who limits himself to abstractions provides neither. Since he does not divulge in specific terms either what he wants or how he expects it to follow from his presuppositions, there is no intelligent way to engage in meaningful dialogue, either on grounds of dislike or of disbelief.

One of the reasons for the often-heated nature of Israeli discussions on the one hand, and the lack of genuine dialogue on the other, is that slogans often substitute for clear formulations. An abstraction functions as a drug: it is either pacifying or arousing, but it is not illustrative. The purveyor of the abstraction is safe, as his readers or listeners concur— however mutually incompatible their individually constructed pictures may be.

Fortunately, however, in recent decades the Israeli social-science community has been vastly enriched by the abandonment of vague abstractions and the confrontation of real issues. It is not a matter of abandoning the high road that Israel's planners charted, for by and large there is no basic disagreement as to ultimate goals. Rather, it is the abandonment of the institutional lockstep that, while feigning societal progress, is at best a marching in place, at worst a retrogression. There is a painful plenitude of societal problems in Israel, and should procedures, definitions, and policies become authoritative, removed from the crucible of continuous testing and evaluation, social thought will harden into intellectual slag. In that case, goals will inevitably recede, for without effective social planning we are at the mercy of most inauspicious forces.

### Kibbutz as Idea and as Reality

Land ownership in the Land of Israel was an indispensable ingredient in the creation of Jewish sovereignty, but in 1948, when the British lowered the Union Jack at Government House in Jerusalem, Jews could show undisputed title to only 780 square miles, less than 14 percent of the minuscule area allowed for the Jewish state in the United Nations partition recommendation. Far more crucial than the size of their holdings, though, was the fact that by and large, Jews had created the kibbutz, a miniaturized, egalitarian society. Based on a love of the Land of Israel, on a new Jewish work ethic, and on the collective ideal, it attracted idealists who literally converted swamp and desert into model farming communities. More than that, the kibbutz itself produced an elite, men and women who were living examples of what the new Israeli Jew could be. Beyond their numbers kubbutzniks were represented among the country's finest military officers, intellectuals, political and social leaders: an aristocracy that even today is still visible.

Yet the kibbutz is not hermetically sealed off from the environment, and today's kibbutz member is profoundly disturbed by the failure to transmit its values to the young, by its detachment from the social ills of the society it had wanted to redeem, and by the inroads of materialism and consumerism. Many kibbutz members lament the loss of their initial vitality. For in the supercharged, expanding Israel economy, where many people had been able to exploit government contracting, military construction, speculative financing, and political corruption to amass personal wealth, the old kibbutz values of hard work, frugality, modesty, and collectivism were sorely tried, often to the breaking point.

To many an Israeli, today's kibbutz is seen as a sort of country club, using hired labor from the Arab and Sephardic towns, and exploiting the kibbutz's favorable tax status and its undue influence in the Israeli Knesset, allowing it to compete successfully against both private farms (moshavim) and private industry. Thus, the kibbutz, which was originally the darling of the Israeli self-image, and an ongoing showpiece on the international scene, fell from grace very suddenly.

Israeli thinkers know, however, that if there is any extant institution that can repair the damages suffered by the Israeli soul, it is the kibbutz, with its traditions as well as its resources. The kibbutzim still produce a voluminous literature, are still value-sensitive, and are still concerned with the quality of Israeli life. Further, in the past they have demonstrated resiliency and adaptability, and it is not farfetched to hope that there will be a renaissance, with the kibbutz reaching out to development towns, urban slums, and other areas, enriching them and themselves by a renewed program of social action. The process has already begun, and the creative discontent of the younger generation is beginning to produce new harvests.

### Education and Inspiration

Like the Jewish people itself, the Jewish state has learned that despite its inner realities, in the international mind it is unique: It remains the incarnation of otherness, a nation mythologized, and the object of metaphor. As a result, many of Israel's hypotheses about itself are, in one way or another, responses to prevailing descriptions of it, whether they express distress over the disparity between these malicious myths and its own sense of self, or whether they are triumphant repudiations of these myths. But what is most essential for Israeli society is not its public relations abroad, but its ongoing efforts at educating and inspiring its own constituency.

Formal and informal education in Israel involves not only schoolchildren in the secular, religious, and independent school networks, not only the universities, seminars and trade schools, but a vast network of educational programs on kibbutzim, in community centers, and in outreach programs. The army, too, is a major educational institution, involving not only young people, in their initial military service, but adults, during their annual reserve duty. In addition to the spectrum of technical knowledge that is conveyed, a major emphasis is placed upon humanism: providing the man, woman, or child with Israel-identification, a sense of Jewish history, a feeling of being part of the homeland, and a desire to participate in building the future.

The task is not an easy one, but it is essential. For if a people is called upon to live dynamically and often heroically, it is dependent upon a vision that has the power of mission. Yet the life-and-death problems that have confronted Israel since its very birth have created an almost compulsive interest in solutions to immediate problems. Further, the undeniable successes of young Israel have sometimes bordered on the miraculous, and therefore it is no wonder that the ongoing necessity to educate and inspire with commitment has been largely overlooked. It was assumed that everything was in order on that front: an atmosphere of portentous wisdom, not the "still small voice" of probing questions.

The past decade (and the Yom Kippur War of 1973 may be identified as the primary stimulus) has seen a revitalization of value sensitivity in Israeli education of thought. Discussion centers on the most basic questions, such as "We are investing ever-increasing efforts in being better equipped to achieve what we want, but what is it that we want?" Or, "We are constantly improving the means of our existence, but what ends should they serve?" Again, "Shouldn't clarifying what we want to be constitute a fundamental cultural-spiritual endeavor?"

There was always Zionist education in Israel; sometimes it was dismissed as boring and archaic, and at other times it proved inspiring in the extreme. Educational theorists and activists today recognize that Zionism, or any idea that unifies the totality of a group's values under one heading, is merely a word. It has no basis in experience except as a generalization; and a loose generalization often substitutes for exactness and depth. Therefore, educators are becoming increasingly wary of the built-in vocabulary that implies content; they mistrust slogans. What they attempt to convey, most of all, is the realization that history is itself a reflection of purpose; it represents the fulfillment of purpose. And Israel itself is a blending of purpose and power. The future Israel will be the result of ideas whose time has come.

The more creative and daring of Israel's educators know that the future is either ventured or it is lost. They know that their role is to analyze Israeli realities, not simply classify them. There is a time-honored tradition of excellence in Israeli education, and it is comforting to discover men and women who dare to encourage fresh insights and creative thought. For it is they who are nurturing the mind and soul of the Jewish state that is still in the making, inscribing new chapters in a saga that is yet in the writing.

### Nostalgia in an Old-New Land

For many young—and not so young—Israelis, the lack of clearly defined images of the life-style they are creating is a source of disappointment and frustration, as well as of anxiety. In a country committed from its inception to personal and collective self-determination, there is an increasing fatalism, a feeling that lives are increasingly controlled by technological-political influences unrelated to choice. It often seems as though foreign policy, life-style, societal norms and even cultural content are being determined by others: We are merely reflexes of Washington, Moscow, Damascus, and Cairo. We are unduly molded by international as well as local media. We are at the mercy of bureaucracies over which we have minimal genuine control. And however unfounded or exaggerated these feelings may be in an era, in which even the superpowers are not entirely independent, the pain and disillusionment are real. Furthermore, there is a vast difference between accepting unwanted realities when they are unavoidable, and abdicating the power to effect change that can be achieved. The morale and spiritual health of any society require its members' sense of involvement in a shared task, yet increasingly one finds the preoccupation with self, an ethic of pure selfishness, with ethical questions regarded as irrelevant. And all this despite the intense self-sacrifice of Israelis during times of immediate national danger.

One of the most familiar refrains heard in Israel today is the plaint "What happened to the good old days?" This is not just a nostalgic urge to return to the camaraderie, simple ethics, and idealism of earlier decades, but more important, reflects a profound sense of frustration at the inability to think, feel, and act as creatively and as nobly as previous generations apparently did. If this problem mattered only to a small coterie of Israeli intellectuals who were distressed by their inability to dream as they once had, the malaise might concern a social psychologist more than a sociologist. Yet to increasing numbers of Israelis—be they academics, farmers, soldiers, or workers—it is the past half of the twentieth century that constitutes Israel's golden age, its classical period.

Israel's clasical period included the years of conquering desert and swamp, gathering the refugees from Arab lands and the survivors of the European Holocaust, and welcoming those idealists from Western lands who raised their feet as well as their hands in affirmation of Zion's call. It was a time of "one hand on the rifle and one hand on the plow," of blue work shirts, khaki shorts, and leather sandals. Today Israel's elders recall the years of sharing, trusting, and building, with the *chevra* in the haystack, the dining hall, and around the campfire, or in the outdoor café. The good old days. Older Israelis often have a double nostalgia: one for the land, language, and culture of their birth, the other for the spirit and life-style of their youth.

Nostalgia, however understandable it may be, is the least adequate response to the challenges of Israel today. Not that it is based on a completely erroneous view of the past. It is not, but it is irrelevant. Yet today, however much Israel may have changed, this imagery retains its hold on the imagination. In song, dance, theater, novel, and school curriculum, these classical descriptions and prescriptions continue to mold thought and feeling. And this in a social context in which the past has ceased to be relevant in many respects.

Israeli language, mental habits, and categories of thought are organically related to a world that was vastly different from that of today, and are therefore not wholly adequate for coping with Israel's contemporary needs and experiences. The young idealist of today must create high-technology industry, not plant vineyards in the wilderness. Industrialization, exporting, business acumen, efficient government, and industrialization are the real desiderata. There is no apparent way of successfully building a functioning Western society without a measure of personal alienation. Stratification, impersonal relations, societal discontent, pragmatic politics, and competition are unavoidable, and old ideologies—however well intentioned—only retard political thinking, social engineering, artistic creativity, and economic weal. It is small wonder that the conflict between nostalgia and need impedes progress, frustrates design, and produces ennui.

Much of the spiritual and emotional frustration in Israeli thought today arises precisely from the conflict between what was to have been and what is, and from a melancholy sense of what will be. For 2,000 years the Promised Land existed as a model, an idealized concept that elicited expectation and contemplation but was not tested in reality. It is therefore not surprising that expectations in Israel are exaggerated. There is a profound radicalism in virtually every dimension, in the sense that all reality is brought before the bar of metahistorical values. Is it any wonder that by the criteria of Isaiah, Hosea, and Amos, and by the criteria of the early pioneers, the fledgling state is found utterly wanting?

The nostalgia that pervades the Israeli psyche is not only the progenitor of frustration, however. It *is* patently exaggerated, but there cannot be any historical consciousness without a profound identification with the past. Nostalgia has its legitimate place in the complex range of responses. "What happened to the good old days!" is a cry. And a cry has genuine import if it does not expect a clear answer but is more of a comment upon an existential situation.

The establishment of the State of Israel caught even the Israelis emotionally unprepared. In the Jewish psyche, a Jewish state was a utopia passionately and ceremoniously wished, but hardly expected. "Next year in Jerusalem" was more a theology than a strategy; a vision of the divinely possible, not the humanly probable. And religious historiography is rarely a basis for realistic expectations, for utopia is literally nowhere, not only geographically but historically. It exists neither in the present nor in the actual past or future. The fascination of a Jewish state is old; the science is new. And the current wave of nostalgia for "the good old days" is the inevitable consequence when a dream is replaced by reality. And Israel *has* profoundly changed: The furious growth in population, expanded economy, and military success (and failure!), have been accompanied by decisive shifts in the character of the nation. There *has* been an erosion of the civic sense and of personal partnership in the Zionist mission. There *has* been a neglect of the original, irreducible first principles upon which Israel was conceived and founded. The fall, unfortunately, is not imagined.

### The Americans in Israel

Israeli thought and behavior have been influenced markedly by a relatively small group, the Americans in Israel. For although they are not an organized ethnic entity their influence is manifold. They have significantly affected all aspects of university, elementary, and secondary education, high-technology industry, public relations, social work, kibbutz life, medicine, and numerous other areas of Israeli life, reflecting American-Jewish values at their best. Often their initial experiences in their new land are difficult, yet many of these new pioneers refuse to equate the easy with the good. And they very soon discover that, in traditional Jewish fashion, Israel welcomes them—socially, professionally, and economically—as much as any country ever welcomed newcomers. And they realize that some adjusting, learning, accepting, and even forgiving on their part is essential.

Americans in Israel generally assimilate into the existing subcultures; some are Orthodox, others function in academe, and still others join kibbutzim and moshevim. What they have in common is intensity and optimism; they invariably have great expectations. And they soon experience the inevitable admixture of fulfillment and frustration. For they are not only a valuable link to the diaspora, and not only a source of Western know-how; they are also products of the society and civilization from whence they came. However invidious comparisons may be, it is well-nigh impossible for Americans *not* to compare the efficiency, affluence, manners, and other aspects of America with those of Israel. And quite often, in these areas and others Israel suffers in the comparison.

On the other hand, the American Jew in Israel knows at first hand that the American Jewish community is a well-organized structure devoid of significant Jewish substance, a structure that is disintegrating and trivialized. He knows that it is fighting a losing holding action against its environment, that it is historically exhausted and functionally anachronistic.

For these as well as for other reasons, the American Israeli is a natural enemy of apathy: The gift of the newcomer is turbulence. He is experiencing a spiritual odyssey, marked by a wide range of emotions as well as insights. Unlike the diaspora Judaism he left behind, his new Israeli identity includes being dreadfully responsible for his own destiny and that of his people, in a land often fraught with fear and trembling. He sees an Israel still in its infancy, and unlike the Israeli-born, he is experiencing for the first time, and at first hand, the pains and the promises of that rebirth. Sometimes he feels that we are standing before an abyss, confronted by the daily potential for tragedy. Invariably his thoughts are marked by an earnestness and honesty that have become distinguishing characteristics of those who left the red white, and blue for the blue and white.

Many Americans came to Israel expecting to find a simple social structure, de-emphasis of property and station, communal cohesion, and commitment to enhancing the social, economic, and political order. That is what they had been taught to expect, and in measure it was valid. But they also discovered a society in which values were disintegrating, in which a social gap was widening, in which Israel-identity was being overwhelmed by cheap Western culture and rampant materialism. As was to be expected, some left the country; others stayed on to play their role in the making of a society that will, by virtue of sustained effort, eventually approximate the high expectations they brought with them.

## A Composite Message

The more closely one examines recent developments in Israeli thinking, the more one becomes convinced that the immediate causes of change are to be found not in the activity of a few speculative minds, but rather in social development. Furthermore, it would appear that Israelis are at their best when, although they cannot make up their own minds, they are courageous enough not to have them made up for them by others. This is a basic trait of a people seeking to fulfill a mission that no one had demanded of it.

The only way to make helpful, valid observations is to make simplifying assumptions, to invent a simplified world. Despite its divergence from absolute truth and specificity, it may be possible to understand how such a simplified world works. The art of practicing good social science (and it *is* an art) is to sense when it is not misleading to extrapolate from the simplified to the real world.

For the average Israeli, reality is that which is spread out before him in his own land. It is the corroboration or refutation of that pervasive Zionist conviction that Israelis had so much wanted to believe, that all Jews could be assimilated into this remarkable little land and all experiences could be weathered, leaving the soul of the people intact. Inner reality is the ability or inability to believe in that Jewish pride that constantly claimed that no people on earth loves its land more than Israelis love theirs. And in his innermost soul the individual Israeli knows that he remains an individual, that his reality is in measure distinct, and must bear its own burden of accountability. Many generalities—some praising and some damning—have been applied to Israel, but a nation or race or people cannot commit a moral or immoral act. Only individuals can be moral or immoral, inspired or cynical, idealistic or materialistic. And no generalization from a sum of particulars can possibly render a judgment about an individual. In so many ways, indeed, the whole differs from the sum of its parts.

If we were to ask thinking Israelis for some message, so that we could then construct a composite portrait, they might well reply, "We are not messengers, we are the message." Or they might elaborate somewhat, along the following lines:

Who are we? We are what we are. And what we are most of all is a busy, struggling nation. Vegetable life begins painlessly; human life begins with a scream. And we were born out of Jewish blood, tears, and sweat. We are yet aborning, for the insecurity of Israeli life is a given. We can either master it or flee from it, but we cannot ignore it. This is the basic given of our existence, and of who we are. It is not all, though. We are a sovereign people living on its historic soil, speaking the language of our ancestors, in dialogue with our tradition, creating the physical and emotional resources of our life. Though internally problematic and externally endangered, we are fully alive. *Am Yisrael hai.* We are fully determined to live, both as a self-evident end in itself and as the only option remaining to the Jewish people.

As a society we have been busy, even frantic, ever since we unfurled the Star of David as the ensign of a Jewish state in 1948. For we exist on the map not by virtue of our neighbors' good will, not by the plenitude of natural abundance, and not by the magnanimity of mankind: We dwell within our narrow borders by the grace of God and by the force of arms. How right were the pioneers: "In blood and fire did Judah fall; in blood and fire will Judah rise!"

Despite a massively orchestrated campaign of vilification, we are an inspiration to peoples the world over yearning to breathe free. A Jewish prophet's message adorns the United Nations, and a Jewish poetess's words adorn the Statue of Liberty. For throughout history we have been a stubborn, subversive, stiff-necked people, insisting that "in the image of God was man created." And the Zionist idea is this: Just as we struggled for the dignity, freedom, and self-determination of those nations among whom we lived, we must struggle to achieve for ourselves.

We Israelis have not had adequate leisure for contemplation, for we have been too busy attempting the near-impossible yet indispensable.

After twenty centuries of being powerless and stateless, living in time rather than space, we have created a strong nation and forged a homeland. We resurrected our ancient culture on our ancient soil, both of which had appeared exhausted. As we converted swamp and desert into meadow and farm, we revived the Hebrew language of antiquity. And we welcomed the tired and the hungry, the dispersed brothers and sisters who came to our shores in wooden boats, along narrow paths, and "on the wings of eagles." They arrived with little more than tattered hopes, frail in body and frightened in soul. And just look at them now!

We are what we are. Within our own limitations we have exerted ourselves and achieved our own successes. To some people they may seem trivial, but they did not seem so in the doing. And they were not. And we have just begun!

# PART I

# Classical Zionism Reconsidered

# 1

# Vision and Redemption

## DAVID BEN-GURION

I will begin with some questions: What are the Jews—a nation like all the nations, a nation with a unique character of its own, a religious community, the fragments of a disintegrated nation? What is Judaism and in what does its uniqueness lie? Is Judaism petrified, rigidly defined, and unchangeable in all generations and all countries, or does it change through contact with others, and assume different forms according to the needs of a particular time and place? How was Judaism preserved in the diaspora when the Jews were scattered among the nations, and will it be preserved in the future? What has brought about the revival of the Jewish state in our day? Is the State of Israel no more than a state like any other, or has it an ideal or a uniqueness of its own? What has the establishment of the State of Israel changed in world Jewry, and what is the mutual bond between Israel and the diaspora? Which problems has the state solved, and which new problems has it created? What light does the state shed on our past, and what does it promise for the future?

I would not venture to offer a reply to all the questions I have put, nor am I certain that there is any definite and certain reply to historical questions in general. Besides, insofar as there are replies to certain questions, every answer arouses new questions. I will try, however, to reply to some of the questions, and if I succeed in clarifying them to some little extent, I shall feel amply rewarded.

If a Jew had been asked two centuries ago: "What is a Jew?" he would have answered simply and with complete inner confidence: "A Jew is a descendant of Abraham our Father, who obeys the commandments and hopes for the coming of the Messiah." At that time this answer would have been satisfactory to any Jew wherever he might live, but today it would not satisfy a large part of our people, perhaps the greater part. Ever since the emancipation, the Jewish religion has ceased to be the force that joins and unites us. Nor is the bond with the Jewish nation now common to all Jews. And there are not many Jews in our time who hope for the coming of the Messiah.

If those who fought for Jewish emancipation in Germany and France had been asked 100 or 150 years ago: "What are the Jews?" they would have replied: "A religious community—the Jews are Germans or Frenchmen of the Mosaic faith." Most of the Jews of Russia, Poland, Galicia, or Romania would have replied a century ago: "The Jews are a minority in exile, completely different from the people among whom they live"; and fifty years ago many of them would have added: "And they aspire to return to Zion." Not many of the Jews of America, even those who continue to call themselves Zionists, would give the last answer today, for it is their desire to become rooted in their new country, as an organic part of America, like all the other religions and national groups that reached America a generation or a few generations ago.

Nor is religious Jewry any longer an integral and internally united entity. The Neturei Karta in Israel and the United States hardly recognize as Jews those who do not think and behave as they do. National religious Jewry of the Mizrahi school does not separate itself from the rest of the nation, and recognizes that all Jews belong to the Jewish people, but it believes that it alone observes truly authentic Judaism, and it aspires to impose its opinions on all other Jews by all possible means. Many observant Jews who do not belong to the Mizrahi believe that the maintenance of religious parties in Israel is extremely harmful to Judaism. They are afraid that the exploitation of religion for political purposes is a danger both to the purity of religion and to the unity of the Jewish people. Then there is Agudat Yisrael, which stands between the Neturei Karta and the Mizrahi, and there are various shades of Reform Judaism. Free-thinking Jewry is no less divided, and the division was particularly great in the period before the rise of Israel, not only in regard to religion and faith, but in the sphere of political concepts in connection with the settlement and the future of the Land of Israel.

### Change and Continuity in Jewish History

Change and continuity are the lot of all nations, just as they are the lot of every human being from childhood to old age. There are nations that have known unbroken continuity and few changes, and there are others that have had the opposite experience. Our share of both change and continuity is perhaps greater than that of any other people, and the vicissitudes did not begin in recent times.

The people that went out of Egypt and wandered in the wilderness was different from the one that conquered and settled Canaan. The people that was split up into tribes in the days of the judges was different from the people that was united under the rule of the first three kings; nor was the people united under one king the same as the people that was divided after the death of Solomon and established the Kingdom of Judah and the Kingdom of Israel. There is a great difference between the people in the days of the first kings of Judah and Israel and the people in the period of Uzziah, King of Judah, and Jeroboam, son of Joash in Israel—the two great kings in whose days there appeared the prophets Amos, Hosea, Isaiah, and Micah. And the Jewish people in all the periods that I have enumerated, from the exodus till the Babylonian exile, was not at all like the people that returned from exile in the days of Zerubavel, Ezra, and Nehemiah and built the Second Temple.

There is a great difference between the period of Persian rule and the period of the Greeks and the Hasmonaeans and the later Herodian and Roman periods. And the greatest changes were yet to come. After the destruction of the Second Temple came servitude to Rome, the great revolts that ended in defeat, and more than 1,800 years of exile and wandering, generations of persecution and conversion, forced and voluntary, in the lands of Christianity and Islam; wandering from one country to another, from regime to regime, tongue to tongue; compulsory and ever-renewing adaptation to the conditions of life, the spiritual climate, and the constantly changing political and economic frameworks in all the countries of the diaspora in every one of the five continents; unceasing political, economic, and spiritual pressure by superior forces. Throughout these prolonged and numerous transformations and tribulations, which have not yet come to an end, the continuous ego of our people was preserved to no smaller extent than the national ego of stable peoples who were never separated from their own land. What was the name of this ego, and how was it preserved throughout all these internal and external changes and transformations, such as no other people has known in the annals of humanity?

One of the most original thinkers and profound scholars who have dealt with the history of the faith of Israel, Professor Yehezkel Kaufmann, states in his book *Golah Venekhar* that "the great rule of history is that every people, when it lives under conditions of exile, is absorbed among its neighbors." And he asks: "How, then, is it possible to explain the fact that the Jewish people clung to the forms of its national existence and maintained its unique national character in spite of the natural effect of social conditions?" And his reply is: "The fact of popular psychology, that the Jewish people saw in its *religious character* the only internal reason for its fight for uniqueness, is of vital importance for the solution of our problem. It was no external factor, nor even the so-called biological urge to survive, but the special power that was latent in Israel's religious culture that was responsible for its unique place among the nations. The true basis for its uniqueness was its religion, for the sake of which it preserved its separateness from the nations . . . [vol. 1, p. 199].

"The idea which acted in the depth of the nation's soul, compelled it to follow its own special path, and marked with its stamp all aspects of its life, was a religious idea." And Professor Kaufmann emphasizes: "A religious idea—and not religion as a regime of laws and commandments, as people are accustomed to think. Hence, it was religion (in the sense of faith, i.e., the faith in one God), which was the only source of their national will" (p. 206).

Professor Kaufmann accentuates the point of his interpretation still further, and declares that "Judaism must not be considered a national religion in its essence because of the national symbols with which it is bound. . . . If we examine the outlook of later Judaism, that a convert became entitled to the name of 'Israel' in its true meaning by accepting the Jewish religion, we shall see that it was a true expression of complete liberation from every ethnic bond" (p. 217).

If this interpretation of Professor Kaufmann's were correct, it would be impossible to understand the reason for the uniqueness of Jewry after the faith in one God had spread to other nations, especially by means of Islam and to a large extent by means of various Christian sects as well, and even among the adherents of the Vedanta in India, according to the interpretation of Shankara and Ramanuja. For Professor Kaufmann emphasizes that it is not the practical commandments but the religious idea of Judaism, namely the faith in one God in opposition to the faith in idols, that united Israel and preserved it in the diaspora.

### Monotheism and Morality

I have no doubt that many have, like myself, eagerly read Professor Kaufmann's monumental work on the history of the faith of Israel, in which he contradicts with convincing force most of the conjectures of the Bible critics of the school of Graf-Welhausen, and proclaims—justly, in my opinion—the originality and antiquity of Israel's faith in one God.

Professor Kaufmann is, of course, aware that the monotheism of Israel is different from the conception of the Vedanta, which in the books of Shankara arrives at an extreme doctrine of pure unity. The difference is in the nature of the One and Only supreme God. According to Shankara's doctrine, Brahma is a purely metaphysical entity; he has to be known and understood, and the redemption of humanity depends on this knowledge and understanding. But while the supreme God of the Vedanta imposes no obligations for right action and he himself has no moral qualities, the supreme God of Israel is the personification of righteousness, justice, and mercy, and only he who cleaves to these qualities is near to God and is truly a religious man.

In his controversy with Ahad Ha'am, in which Kaufmann insisted that not only justice but kindness and mercy, as well, are basic elements of Judaism, the truth is certainly on Kaufmann's side, although in my humble opinion Kaufmann is mistaken in imputing the ethics of lovingkindness and mercy only to later Judaism and not to the Judaism of the Bible (p. 203). Insofar as the qualities of lovingkindness and mercy are concerned, there is no difference between the prophetic morality and that of later Judaism, as Kaufmann implies. The God of Israel in the Bible is long-suffering and of great mercy (Num. 14:18). Micah the Moreshtite states: "He hath showed thee, O man, what is good; and what does the Lord require of thee, but to do justly, and to love mercy, and to walk humbly with thy God." (Mic. 6:9). Hosea denounces Israel because "there is no truth, nor mercy, nor knowledge of God in the land" (Hos. 4:1), and when he wishes to comfort this people he says: "And I will betroth thee unto me in righteousness, and in judgment, and in lovingkindness, and in mercy" (Hos. 2:21). Jeremiah, the prophet of the destruction, proclaims in the name of the Lord: "I am the Lord which exercises lovingkindness, judgment, and righteousness, in the earth: for in these things I delight, saith the Lord" (Jer. 9:23), and the Psalms constantly repeat and emphasize the quality of mercy: "The Lord is merciful and gracious, slow to anger and plenteous in mercy" (Ps. 103:8); "For Thou, O Lord, art good and forgiving and plenteous in mercy to all them that call upon thee" (Ps. 86:5); "For I have said: The world shall be built in mercy" (Ps. 89:3). And Zechariah, the prophet, calls to his people: "Execute true judgment, and show mercy and compassion every man to his brother" (Zech. 8:9).

For this reason it is surprising to find Professor Kaufmann stating that "it was not morality but religion that served as the basis for the uniqueness of Israel in the diaspora" (p. 204). The distinction between morality and religion is foreign to the spirit and the character of the faith of Israel, both that of the Bible and that of later times, in my humble opinion, but the fundamental error of the author of *The History of the Faith of Israel* and of *Golah Venekhar* lies in the fact that he does not adequately appreciate the central national factors that were active in the life of Israel, both while it lived in its own land and while it was in exile, aside from "the religious idea," i.e., monotheism, which after the spread of Christianity and Islam was no longer specific to Israel.

Professor Kaufmann, who see the uniqueness of the Jews in monotheism, was unable to ignore entirely the national factors that were active in Jewish history, and he says that "in the consciousness of the Jewish people the racial religious concept indeed occupied a considerable place," and "Israel was not merely a religious community but also a nation, a specific racial and national entity" (p. 217). But even with this addition, it seems to me that this great scholar of the faith of Israel misses the target of historic truth. Kaufmann apparently completely ignores the profound spiritual attachment of the Jewish people to its ancient homeland even while it lived in exile; he does not realize the bond of the nation to the Hebrew language; and, what is even more remarkable, he does not appreciate the messianic vision of redemption, which fills the very air of Jewish history and which, in various periods, aroused mighty, tempestuous movements in Israel and in our own day has led to a revolution in the history of our people.

On the threshold of Jewish history stood three central events, the memory and the influence of which have not passed away among us even to this day—the exodus from Egypt, the revelation on Mount Sinai, and the conquest of the Land of Israel. The will for redemption preceded these three decisive events. According to tradition, which undoubtedly contains a grain of truth, our people spent its infancy in exile, in the Egyptian house of bondage; and without the will for redemption, the departure from Egypt would have been impossible. Without this will, they would not have conquered the Promised Land. As for the prophets who molded the ancient character of our people, the will for redemption and the vision of redemption pulsate in all their prophecies, ideals, commands, and visions.

### The Vision that Revived Israel

In our day we have seen a number of nations in Europe, Asia, and Africa that have emerged from bondage to freedom. India, Burma, Ceylon, and other countries gained their independence almost simultaneously with the State of Israel. But everyone knows the fundamental difference between the rise of Israel and that of those countries. The nations of India, Burma, and Ceylon lived on their own territories all the time; but at certain periods they fell under the domination of foreign conquerors. When they cast off foreign rule, they were left independent. Not so with Israel. Nor does the rise of Israel resemble the rise of the United States, Canada, Australia, or the Latin American countries. These countries were rediscovered by conquering voyagers from Spain, Portugal, and Britain. The metropolis in Europe sent them emigrants whom they settled, and after the settlers had arrived at a certain degree of development, they split off from the metropolis by force or by agreement, and took over command of their own affairs. The rise of Israel, like the survival of Israel in exile, is a unique phenomenon in world history, and it can shed light on the riddle of the survival of Israel in exile.

The Jewish state was revived in a period when the House of Israel in the diaspora was not as wholehearted and united as it was 200 years ago in its faith, neither in the observance of the laws and commandments nor in the "religious idea," in which Professor Kaufmann sees the secret of the survival of Judaism. There is no doubt, however, that without the forces that preserved Judaism in the diaspora, we would not have achieved the revival of Israel. It was not a conquering and settling power, nor an enslaved nation in its own land casting off the foreign yoke, that revived Israel. *In the beginning of our revival was the vision.*

The State of Israel was established in a country that had been inhabited by Arabs for 1,400 years, and it is surrounded on the south, the east, and the north by Arab countries. The Land of Israel itself was ruined and impoverished, and the standard of living in it was lower than that of the countries from which the Jews who began to rebuild it came. As late as 1918, at the end of World War I, there were fewer than 60,000 Jews in this country, i.e., fewer than 10 percent of its non-Jewish inhabitants. And yet in this land there has arisen in our days the Jewish state. The second thing that has happened is also unique: the Hebrew language, which the people appeared to have laid aside for 2,000 years, came to life again and became the language of speech, life, and literature, and of the revived State of Israel. Nothing like this has ever happened in the history of language. We know of the tremendous effort that the Republic of Ireland has been devoting for decades to the revival of the Gaelic tongue, and yet all these efforts have utterly failed, although the Irish people has been living in its own land all the time, and this nation—which is not yet entirely free from its profound hatred of the English who ruled it so long—continues to speak the English language. Still a third thing has happened in Israel: In this country the Jews have fundamentally transformed their economic way of life and taken up manual labor and the tilling of the soil.

What, therefore, is the explanation of this extraordinary political and cultural phenomenon, which has no parallel in human history?

The messianic vision of redemption, the profound spiritual attachment to Israel's ancient homeland and to the Hebrew language, in which the Book of Books is written, were the deep and never-failing springs from which the scattered sons of Israel in the diaspora drew for hundreds of years the moral and spiritual strength to resist all the difficulties of exile and to survive until the coming of national redemption.

Anyone who does not realize that the messianic vision of redemption is central to the uniqueness of our people does not understand the basic truth of Jewish history and the cornerstone of the Jewish faith. The spiritual and political transformations that have taken place in the Jewish people in the course of thousands of years have affected the characteristics and the expression of this vision. It did not assume the same form in all periods, just as Judaism as a whole assumed different forms at different times. But through all these changes the inner kernel was preserved, the kernel whose first germination we see in the State of Israel.

Within the consciousness of the Jewish people there were indissolubly combined special and distinctive national elements, confined to the Jewish people, and cosmic, human elements that are outside of any national, or even human, framework, for they embrace the entire universe. The supreme expression of this combination was the messianic vision of redemption; the people's prophets and teachers aspired to complete national redemption in the Promised Land, but this aspiration was not limited to the Jewish people. It brought tidings of peace, justice, and equality to all the peoples—tidings of complete redemption for humanity and the ending of all cruelty and tyranny the world over.

In the messianic vision of redemption an organic bond was woven between Jewish national redemption and general human redemption. The inner necessity of this combination will be fully understood in our own days. In this generation more than at any other period in the history of mankind, nations are interdependent, and even the mightiest of nations cannot safeguard its sovereignty, security, and peace without bonds with other nations. Although the world is in a state of division and disintegration, it is in fact one world; and in spite of numerous and bitter conflicts, its oneness and its unification are gathering strength with the achievements of science and technology and modern means of communication, which abolish distance. The redemption of our people, therefore, is impossible, and its peace and security cannot be safeguarded, without the redemption of the world as a whole, without the achievement of general international peace, and without the establishment of peace and equality among the nations. For this reason the prophets and teachers of Israel did not promise redemption alone, but demanded that their people be a chosen people. The prophet Isaiah denounced his people with all the implacability of a man who was bound to the truth, and foretold the destruction of cruelty and tyranny in the world and the exaltation of all men when he said: "And I will punish the world for their evil, and the wicked for their iniquity; and I will cause the arrogancy of the proud to cease, and will lay low the haughtiness of the terrible. I will make a man more precious than fine gold; even a man than the gold of Ophir" (Isa. 11–12). Yet he believed in the great mission of his people, and said in the name of God: "I the Lord, have called thee in righteousness, and held thee by the hand, and made thee a covenant for the peoples" (Isa. 42:6).

These two motifs—the vision of redemption and the chosen people—are repeated in the books of the Bible and the apocryphal literature, in the Mishna and the Midrash, in the Jewish liturgy and in Hebrew poetry. The greatest of Jewish philosophers—who seemed to have become estranged from his people after he had been excommunicated by the Amsterdam community, who denied religious tradition and laid the foundation for the criticism of the Bible on the basis of reason and logic—even he expressed, in his *Tractatus Theologicus-Politicus* 300 years ago, his absolute confidence that the day would come when the Jewish people would reestablish its state and God would choose it afresh. In other words, upon the renewal of its national sovereignty the Jewish people would again be a chosen people, showing the way to the world. The men who saw the vision of the Jewish state in the nineteenth century, Moses Hess and Theodor Herzl, also believed that it would be a moral state.

Naturally, so long as all Jewish communities were immersed in religious life, both the vision of redemption and the idea of a chosen people, as well as the attachment to the land, also took on religious characteristics. The history of our days has shown that neither the vision of redemption nor the attachment to the land and the Hebrew language are conditional on attachment to tradition and religious law. In the building and defense of the Jewish state, religious and freethinking Jews took part with equal devotion, and the opposition to the work of settlement that brought about the creation of the state came with considerable force from both Orthodox and nonreligious circles.

The former saw in the attempts to establish the state by natural means a dangerous divergence from the traditional faith in the coming of the Messiah, while the latter saw in the return to the ancient homeland a danger to emancipation and the status of the Jews in the diaspora. Although the anxieties of both sides were not entirely baseless, the revival of Israel aroused joy and pride in all sections of the Jewish people, wherever they lived, and apart from the opposition of the two extremes—Neturei Karta and the Communists—there was no Jew in the world who did not enthusiastically welcome the establishment of the state.

On this occasion I will not renew the argument as to whether the state was created by the immigrants or by the Zionist organization. I will say only that it is now the greatest asset, and perhaps the only common asset, of the entire Jewish people, for in most of the values of Judaism the Jewish people in our day is divided and splintered. In the diaspora,

Jews have no common language, no specific way of life, no general attachment to the Jewish law and tradition, no common conception of the nature and the future of Judaism.

### Jewish Demography

In order to understand the function of the state in Jewish history from now on, it it necessary to discuss two further changes that radically altered the nature of the Jewish people in the first half of the present century, before the rise of the state.

At the beginning of the twentieth century there were ten and a half million Jews in the world. More than 80 percent of them (8,673,000) were concentrated in Europe, and fewer than 10 percent lived on the American continent: about one million in the United States, and about 50,000 in the other countries of the New World. At that time, about 700,000 Jews lived in Asia and Africa, and about 55,000 in the Land of Israel. Before the beginning of World War II, the Jewish people numbered about sixteen and a half million, and although in the meantime millions had emigrated overseas, the great majority of the Jewish People, almost nine million souls, lived in Europe. European Jewry, especially that of Eastern Europe, had been for the previous three centuries the Mother of Jewry: It housed the centers of learning; within it there arose the emancipation movement; in it there were born the Haskala and modern Hebrew and Yiddish literatures. In its midst Jüdische Wissenschaft flourished; from it there grew the Hibbat Zion movement and the Jewish workers movement; and when the First Zionist Congress was convened at the end of the nineteenth century by the creator of political Zionism, Dr. Theodor Herzl, European Jewry was the major part, the fortress and support, of the Zionist movement.

In the Zionist movement we must distinguish between ancient sources, almost as ancient as the Jewish people itself, and new circumstances and factors that grew on the soil of the modern era in Europe in the nineteenth century and the beginning of the twentieth. These ancient sources are the profound spiritual attachment to the ancient homeland and the messianic hope. Their beginning is bound up with the life of the first Hebrew, to whom, according to tradition, the promise was given: "And I shall give thee and thy seed all the land of Canaan for an everlasting heritage." It was neither Herzl, nor Hess, nor even Baruch Spinoza who invented the idea of a Jewish state. For thousands of years Jews prayed three times a day: "Blow the great trumpet for our freedom and raise the banner for the ingathering of our exiles, and gather us together from the four corners of the earth, and may our eyes behold the return to Zion in mercy." The sporadic waves of immigration from various countries, the visits of emissaries from Palestine to the various parts of the diaspora, the messianic movements that arose from time to time, from the period following the destruction of the Temple to the eighteenth century—all these were a real and living expression of the attachment and the longing for the homeland, and the hopes that throbbed in the hearts of the people for national redemption and salvation.

Until the beginning of the emancipation in the nineteenth century, all Jews, wherever they were, knew that the places where they lived were only temporary exiles; and it did not even occur to them that they were a part of the peoples among whom they lived, just as such an idea was foreign to those peoples themselves. This feeling of being foreign existed in East European Jewry till the last moment. The Jewries of Russia, Poland, Romania, and the Balkans knew all the time that they were a minority people in a foreign land, and in the 1880s there began a mass migration from the countries of the East to lands overseas.

This feeling of foreignness, which was expressed in the word galut existed in all the generations after the destruction of the Second Temple. The Jewish faith, the messianic hope, and the feeling of moral superiority, enabled the Jews to overcome all the troubles and persecutions and sufferings that were their lot in most countries and in most historical periods. In this capacity for resisting external pressure there was a kind of great moral heroism, but it was a passive heroism, for it was accompanied by a submission to fate and a feeling of helplessness. The longed-for redemption was to come by supernatural means.

### The Modern Movement of Redemption

The revolutionary events of the nineteenth century, the movements of national revival that arose in several European countries, aiming at unification and independence (in Italy, Germany, Poland, and the Balkans), the wakening of a working class to fight for a new social system, the mass migration from Europe to countries overseas—all these opened up in the nineteenth century a new road for the vision of messianic redemption, straightened the backs of the Jews, strengthened their consciousness of their own value and standing, and revealed the possibilities of redemption that were latent in Jewish migration. Faith grew in the capacity of the Jew to rebel against his destiny, to liberate himself by his own strength from the bonds of exile, to bring the redemption nearer by natural means, by a planned effort of settlement.

A new phenomenon appeared that changed the course of Jewish

history: the phenomenon that we call *halutziut* (pioneering)—the creative and revolutionary capacity for action that brings into play the human faculties for realizing the ideal without recoiling from any difficulty or danger; that brings into action all the physical and spiritual powers, and strives with every ounce of energy toward the goal of redemption. This creative and active faith was at first the heritage of a few, but the life's example of those who began the work of implementation slowly influenced hundreds, thousands, and later even tens of thousands, and the impetus of *halutziut* transformed Hibbat Zion and the Zionist movement into historic forces.

There were also pioneering phenomena in previous centuries—in the days of Don Josef Nasi in the sixteenth century; in the days of the immigration to the Land of Israel of Rabbi Judah Hasid and his companions at the beginning of the seventeenth century; and in the days of Rabbi Hayim Abulafia in the middle of the eighteenth century. These, however, were sporadic phenomena that were not continued. Only in the last quarter of the nineteenth century did the pioneering spark flame up and grow and incessantly gather strength, until it arose like a pillar of fire lighting the way for the loyal sons of the Jewish people in all parts of the diaspora to the establishment of the Jewish state.

Without the guidance of a social ideal, which was also born in the nineteenth century, the pioneering impetus would have lost its way and wasted its efforts, and the Jewish state would not have been established: This was the idea that labor is the principal foundation for a healthy national life. Not only did the Jews in the disapora live in exile and depend on the decisions of others, but the structure of their economic and social life was different from that of any independent people living in its own land and controlling its own destiny. The Jews were landless, and were not employed in the principal branches of the economy on which the self-supporting existence of a nation depends. Without a mass return to the soil and to labor, without the transformation of the economic and social structure of the Jewish population in the Land of Israel, we would never have arrived at a Jewish state. It is impossible to conceive of a state the majority of whose people does not work the soil and carry out the types of work required for its economic survival.

The feeling of foreignness, either as a reaction to anti-Semitism in central and western Europe or as the outcome of the consciousness of a specific Jewish character and the absence of a traditional bond with the gentile nation and its culture, as in Eastern Europe; the example of the national and social liberation movements; and the recognition of the value of labor as the main basis for national life—all these were common to large parts of European Jewry, and almost only of European Jewry. It was there that there appeared the pioneering movement that transformed the aspiration of generations into an act of daily implementation; it was this movement that laid the foundations for the Jewish state, the most wonderful event in the life of the Jewish people since the conquests of Joshua, son of Nun.

But during the twenty-eight years between the end of World War I and the end of World War II, European Jewry was visited by two appalling disasters: One-third of East European Jewry was cut off from world Jewry by force about forty years ago, at the end of World War I, by the Bolsheik regime in Russia; and about two-thirds were slaughtered by the Nazi butchers during World War II.

This was a double disaster, unparalleled even in the history of our people, that visited us in the first half of this century, before the establishment of the state. Only scanty fragments of European Jewry were left in freedom, and the period of European Jewry in the life of the Jewish people came to an end, never to return. In the second half of this century, however, there was a second change, a fruitful and beneficial one, in the growth of the great Jewish center in the United States of America, from one million at the beginning of the century to more than five million in our own day. And this was not only a quantitative growth. In the foremost country of the New World there grew a Jewish center, the likes of which was never seen in the diaspora for wealth, influence, and power, for political and spiritual capacity. And this Jewry, which had first considered itself a spiritual "colony" of European Jewry, has become in our own day the political, material, and cultural metropolis of diaspora Jewry.

Here there arose a great labor movement, though it is now shrinking as the second and third generations of the immigrants go over to trade and industry and the free professions. Here there arose important centers of Jewish scholarship, Jewish universities and academies for teachers and rabbis. Here the feeling of exile and foreignness grew weaker and disappeared completely, and although the ideology of assimilation struck no roots in American Jewry, assimilation in practice—in language, culture, manners, economy, and political life—is constantly growing. The Jews of America, including the Zionists among them, see themselves as part of the American people, while at the same time they consider themselves a Jewish community; their hearts are alert to every Jewish cause, and their material and political assistance in the building of the *yishuv* and the establishment of the state have been of inestimable value.

When the Jewish state arose in the middle of 1948, the character, status, distribution, and conditions of life of the Jewish people were completely different from what they were at the end of the nineteenth and the beginning of the twentieth centuries.

### The State—A New Chapter

The rise of Israel opened a new chapter not only in the history of this country, but in the history of Jewry as a whole. It straightened the back of every Jew wherever he lived; in the course of a few years it redeemed hundreds of thousands of Jews from poverty and degeneration in exile, and transformed them into proud, creative Jews, the builders and defenders of their country; it poured new hope into the hearts of the helpless and muzzled Jews of the Soviet bloc; it revealed the extraordinary capacity of Jews for accomplishment in all spheres of human creative work; it revived Jewish heroism; it assured every Jew who enjoys freedom of movement of the opportunity to live in his independent homeland if he chooses to do so, thus ensuring potentially, if not in practice, a life of independence for the entire Jewish people.

On the international scene there appeared a free Jewish nation, equal in rights to the rest of the family of nations. It is not remarkable that all parts of the Jewish people in the diaspora—whether they called themselves Zionists or non-Zionists, Orthodox or nonreligious, whether they lived in lands of prosperity and freedom or in lands of poverty and enslavement—welcomed the rise of the state with love and pride, and the state became the central pillar on which the unity of diaspora Jewry now rests. Let us not, however, be overconfident; the vision of redemption brought forth the State, but the state is still far from the realization of the vision.

The state has solved a number of problems, and also produced new ones. Jewish sovereignty enables the Jew in Israel to mold his own needs and values, in loyalty solely to his own spirit, his historic heritage, his vision of the future. In Israel, the barrier between the Jew and the human being has fallen. The Jews in their own state are no longer subject to two opposing and conflicting authorities: on the one hand, the authority of the gentile people in all economic, political, and social matters and in most spiritual and cultural questions, as citizens and subjects of a state with a non-Jewish (or even anti-Jewish) majority; and on the other hand, their own authority in the one small and poor corner that draws its sustenance only from the past, in which they function as members of the Mosaic faith or of the Jewish people in the world.

Israel has restored to the people living in its midst their wholeness as Jews and human beings; the sovereign Jewish authority covers all the needs, acts, and aspirations of man in Israel. In Israel the profound cleavage, which in the diaspora split, and still splits, the lives and souls of Jews, has been healed—the cleavage that impoverished both the man in the Jew and the Jew in the man. Our lives have again become, as in the days of the Bible, a complete unity of existence and experience that embraces in a Jewish framework all the contents of the life of man and people, all his acts, needs, aspirations, cares, problems, and hopes.

In Israel there has been created not only the Jewish field, the Jewish sea, the Jewish road, the Jewish factory, the Jewish laboratory, Jewish science and research dealing with all that the world contains and not only with Jüdische Wissenschaft. Here there has arisen a Jewish political life, and Jewish literature, poetry, and art once again draw their sustenance from all the natural and living sources that sustain us. The single, complete authority makes everything human Jewish, and everything Jewish human.

Only here, where we have become free citizens in the State of Israel, have we become citizens of the world, with equal rights, who must adopt an attitude of our own on all the problems of the world and the relations between nations. This sovereignty also imposes on us heavy responsibilities that were unknown to Jews in the world for many centuries: We bear full responsibility for our fate and our future, and we have a heavy price to pay for this responsibility.

I will not go into Israel's political and economic problems, but I must deal with its internal problems and its bonds with world Jewry. I will say only a few words on the decisive and fateful political problem of Israel: the problem of security. The solution of this problem does not lie in the organization of a first-class army—and no one will suspect me of any desire to belittle the value of the Israel Defense Forces. The survival and the peace of the State of Israel will be safeguarded by one thing and one thing alone—large-scale immigration. For the safeguarding of its security, the state requires an addition of at least two million Jews in the coming period.

### The State's Two Supreme Laws

This state has been established by the strength of the entire Jewish people, not only that of the Jewish people who live in our own generation; I have no doubt that all generations of Jewry have a share in the extraordinary and tremendous accomplishment of our day: The state has been established for the entire Jewish People. But in practice the state is today inhabited by about 20 percent of the Jewish people. For this reason alone, the state considers itself no more than a beginning. The State of Israel has two central objectives that were laid down in the Proclamation of Independence and in two special laws that—although they are not called basic laws—I consider to be the supreme laws of the State of Israel, destined to be a light for the generations. Until these are fully implemented the work of the State of Israel will not be completed.

The first is the Law of Return, which contains the objective of the ingathering of the exiles. This law decrees that it is not the state that grants a Jew the right to settle in Israel, but that this is his right by reason of the fact that he is a Jew, if only he wishes to join the population of the country. In Israel a Jewish citizen has no privileges over the non-Jewish citizen.

In the Proclamation of Independence we laid down that "the State of Israel will uphold the full social and political equality of all its citizens, without distinction of religion, race, or sex," but the state sees the right of Jews to return to the Land of Israel as preceding its foundation, and having its source in the historic and never-broken bond between the Jews and their ancient homeland. The Law of Return is not like immigration laws existing in other countries, which lay down the conditions under which the state receives immigrants from abroad. The Law of Return is the law of the historic permanence and continuity of the bond between the land and our people; it lays down the principle of state by virtue of which the State of Israel has been revived.

Within the few years in which the state has been in existence, complete communities, from Asia, Europe, and America, have returned to Israel, but we are still at the beginning of the process of the ingathering of the exiles. None of us can foretell the potential scope of this ingathering. There are Jewish communities that wish to come here and are not permitted to do so. There are Jewish communities that have the permission, but do not have the will. But there is not a single Jewish community in the world that does not send some Jews to Israel, whether the number is small or great. The two forces that were active in the process of aliyah before the rise of the state—distress and the vision of redemption—have now been reinforced by the attractive power of Israel, its freedom and independence, and its creative momentum. Only the future will show what parts of our people will return to the homeland, but we are certain that the millions of Jews who long to come to Israel and who for decades have been deprived of the right to do so will surely come in the end.

The second law determines the social direction of the state and the character to which we aspire for the people of Israel—and it is contained in the State Education Law. Paragraph two of this law says: "The object of State education is to base elementary education in the State on the values of Israel and the achievements of science; on the love of the homeland and devotion to the State of Israel and the Jewish people; on training in agricultural labor and handicraft; on pioneering implementation; on striving for a society built on freedom, equality, tolerance, mutual assistance, and love of humanity." This law lays down the main themes for making us into a model people and a model state, and asserts our unfailing bond with the Jewish people in the world.

Our historic goal is a new society built on freedom, equality, tolerance, mutual assistance, and love of humanity—in other words, a society without exploitation, discrimination, enslavement, the rule of man over man, the violation of conscience, and tyranny. This law also expresses our aspiration to develop in Israel a culture built on the values of Judaism and the achievements of science. And the law demands devotion not only to the state but also to the Jewish people.

Both this law and the Law of Return are far from a state of complete realization; they are only signposts by which the state wishes, and is bound, to be guided, so that it may survive and achieve its historic aim.

We cannot boast that the people of Israel are today a model people, although within our short period of independence we have perhaps made relatively more progress than any other country in a similar period. Our society is far from perfect, and it needs reforms. Nor can we congratulate ourselves that by our ingathering of Jews after the rise of the state we have carried out "the ingathering of the exiles." But I shall try briefly to describe both the historic necessity of making this country into a model state, and the qualifications we possess to carry out such a great ideal, as well as the need and the prospects for the ingathering of the exiles to the maximum extent.

### Israel's Faithful Ally

Israel has one faithful ally in the world: the Jewish people. Israel is the only country in the world that has no "relatives" from the point of view of religion, language, origin, or culture, such as are possessed by the Scandinavian peoples, the English-speaking peoples, the Arab peoples, the Catholic peoples, the Buddhist peoples, etc. We are a people that lives alone. Our nearest neighbors, both from the geographical point of view and from the point of view of race and language, are our bitterest enemies, and I am afraid they will not speedily be reconciled to our existence and our growth. The only loyal ally we have is the Jewish people.

Considerable parts of scattered Jewry will join us in the near future: both Jews from the Islamic countries and Jews from Europe, as well as no small number from the Jewries of the prosperous countries. But there was a Jewish diaspora as early as the days of the First Temple, which preceded the Babylonian exile; this diaspora was in Egypt. During the period of the Second Temple the diaspora grew, and it is hard to imagine that the Third Commonwealth will absorb the whole of the diaspora of our day. The survival of Jewry from now on is inconceivable without the State of Israel and an inner attachment to that state. But the survival of the state is also inconceivable without a loyal partnership between it and all the Jewries of the diaspora. Without a moral, cultural, and political illumination that will go out from Israel to all parts of the diaspora, this partnership may be undermined. The War of Independence and the Sinai Campaign aroused Jewish pride and raised the status of Jews among the Jewish people and in the whole world. But the State of Israel was not created to be a Jewish Sparta, and it is not by military heroism that it will win the admiration of the Jewish people.

Only by being a model nation, of which every Jew, wherever he is, can be proud, shall we preserve the love of the Jewish people and its loyalty to Israel. Our status in the world, too, will not be determined by our material wealth or by our military heroism, but by the radiance of our achievements, our culture, and our society—and only by virtue of these will we acquire the friendship of the nations. And although there is no lack of shadows—most of them heavy—in our lives today, we have sufficient grounds for the faith that we have it in our power to be a model people.

It is already possible to point to three elements in Israel today that give clear indications of the moral and intellectual capacities latent within us: They are the labor settlements, the Israel Defense Forces, and our men of science, research, literature, and art, who can bear comparison in their relative quantity and high quality with those of any other people in the world.

The labor settlements have marked new roads toward a society built on liberty, equality, and mutual assistance that have no parallel in any country, in the East or the West. The Israel Defense Forces are not only a loyal and effective instrument for defense, but an educational framework that raises human standards, breaks down communal barriers, and gives the youth of Israel self-confidence, responsibility to the community, and a vision for the future.

And although in the few years of our sovereign independence we have been compelled to invest tremendous resources in defense, in the absorption of immigrants, and in the building of our economy, and we shall have to continue to do so for many years to come, we have succeeded in establishing institutions of science and research and development, literature and art, on a level as high as that of the most developed countries.

I am not one of those who engage in destructive criticism of science, as if the law of causality had been abolished and there was a doubt of the existence of matter, and the undermining of science had restored us to faith in the miracle of revelation. I am one of the "conservatives." Einstein, it will be remembered, continued to believe in the law of causality even after the quantum theory. And in my humble opinion, if I may say so, matter has not been abolished, but the identity of matter and energy has been revealed. It may be said that in a way the duality of matter has been broken down by science, and we still remain within the bonds of experience and the reign of material laws. Science, however, does not tell man what path to choose in life, for science is beyond good and evil. Without religious or moral or spiritual values, man has no reliable guide in life, and the human race has no more exalted values than those bequeathed to us and to the world by the prophets of Israel.

Just as we must not belittle the tremendous difficulties that face Israel in the political and economic spheres, so we must not ignore the moral difficulties that are strewn in our path: the habits of diaspora life; the lack of education and political capacity, our overfragmentation; our exaggerated partisanship; the undermining of tradition; absorption difficulties; the influence of inferior books and periodicals from within and without; the numerous crimes among immigrants who have not become integrated, and Israeli youth who have lost all spiritual and social values.

We shall not consolidate our national standing and security in one day, nor shall we achieve our economic independence without difficulty, and certainly we shall not become a model people without constant effort and social struggle. There is also a mutual influence between our economic position and our political status on the one hand, and our capacity for spiritual and social advancement on the other. Matter and spirit are not two separate realms. The creation of the body and soul are dependent on each other. We have in store a difficult and prolonged effort in all spheres—economic, political, social, and cultural. But the history of the Jewish people in all periods, and the capacity that has been revealed since the establishment of the state, the extraordinary transformation that has been achieved among hundreds of thousands of immigrants in a short space of time—all these may strengthen our faith that in the end we shall accomplish our aim, though much depends on the attitude, the cooperation, and the will of the diaspora.

## The Diaspora of Today

We are now faced with a Jewish diaspora that is radically different from that which existed fifty years ago. The two largest and most important centers of Jewry in the diaspora are in the United States and the Soviet Union. The greater part of the Jewry of the Moslem countries has already come to Israel, and it may be assumed that most of the remainder will also come here within the next few years. American Jewry is different from any Jewish community we have known so far in our history, from Babylonian Jewry in ancient times to Russian Jewry in the days of the tsars. It has grown up in freedom and equality, and all those among whom American Jews live are descendants of immigrants like themselves. In one thing alone does it resemble all the other Jewish communities in the diaspora: Its economic and social structures are different from those of the majority of American people. The Jews of America belong more and more to the middle and upper classes; the number of farmers is almost nil, and the number of workers is constantly declining. Jews are being absorbed in trade, industry, and the free professions, and they are making great material progress in these vocations. How this will influence their situation and the attitude of the majority to them time alone will tell.

In all other respects there is no difference between Jews and non-Jews. There is no ideology of assimilation among the American Jews, but there has been an increase in assimilation in practice, although this assimilation does not involve the denial of Jewishness. This Jewishness, however, has few and feeble foundations. There is an increase in religious worship, but it is doubtful whether it involves an intensification of religious consciousness. Membership in a synagogue or a temple is not identical with an attachment to traditional law or to the spiritual values of the prophets of Israel. Members of the bodies that belong to the Zionist Organization are no different from those Jews who do not belong to that organization. Zionism in America is not based on the consciousness of exile and foreignness, or on the will and the need to turn to Zion. Any comparison between the fate of European Jewry and that of Jewry in the United States—whether for good or for ill—is baseless. There is nothing to prevent the Jews in America from preserving their Jewishness and their bond with Zion, but at the same time there is no internal or external obligation to do so. Any scientific prognosis based on historical necessity—if scientific prognoses are possible at all in history—is likely to be disproved. There is no particular usefulness in abstract discussions of the future of Jewry in America—but we should discuss what is to be done to safeguard its future in accordance with our Jewish aspirations and needs.

The position of Jewry in the Soviet bloc, and especially in the Soviet Union, is different. This Jewry has been condemned to disintegration for about forty years by a hostile, totalitarian regime. The generation that has grown up under Bolshevik rule cannot receive any Jewish education, and it has been forcibly severed from its historical tradition and its bonds with the Jewish people and the Land of Israel. It cannot read and write either Hebrew or Yiddish. It is forbidden to leave Russia. And had it not been for the rise of Israel, it would have been condemned sooner or later to disappearance, in the Jewish sense.

But even a totalitarian regime is neither all-powerful nor safe against change and fluctuation. In contradiction to the declared theory of self-determination for all the peoples in the Soviet Union, the Jews, although they officially belong to a Jewish nationality, do not enjoy this right. The Birobidzhan experiment was a complete failure, and anti-Semitism in the Soviet Union, although it is forbidden by law, has neither ceased nor weakened. This fact, no less than the fact of the existence of the State of Israel, encourages and strengthens Jewish feeling, although under the conditions of the Communist regime they have no organized or cultural expression. The Jewish problem in Russia becomes more and more troublesome even from the point of view of the Russians, and it is not impossible that ultimately, and perhaps even in the next few years, they may arrive at the only real solution: the opening of the gates for the aliyah of these Jews to Israel. According to reliable information, the number of Jews in Russia is from three million to three and a half million. If the gates are opened, it may be assumed that at least half of Russian Jewry will come to Israel, and the State of Israel and the entire Jewish people must prepare for this possibility—a possibility that involves both tremendous difficulties and beneficial prospects such as we have not yet known for the state and the future of the Jewish people as a whole.

Even though more than 80 percent of diaspora Jewry is concentrated in the two great world powers, we must not neglect the Jewish communities in the other prosperous countries—in Western Europe, Canada, Latin America, South Africa, Australia, and New Zealand. Conditions in these countries are not exactly identical with those in the United States, but there is a considerable resemblance. Here, too, there is no point in engaging in abstract prognoses. What we have to deal with are methods of work and the means of deepening the consciousness of the Jewish mission and Jewish unity. In my opinion these methods are threefold:

1. Hebrew education, the central place in which will be held by the study of the Book of Books.
2. The intensification of the personal bond with Israel in all forms: visits; investment of capital; education of children, youth, and university students in Israel for longer or shorter periods of time; training for the best of the youth and the intelligentsia to fit them to join the builders and the defenders of the country.
3. Deepening the attachment to the messianic vision of redemption that is the vision of Jewish and human redemption held by prophets of Israel.

These three elements are the common denominator that can unite religious, Orthodox, Conservative, Reform, and freethinking Jewry, and give Jewish meaning, purpose, and significance even to those Jews who will not join in the process of the ingathering of the exiles. It is these three elements that can serve as a moral and cultural bond between diaspora Jewry and Israel. Attachment to Hebrew culture, and first and foremost to the Book of Books, in the original; attachment to Israel; and attachment to the messianic vision of redemption, redemption both Jewish and human—that is the threefold cord that can unite and bind together all sections of Jewry, of all parties and of all communities. And if we will it, it shall never be broken.

# 2

# Israel's Mission and Zion

## MARTIN BUBER

It seems to me that Ben-Gurion was justified in taking issue with the view that monotheism is the distinguishing feature that separates Israel from all other nations. He was not justified, however, in maintaining the thesis that the combination of religion and ethics distinguishes Israel from all other nations.

Monotheism, that religious view which holds that there is only one God, developed among a number of peoples, albeit in varying degrees of intensity and emphasis. And there is no need to assume that one people borrowed the idea from another. The combination of religion and ethics is also to be found, for example, in the early teachings of India and Persia. What is peculiar to Israel is the demand that the people submit its entire life, including its social and political activity, to the will of God as the true King. We have here not a combination of religion and ethics, but a complete, all-pervading unity.

That which distinguishes the monotheism of Judaism from all other monotheisms is the all-embracing subservience to the divine Ruler, extending, without exception, over all areas of national life. It is the will of this God that the human world recognize his sovereignty freely and in deed. And of Israel He requires that it begin to give exemplary expression to His kingdom by subjecting its whole social life to His rule, which means the realization of justice and truth both in its internal and external national relationships, and in the private conduct of the individual in Israel, especially in his behavior as a member of society and as a citizen of the state.

### Not a Theocracy

This aspiration, and the social order at which it aims, cannot be called a theocracy in the ordinary meaning of that term, which, as is well known, originates in Josephus and refers to the hegemony of the priest-hood. Biblical theocracy appeared in two forms: The first was primitive rule, as described in the Book of Judges, according to which, in those early days, in times of crisis men, seized by the spirit, pronounced judgment in the name of God who alone is the Ruler. The second was the historical form, whose essence found expression in the fact that the prophets anointed the kings to be God's representatives, and in the repeated demand of the prophets that the kings fulfill the obligation imposed upon them at the time of the anointing, the obligation to incorporate the divine ideals of justice and truth in the social and political life of the people. These prophets are men bereft of all political power and able only to protest. Thus they stand before the rulers and protest in the name of their God, and in His name they confront the rulers with the fateful choice.

True, other peoples of the ancient East also believed that the king was responsible for his deeds to "his father," the God who adopted him and gave him dominion. But this relationship of responsibility was expressed only in symbolic form. We know, for example, that in Babylon the high priest approached the king on New Year's Day and slapped him, and immediately after this ritual everything returned to its former state and the king continued to act as before.

In biblical religion, however, you will find no symbolic rite performed with regard to the kings outside of the solitary rite of anointing. Thus, "for his iniquities," for the iniquities of the king, called "the son of God" (2 Sam. 7:14), God commands him to be chastised "with the rod of men," and this is actually carried out; and the prophets come as messengers of heaven and censure him for betraying his mission, and prophesy that calamity will befall him and his people if he does not mend his ways and does not fulfill the obligations assumed in the act of being anointed. This mission they performed at the risk of their lives. This is the transcendent realism that distinguishes the faith of Israel: There is no room here for empty symbols.

## The Glory of Israel

What exactly was it that the prophets censured when they faced the rulers? It was the means that they used to arrive at their ultimate goal, concerning which the prophets did not differ—the glory of Israel. These means contradicted the ends, and one of the unexpressed principles of prophecy is that ends do not justify the means. And if the nature of the means is in contradiction to the nature of the end, they desecrate it, poison it, and make of it a thing of horror.

Youth in Israel *is* very much interested in certain parts of the Bible, especially in the stories about the conquest of the land, in the stories of hero-kings, and also in some words of the prophets. But on no account are the prophets to be regarded apart from the historic mission that sent them to those men who had seized the reins of power, in order to summon them to stand in judgment before their God who made them king provisionally.

Ben-Gurion rightly sees in the messianic vision the second cornerstone of living Judaism. But this also is in need of greater concreteness. It is not enough to set "the redemption of Israel" side by side with "the redemption of the human race." The messianic message is unique in the demand God makes upon the nations of men to realize His kingdom and in this way to take part in the redemption of the world. The message is applied especially to Israel, and demands of it that it make an exemplary beginning in the actual work of realization, that it be a nation that establishes justice and truth in its institutions and activities. Therefore, Isaiah not only calls upon the gentiles to stream to Mount Zion and there receive the second Torah, the universal one; he supplements this by his summons to the House of Jacob to walk before them in the light of the Lord.

### The Life of Service

Just as the monotheism of Israel differed from the others in that, according to it, the people should live their whole lives as one great service of God, so did the tidings of redemption differ in Israel from all others in that they summoned the people to begin doing their part in putting this idea into actual practice. We do not have here only thoughts and visions, but actual demands on whose fulfillment hangs the destiny of the people. These demands are not only directed to the generations to whom they were first presented, but to all the generations, and especially to ours, the first generation after 2,000 years that has the prerequisite for fulfilling its task—that is, independence of a strong nucleus. This gives our generation at long last the power to determine for itself in no small measure its institutions, its modes of life, and its relations to other nations.

Behind everything that Ben-Gurion has said on that point there lies, it seems to me, the will to make the political factor supreme. He is one of the proponents of that kind of secularization that cultivates its "thoughts" and "visions" so diligently that it keeps men from hearing the voice of the living God. This secularization takes the form of an exaggerated politicization. This politicization of life here strikes at the very spirit itself. The spirit, with all its thoughts and visions, descends and becomes a function of politics. This phenomenon, which is supreme in the whole world at present, has very old roots. Even some kings in Israel are said to have gone so far as to employ false prophets whose prophesying was merely a function of state policy

## The Zionist Mission

Closely connected with all that I have been saying is the problem of Zionism in our day. Ben-Gurion has stated that this no longer has a real or positive content, and that in the eyes of the Israeli generation, in whose name he speaks, it has become an ideological anachronism. Zionism, so his argument runs, means a longing for Zion, and since this longing has already attained its goal, there is no rhyme or reason for Zionism any more. But those who inscribed the name Zion on their banner, first calling themselves Lovers of Zion and thereafter Zionists, did not have in mind something that existed and needed only to be repossessed.

I still recall what this circle of young Zionists to which I belonged some sixty years ago meant by the name. Had we been asked: "Are you striving for a country of Jews in Israel?" we would have answered: "We are striving for Zion and in order to establish Zion we desire independence for our people in our country." Even today there are many Zionists who share this feeling, not only the older ones; I myself know a number who came to the country and who continue to dream this dream that has as yet found no fulfillment, the dream of Zion. They hope with all their hearts that this country, as it is, is the first step in the direction of Zion.

This quasi Zionism that strives to have a country only has attained its purpose. But the true Zionism, the love of Zion, the desire to establish something like "the city of a great king" (Ps. 48:3), of "the king" (Isa. 6:5), is a living and enduring thing. Come, let us awaken this Zionism in the hearts that have never felt it, in the diaspora as well as here. For here in this country also we need a movement that strives for Zion, aspiring toward the emergence of the rebuilt Zion from the materials at our disposal. We need "Zionists of Zion," here and abroad.

## The New Generation

What Ben-Gurion has said about the present Israeli generation is no doubt true of its majority. A remarkable, and at the same time understandable, change has come over us, as over the whole world in our day. After a generation that, though it had performed great things, was unable to confront the catastrophe, there came another generation that clings to the practical execution of great ideas—the execution that took place in our time whether on a large or a small scale (and certainly what was done by us was by no means small). The members of this generation, whether openly or secretly in their hearts, suspect ideas as ideas and put their trust only in tangible reality as such. Is it desirable to advocate such emphasis on the material, which threatens to swallow up the ideas that are still alive, or is it our duty to subdue this trend?

And now Ben-Gurion tells us that Zionist thought is dead but the messianic idea is alive and will live until the coming of the Messiah. And I answer him with the question: "In how many hearts of this generation in our country does the messianic idea live in a form other than the narrow nationalistic form that is restricted to the ingathering of the exiles?" A messianic idea without the yearning for the redemption of mankind, and without the desire to take part in its realization, is no longer identical with the Messianic visions of the prophets of Israel, nor can that prophetic mission be identified with a messianic ideal emptied of belief in the coming of the kingdom of God.

# PART II

# Life After Death: Confronting the Holocaust

# 3

# Lessons of the Holocaust

## ABBA EBAN

### Relevance of the Holocaust

There is little reason why audiences that do not bear a judicial responsibility should hear what three judges in Jerusalem have been called upon to hear about medical experiments, compulsory abortion, sterilization, and skeletons deliberately made available for "racial anthropological research." If the statistics could be translated into human images they would have stunning effect: Maidanek, 200,000 exterminated; Treblinka, 750,000; Belsen, 600,000; and looming above them all, Auschwitz, two and a half million.

This is the story in its barest outline. But the question arises: Why enact it at all? Is it not better to forget? Does not the tormented human imagination deserve respite from the assault of such memories? There are many people of impeccable sincerity who advocate this oblivion. Victor Gollancz, for example, has written, "The sooner we forget the cruelties of the past, the better."

After millions of years of evolution, a species emerges on this planet endowed with the gift of memory and articulation. Man is the only animal able to transmit its experiences and values. The transmission of experience is the central core of education and moral progress. Memory is the father of conscience. Whosoever flees from his memory runs away from the dictates of conscience. It is startling to hear it said that man would be better for the abandonment of his historic experience. Moral and legal concepts have evolved in human society through the incessant exercise of memory in the appraisal of conduct. We are here being asked to wipe from the tablets of memory the most trenchant and illustrative evidence of the consequences flowing from inhumanity. And we are asked to do this within a lifetime of the very generation that performed or witnessed or suffered these acts.

It is no answer to assert that there are other schools in which the lessons of inhumanity may be learned. The element of quantity is decisive in commanding our attention to this, rather than to any better illustration. I dismiss as unworthy of scientific or moral discussion Toynbee's belief that there is no element of quantity in moral judgment and that murder of one and of a million are equivalent in a strict moral perspective.

You have to think of a bureaucratic system under which men arise in the morning, carry out their quota of executions, have lunch, pursue their toil in the afternoon—and then return home to surround their families with a moving affection. Out of the darkest depths of man's divided nature there springs this terrifying organization of cruelty to a point of detachment in comparison with which sheer hatred would almost be a saving grace.

Surely there are lessons to be learned here about the social implications of human nature. The patron saint of this series of lectures on tolerance has been John Stuart Mill. You have heard his optimistic concept of human nature as the basis for his social thought: "Let us emphasize the importance to man and society of giving full freedom to human nature to expand itself in innumerable and conflicting directions."

The assumption is that "the full freedom of human nature to expand itself in innumerable directions" is bound to give a positive direction to moral development. The corollary is the need to offer complete tolerance within society for all ideas, even those whose evolution becomes an assault on society itself. This is the oldest dilemma of liberalism. If a society is free and dedicated to tolerance, must it even tolerate attacks on its own tolerance? Must it give shelter in the name of liberty to the propagation of ideas the ultimate conclusion of which is the destruction of all its higher values? The answer to this problem after the Nazi tragedy cannot be the same as it might have been before. It is demonstrable that this episode could not have reached its plenitude of horror if license had not been given, presumably in the name of liberalism and democracy, to the propagation and publication of Nazi doctrines. Surely we must conclude that even the most liberal of societies is entitled to establish a limit beyond which the dissemination of ideas cannot be protected. If a society can suppress pornography without ceasing to be free, why is it forbidden to establish some criterion whereby ideas fatal to social morality may be denied the sanction or shelter of the law? If the Nazi ideology had been proscribed or even ridiculed in its earliest phase on the plane of academic discourse and public opinion, it is doubtful whether the Nazi movement could have won such massive credibility and support. There may have been some in the universities and academies of the world who thought that Nazi ideas were so grotesque that refutation was not required. The study of the academic movements in Europe during the rise of the Nazi regime reveals a paralyzed failure to quench the flames. The ideological basis of Nazism had been firmly laid before the intellectual community arose to its peril.

Another lesson is that large conclusions flow from small beginnings. It is the small discriminations that begin the sequence. Some of these seem very harmless: the contemptuous reference to an ethnic or religious group; the assumption that they are not endowed with a humanity common to all; that they are rather outside the pale and not human in the fullest sense. These mild expressions of prejudice soon become deadly. They are the beginnings of an evolving process. The outrage of Treblinka and Auschwitz could not have taken place had there not been tens of thousands of men who had grown accustomed to looking at other men as though they were not human at all. A man cannot murder others in cold blood, he cannot dash a baby to the ground, or fling children into a furnace unless he is first convinced that, despite external evidence, they are not a part of his own humanity.

There is another lesson that belongs uniquely to our age. Germany before and during the Nazi regime fostered a highly advanced science and technology. Surely this Nazi tragedy, springing from the center of European civilization, teaches us the fallacy of scientific rationalism uninhibited by moral restraint. There are many who, dazzled by the potentialities of the scientific revolution, demand a shift of emphasis in the educational movement from the human to the natural sciences. The contrary lesson should be drawn from the events that we have here reviewed. The Nazi assault was a unique synthesis between scientific skill and moral degradation. We should not draw back from our admiration of scientific method because it has sometimes been put to perverse use. The critical temper, the constructive rationality, the intellectual humility that are essential in the practice of scientific method are not simply adornments of a well-balanced mind. They are of its very essence. The career of science is a continuing exchange of ideas, and its enduring products are in the end the fruit of a refining process of mutual criticism. But surely in the age of high-energy physics and the conquest of outer space, the problem is not how to generate greater concentrations of power.

The issue is how man can learn to live with the power that science has already generated. Man has probed deeply into the spectacle of nature but stands baffled before the incalculabilities of his inner character; he has exercised dominion over his external realm, but stands helpless before his internal domain. Thus the age of scientific triumph is also the age of anxiety. Man is conscious of his loss of outward and inward wholeness, obsessed by the sense of being a fragment in a fragmentary world. The educational lesson points toward a more humane emphasis. It demands a greater harmony of the scientific and humanistic disciplines. Science creates problems that only the humanities can solve. The humanities transmit to us visions of human excellence that have stirred man throughout the centuries. The purpose must be to remind man of his distinctively human endowments, to multiply and refine his moments of vision. The leaders of the contemporary scientific movement speak with a deep humility about their limitations, and can often be heard urging a greater concentration of research upon the examination and analysis of man's inner domain. The era of high-energy physics was born in fear and havoc, but its destiny is hope and peace. The destiny will be fulfilled only if we avoid distortion of the educational process by the creation of a technocratic race skilled in the manipulations of natural force but lacking the moral force that gives direction to their insights.

### International Consequences

I have spoken of social and educational consequences to be drawn from this lesson. There are, I suggest, international consequences as well. The life of our time is caught up in a strange paradox. Forces are alive in the world moving inexorably toward the unification of humanity; these comprise science and technology, the conquest of distance, the equalization of national rights within the international family, and the trend toward larger regional groupings for economic and political cooperation. The common nuclear peril is also a potent unifying force. But precisely at the time when science and technology require the unification of humanity, there has taken place a new fragmentation of the political map. These small nations have no prospect of assuring their safety except within an international system of security and economic cooperation. The central international issue today is to reconcile the triumph of nationalism with the new impulses of universalism. This seems to me to have very concrete implications for the United Nations, which mirrors the diversity of the international community.

The problem is the role of the United Nations in defense of human rights when these are violated by action of sovereign states.

The pivot of the controversy is Article 2, paragraph 7 of the Charter, which forbids international intervention in matters that fall within the domestic jurisdiction of states. Two views have arisen within the first decade of United Nations jurisprudence. There is the formal view, which recoils from any intervention in whatever goes on within sovereign frontiers of sovereignty; and there is the broader view, expressed in the Covenant of Human Rights and in the growing tendency of the United

Nations to intervene on behalf of world opinion against discrimination and persecution.

It seems that the Nazi tragedy illustrates the necessity for emphasizing the broader view. However the scales were poised before, no one who recalls the Nazi decade can support an unduly formalistic and restrictive interpretation of this Article in the United Nations Charter. As one looks back upon the operation of world opinion in the middle thirties of this century, it is difficult not to be appalled by the docile acceptance of sovereignty as an excuse for inhibiting action and even opinion against the horrors that were taking shape in the Nazi system. With dreadful speed the Nazi administration became an acknowledged part of the international landscape and an accepted subject of international law and relations; reluctantly accepted, perhaps, but accepted nonetheless. The authors of these doctrines and persecutions were not ostracized or submitted to an overwhelming pressure of opinion at the early stage, when that regime could not have survived a purposeful and universal expression of indignation. There were some eloquent manifestations of indignation, but international institutions did not organize a constant and intensive pressure. There was no impression that the regime would suffer in its international and economic position to the point at which the renunciation of these policies might have appeared the most expedient course. For after all, the regime gained nothing from this. It did not even gain strategically. The slaughter was senseless and tragically useless. One of the most extraordinary features of the whole business was the execution of the Final Solution from 1944 until the summer of 1945, when it must already have been evident that the defeat of Germany was assured. Nothing was now to be gained. But the agents of the massacre accelerated the machinery with ardent zeal, as though it was vital that at least this part of the Nazi design should not remain unfulfilled.

I do not dispute that there was sacrifice and solidarity in many lands. But as we look back over the literature and international discussion of the early thirties, we see little in which the leaders of the free world can take pride. We constantly find the slogan about the rights of sovereign states. Mechanistic and formal arguments were raised even against the granting of asylum to the victims. The question whether 10,000 children could be saved was weighed against the transient annoyance of Arab governments. Surely the history will have been in vain if it does not lead to a greater intensity of intervention in defense of human rights.

There are varying degrees of sensitivity to world opinion. But the government has not yet existed that has been able to evince total insensitivity to the expressed view of world opinion. Governments ostensibly totalitarian and immune from the penetration of ideas go to extreme lengths to secure support and approval of their acts. This does not mean that international discussion of violations of human rights should be conducted in anarchy. There are boundaries of moderation here as in everything else. But if we witness a tendency in the work of international organs to transcend the formalistic argument of domestic jurisdiction and to bring the weight of world opinion to bear upon racial discrimination, then there is a salutary and legitimate consequence to be drawn from this tragedy.

There have been other international consequences of the tragedy. Perhaps the very existence of Israel is one of them. One of the impulses that led to Israel's establishment was an awakening of the world's conscience to the necessity for an independent domain of Jewish freedom. This people at the depth of its agony gained nothing that other nations, and especially the neighboring nations, did not obtain with much less sacrifice and in far more lavish measure. But it is an act of requital nonetheless; a burden removed from the international conscience. While Israel is many things in the political and cultural life of our times, it also represents an act of minimal retribution for the Holocaust. If one hears threats to "throw into the sea" or annihilate a people which is but the remnant of those already annihilated, a shudder should pass through the conscience of this generation. The issue of Israel's physical security is not only a part of the general problem of international security and law. It also has a special dimension arising from this particular lineage of history. The civilized world must decide whether it can stand by and add to its burdened conscience another weight of international negligence and sin.

There are religious consequences, too. The necessity is surely to emphasize the common origins of these historic faiths. The river of Judaism sustained the currents of Christianity and Islam while keeping its own native water perennially fresh. The gift of this small people to history lay in its revolutionary doctrines of individual morality, social justice, and international peace. These insights may answer the question of why this people became the target of frenzied assault. Judaism is the parent source of the ideas that are the ideological antithesis of Nazi and cognate doctrines. There is a strong case here for the solidarity of religious faiths. The differences between Jews and Christians are not unimportant, and we should not be disposed to underestimate them. The elements that are distinctive to each tradition may be precisely those that are of special value to the common reservoir of thought. But the frontier in our times is not drawn between Judaism and Christianity. It lies between those who uphold, and those who reject, the supremacy of moral law. We occupy different areas of thought and experience, but we occupy them on the same side of that crucial line of demarcation.

### *Will It Happen Again?*

The question is whether we are safe against the renewal of the tragedy. We may become so if we save it from oblivion, and deduce its lessons in the political, social, religious, and educational domains. This is the justification for reopening the wound. It is the affirmative therapeutic side of a coin that, on its other face, is impregnated with agony and pain. If the lessons are deduced then the victims whose fate is beyond consolation may, in their immaculate sacrifice, have served a historic design.

The Renaissance artists portrayed the human soul as being drawn upward and downward by elements in its own nature. Both the upward and downward pull can be discerned in the life of our times. There is reason to believe that the instinct for survival will drive the human race to unification. Modern diplomacy is largely a holding action designed to avoid a premature explosion, until the unifying forces of history take all nations into their embrace. The story of this dark and evil assault enters the literature and the memory of man as one of his weapons in the struggle for the vindication of his humanity. A modern humanist, Julian Huxley, has expressed the scope of our opportunity in incisive words: "Floating in a sea of thought there are for man's taking the daring speculations and aspiring levels of men long dead, the organized knowledge of science, the hoary wisdom of the ancients, the creative imaginings of all the world's poets and artists. And in his own nature there are waiting to be called upon an array of potential helpers, all the possibilities of wonder and knowlege, of delight and reverence, of creative belief and moral purpose, of passionate effort and embracing love."

# 4

# Holocaust Education in Israel

## CHAIM SCHATZKER

In 1943, in the thick of World War II, before the fate of European Jewry had become known to the general public, an article—perhaps the first of its kind—was published by M. Avigdal, entitled "Ba'ayot Hinucheinu Bish'at Hashoah" ("The Problems of our Education During the Holocaust"), calling for an evaluation of events from an educational standpoint.

The Jewish educational system realized, more as an outcome of emotional-intuitive distress than, as yet, from a clear-cut awareness, that it could not ignore the Holocaust. Yet, for the following eighteen years, during which the extent and results of the Holocaust were revealed, educational literature failed to deal with the problems of teaching the Holocaust, and the topic was hardly broached in educational discussions and debates held throughout the country. Perhaps this is because these were also the years that witnessed the immigration to Israel of Holocaust refugees, and their absorption within the country; years of war and struggle for independence; and the establishment of a new state.

It was only in 1961–62, during the Eichmann trial, that we were witness to a wave of publications dealing with the Holocaust as a didactic-educational problem.[1] Educators suddenly found themselves sharing the surprising discovery that the Israeli educational system had not fulfilled its duty in teaching the Holocaust, thus leaving the Israeli student unprepared for the confrontation with the problems and revelations raised by the trial.

Since the Eichmann trial, however, educational literature has constantly addressed the topic,[2] with a marked rise in the number of publications since the Six Day War and the Yom Kippur War.[3] Among the latest wave of publications are a considerable number of tested and fully articulated study programs and teachers' extension courses. These generally surpass those of past years in both scope and frequency of appearance.

All these newer educational studies and publications were based on two components: the contemporary discoveries and conclusions of Holocaust research, which they sought to integrate into study programs, and the various ideologies and world views within our society, as well as changes wrought in them by the passage of time. They were also influenced by innovations in the field of didactics and by research on curricula and curriculum planning that had developed greatly during the last decade.

### Educational Trends

Historical treatment of the fate of the Jews at the hands of the Third Reich has been influenced greatly by the fact that though the *yishuv* (Jewish community in *Eretz Yisrael*) suffered a traumatic experience that rocked the very core of its being upon hearing the news of the Holocaust, at the end of World War II, they failed to grasp the situation from a rational point of view. For this reason, the Holocaust has always been perceived as a catastrophe and not a continual historical process lending itself to research through historical, rational, and causative reasoning. This has had weighty implications with regard both to our lives and our attitudes to the Holocaust—implications that have determined four trends in Israeli society in its approach to the Holocaust and, willy-nilly, in its treatment of the subject in the fields of education and instruction:

1. Our fundamental despair in the face of the vastness of the phenomenon led to a demonization of German murder campaigns, similar to the Middle Ages' conception of Satan as the source and essence of all evil, an entity which man fears, rejects, hates, despises, and constantly fights, but which remains beyond his comprehension and perception.
2. The blow to the national and human pride of the Jewish nation inflicted by the extermination of one-third of its people hardened the remainder to any logical and rational argumentation on the subject of the Holocaust.
3. The undefinable and incomprehensible element that causes fear and negates the very essence of self-existence was not included as an actual part of our lives—or of our school curriculum—despite its continuous existential presence, but underwent a process of psychological repression.
4. The shocks of the Eichmann trial, made vivid by the trial itself, and the danger and tension of the Six Day War and the Yom Kippur War reversed the repression process. The repressed consequently resur-

faced suddenly, finding compensation and even overcompensation in the deep emotional and spiritual reaction conveyed on memorial days by symbolic expressions of mourning and solidarity.

These four trends—each one understandable on its own—constituted, at the same time, an obstacle to any organized learning process that hoped to achieve rational ends through controlled means and was guided by considerations relating to professional didactics and educational psychology.

There is no reliable research available regarding the extent, program, and methods of Holocaust education in Israeli schools. The sole indications we have are the chapter headings appearing in the school curricula of the Ministry of Education and Culture and the relevant texts in history books. Both are unreliable sources for gauging the degree of actual classroom instruction given in the schools, since the teacher can ignore them and assign the topic to the students within the framework of individual study. When students at a large number of secondary schools were asked if they had studied the Holocaust and, if so, what they had learned, many replied that they had never studied the topic in school, even in a superficial manner; the teacher had never gotten to it and had assigned it, instead, for individual study by the students themselves. In contrast, there are many students who have studied the subject thoroughly, and this seems to point to the fact that the influence of the teacher is far greater than that of any curriculum or textbook. What is significant in our case is the reality that it is possible to graduate from an Israeli school without having learned about the Holocaust.

### Levels of Study

Both in historical texts and within the framework of history lessons, the events relating to the Holocaust are studied at two different stages and in two different places, in accordance with the accepted division in the Israeli school system between world history and Israeli (Jewish) history. In this particular case, the division proves a stumbling block, since it disassociates the Holocaust from its general background, without which it is not properly understood, and it appears, instead, distorted and unhistorical, through a conscious surrender of historical and causative reasoning.

Within this framework, the periods of the Weimar Republic and World War II are learned independently—and sometimes at a time lapse of even a full school year—from parallel events in Jewish history.

In all the relevant textbooks, the Holocaust assumes an important role. In the widely used book written for secondary schools by Zvi Ettinger, thirty-one pages are devoted to the Holocaust, while thirty-seven pages in Aviva Persky's book for primary schools are devoted to it. The descriptions are distorted, with some authors writing in a practical and restrained manner and others writing more emotionally, yet with none fully able to reflect the society in which and for which their works are being written. Therefore, too much is described and too little explained; the terrible and incomprehensible are judged, but they remain incomprehensible.

## Demonization

There has already been discussion of the demonization trend stemming from our conceptual helplessness in the face of the grimness of the Nazi phenomenon. Not only is this inclusive approach at odds with scientific research, but it poses an obstacle to our deriving any possible lessons or conclusions from the events of the period. Since one cannot draw an analogy between Satan and man, any demonization is in the nature of a fixation of evil in an external object instead of a search for it in the soul of man.

One must understand the origins of evil and the atmosphere in which it thrives and acts, so as to frustrate any such phenomenon in the future. Such an understanding can be reached through a system of education that derives its orientation, in part, from past mistakes and blunders. If any lesson is to be learned from the Holocaust, there is no sense in imputing its execution to demonic monsters. For then it becomes both impossible and irrelevant to underline a common human approach to their actions. Such a reading of Nazis out of the common human condition is precisely the obverse side of the Nazis' attitude toward the Jews.

## National Pride

It is the nagging problem of wounded national pride, rather than any other, that has constituted the focal point of interest, and it has determined the drawbacks of study books, professional didactic literature, and the instruction given in the classroom over a long period of time. The very essence of the Holocaust has not penetrated consciousness as a sequence of events related to causes conditioned by certain events, background, and data. Jewish resistance, or talk of it, during the Holocaust has not been relayed as a realistic reaction to the situation but as behavior that has immersed us in national disgrace (dishonor) and given rise to such questions as: "Why didn't they immigrate to Israel?" "Why didn't they see the obvious?" "Why didn't they defend themselves?" and "Why did they go like sheep to the slaughter?"

A generation of teachers and educators have been struggling with these questions, and they have been hard put to answer them in a convincing manner, since the students tend to regard such answers as apologetics. It is noteworthy that these problems have often become the center of any discussion on a subject connected with Holocaust education, shifting the focus from other, far more important problems. It seems that the addition of the word *gevura* (heroism) to *Shoah* (Holocaust) has not contributed a great deal to Holocaust education, since often the schoolroom discussion focuses upon Jewish resistance during the Holocaust, with the teacher being pushed into a tight corner by students assuming the dual role of prosecutor and judge of matters that are totally beyond their empathic judgment and with which they cannot possibly identify. Such discussions usually result in each side emerging with renewed belief in its own argument. Very rarely does a change in position occur as a result of another's relevant or practical arguments.

This complication has long constituted the most widespread motif in the didactic literature dealing with the subject. Ostensibly, the Yom Kippur War, with all its ramifications, brought about a spiritual readiness and a greater empathic ability on the part of students to delve into the problems of Jewish resistance during the Holocaust. We have indicated the process of repression, which has been reflected in the field of education by the silence or disregard with which the topic had been treated for many years. The titles of articles written on the subject easily attest to this fact:

"What Has Been Done To Teach the Lesson of the Holocaust?"[4]
"The Mystery Concerning the Ignorance of Holocaust History (Among Students)"[5]
"Growing Weary of History"[6]
"Holocaust Education Should be Integrated Into All Subjects"[7]
"How Shall We Give Expression to the Holocaust?"[8]
"The Youth Have Been Reared On a Negative Attitude Toward the Diaspora"[9]

### Repression and Compensation

For many years Israeli society has sought in a number of ways to compensate—even overcompensate—for this process of repression: in memorial ceremonies and symbols, rather than in didactics; in the martyrology of perpetuation of the memory of the fallen, rather than in education; and in institutions such as Yad Vashem, Kibbutz Yad Mordechai, and Kibbutz Lohamei Hageta'ot, rather than in university faculties.

Without detracting from the importance of memorial ceremonies and symbols, let us deal with their value in terms of the psychology of learning.

The various facets of the learning process, such as cognition, perception, conceptualization, analysis, recognition of causalities, synthesis, generalization, and deduction, differ from the psychological mechanism rooted in memorial days and ceremonies. By their very nature, the latter are not analytical events. Quite the contrary. Their purpose is to induce a sense of sublimation amid the pain and the grief, to raise events onto a plane where they can be viewed in a comprehensive and inclusive manner, from the distance of time—a metaphysical experience. All this is to enable man to come to terms with fate—often inexplicable and uncompromising—over which he has no control yet cannot but face, aware of and wondering at the helplessness born of his mere mortality.

Both education and ceremony play essential parts in the lives of men, societies, and nations, but we must differentiate between them for the sake of our discussion. A school can hold assemblies and ceremonies on Holocaust Day and should teach about the Holocaust, but to confuse these two trends would be to harm them both. One cannot be substituted for the other. It seems, however, that the Israeli school has acted otherwise. The conception of practical learning aimed at awakening and heightening emotions and feelings has given rise to the dubious concept of "emotional study." This approach seemed to suit the subject of Holocaust education, because it perceived emotion as the cornerstone, motivation, content, and method of education. There seemed to be a dissatisfaction, born of impatience, with awaiting the emotional response to the relevant study process. There are those who feel that this has brought no good either to the educational process or to the emotional response it sought to engender. Indeed, in recent years there has been a trend to adopt these two separate concepts as complementary, yet clearly individual, didactic concepts.

Another danger likely to cause the shelving of Holocaust education in the school curriculum has arisen from certain developments in the educational sciences themselves. This follows their attempts to become integrated within the social and behavioral sciences by turning their backs on any humanistic, normative, or moral concept.

## Developing Thought Processes

There is no doubt that the last decade has been witness to new, praiseworthy trends in educational theory, stressing the development of the thought processes rather than the accumulation of information. These trends seek significant clarification and content, rather than prescriptive moral attitudes; individual activity, rather than frontal teaching and superficial learning; and democratic selection of content, using criteria of relevance aimed at motivating the student.

It seems as if a curse hovers over conceptual principles when they sever themselves from historical cultural heritage, from social contexts of time and place, and become absolutes, each with its own abstract vitality.

For example, through context it is possible to reach the individual thought processes of the student—a positive accomplishment in itself—and subsequently make the educational process into an instrumental one by totally depleting it of any normative and moral significance. The result is all content, having no value other than that of developing the child's thinking faculties. According to this concept, there is no value difference between one program and another, and all are interchangeable as long as they achieve the above-mentioned aims. In our case, this would be like equating the Holocaust with, for example, the reign of Louis XIV in terms of educational significance, as long as each served as a means through which the student could acquire practice in historical thought and research.

### The New History

The Ministry of Education and Culture has outlined a new concept for teaching history in the upper grades of primary school. Under this system, history would be studied not in chronological order, but according to topics chosen by the teacher and the students, in an attempt to encourage free thinking and research through individual activity, rather than the mere memorization of information by the students.

All but the following three compulsory topics will be left to the choice of either the teacher or the school:

1. The principal Jewish communities of the last generation
2. The Jewish National Revival and the establishment of the State of Israel
3. The Israel-Arab confrontation

Despite continuous appeals, the Holocaust has not been included among these topics.

Thus, the members of the committee who decided upon the above have become slaves to their own concept, and the championing of this abstract principle to its very extremes has assumed greater importance to them than has the sense of natural awe that should have been accorded certain topics—first and foremost among them, the Holocaust.

## *Flaws in the System*

This decision will probably result in the selection of topics other than the Holocaust (unattractive by its very nature) by the students, who will thus complete secondary school without ever having learned about the Holocaust in a methodical and in-depth manner. Moreover, this decision undermines the moral basis of Israel's demand to other nations and countries to include study of the Holocaust as a compulsory part of their school curriculums. The Israel Ministry of Education and Culture has put its own seal of approval on the process of allowing the Holocaust to be forgotten by the world.

This decision has widespread public ramifications, as well as educational and didactic aspects, and it is doubtful whether the Israeli public will accept it.

Another danger stemming from inordinate ahderence to innovation arises from the attempt to engender among students identification and involvement with Holocaust topics through simulation—a method based upon the assumption that there exists a fundamental similarity between the simulator and the subject of simulation. Effective simulation can be achieved only in the presence of such a basis of similarity—be it similarity of situation, similarity of systems of thought, logic, and rules of play, or the similarity arising from the fact that all men are human beings whose instincts and reactions bear a certain resemblance to one another. By its very definition, the term Holocaust cancels out the possibility of simulation, since the subject is outside the realm of one's experience and system of terms, imagination, and logic. Moreover, every attempt to simulate "another planet"—possessing a logic and legitimacy of its own and a uniqueness born of its deviation from norms accepted and recognized by the human race since the beginning of time—is none other than an infantile attempt to follow current trends in the world of didactics. Such an attempt will either diminish the seriousness and significance of the Holocaust or result in emotional and intellectual deception.

It seems to me that in the entire Israeli school curriculum there is no other topic so saturated with unresolved emotional and spiritual conflicts—fluctuating between self-accusation and the accusation of others and the necessity for defensiveness and apologetics, between a readiness to cope with and attempts to repress the Holocaust.

This is all due to the fact that the Holocaust still casts a shadow that darkens our lives, and, paradoxically, the further we get away from it, the more it constitutes a reality that governs our reactions, especially in times of stress and danger.

CHAIM SCHATZKER

## *Notes*

1. See, e.g., *Hora'at Hashoa B'beit Sefer, Diyunim Velyunim,* Ministry of Education and Culture, 1961. See also:

   Arieh Bauminger, "Hashoa VeHameri B'aynei Hanoar Hayisraeli", *Hahinuch* 34 (1962).

   Yisrael Gutman, "Hashoa VeHameri, Noseh Limudi," Hakibbutz He'artzi, Hashomer Hatzair, 1961.

   Michael Hendel, "Lehora'at Hashoa VeHameri," *Urim* 19 (1962).

   Eliezer Yerushalmi, "Al Tochnit Hashoa," *Ma'alot* 5 (1962).

   Fredka Mazja, "Ba'ayot Hahora'a shel T'kufat Hashoa," *Alon Hahonchot* 2 (1961).

   Sarah Neshamit, "L'toldot Hashoa VeHameri," Hakibbutz Hameuhad, 1961.

   Sarah Neshamit, "Limud Korot Hashoa, Ma VeKaytzad," *Urim* 18 (1962).

   Haim Schatzker, "Ba'ayot Didaktiyot B'hora'at Hashoa," *Yedion Lamoreh L'historia* 2 (1961).

   Ya'akov Shalhev, *Mifneh B'hora'at T'kufat Hashoa VeHagvura,* Yad Vashem, 1972.

2. The following should be noted:

   S. Cohen, "Arachim Hinuchiyim B'limud Noseh Hashoa," *Urim* 21 (1964).

   Fredka Mazja, "L'Ba'ayot Hora'at T'kufat Hashoa Ulekaha", *Hahinuch* 3 (1968).

   Aryeh Mencher, "L'hora'at Hashoa Vehagvura" *Hed Haninuch* 39 (1965).

   Haim Schatzker, "Ba'ayot Didaktiyot B'hora'at Hashoa," *Hahevra L'hinuch,* Haifa, 1968.

   *Hora'at Hashoa B'beit Sefer Tichon,* Yad Vashem, 1969.

   *Yom Hashoa Vehagvura,* Ministry of Education and Culture, 1966.

3. See, for example:

   Zvi Bachrach, "Hashoa K'ba'aya Historit," *Ma'alot* 5 (1976).

   H. Shadmi, "Implikatziot Hinuchiot B'hora'at Hashoa," *Hahinuch* 2–3 (1975).

   *"Hatzaot Tochniot Avoda B'noseh Shoa Utekuma,"* Ministry of Education and Culture, 1974.

   Aryeh Kermon and Yair Oron, *Hiyuniyut Yehudit Bashoa, Tochnit Hinuchit,* Ministry of Education and Culture, 1974.

   *Madrich L'emtzaei Hora'ah B'noseh Mishoa Lagvura,* Ministry of Education and Culture, 1976.

   David Pri-Hen, *Mishoa Litkuma, Hatzaot L'peiluyot B'beit Hasefer Hamamlachti,* Ministry of Education and Culture, 1975.

   Haim Schatzker, "Ekronot Umivhanim, He'arot L'tochnit Limudim Hadasha shel Hora'at Hashoa," *Ma'alot* 4 (1975).

4. A. Dushkin, *Hora'at Hashoa B'beit Sefer.* See footnote 1.

5. M. Dworzecki, Ibid.

6. M. Hendel, Ibid.

7. D. Ochs, Ibid.

8. A. Simon, Ibid.

9. S. Nehamit, Ibid.

# The Death Taint and Uncommon Vitality: The Case of the Ever-Dying Jewish People

## EUGENE C. WEINER

There are existences that seem to be tainted in some ominous way by a kind of living death (Heidigger 1962; Demske 1970; Lifton 1973). These attenuated lives can occasionally be amazingly vital and creative. It is our aim to explore briefly, and in very broad outline, one of these vital but attenuated existences—the case of the Jewish people.

In its essence, the continuity of the Jewish people is a heroic, unprecedented, existential hyperbole, a tour de force of religious, cultural, and national assertiveness. And the State of Israel is one of its most impressive recent achievements. Israel, even with its present existence a certainty, still *seems* unlikely. It is based on what may appear to be excessive resoluteness, unique claims about the continuities of national consciousness, and an exaggerated expression of collective will to reembody religious culture in national identity. It is a strange phenomenon. Because while statements about facts are sometimes exaggerations, facts themselves generally are not. The factuality of this latest manifestation of Jewish resoluteness—Israel's existence—still has not dispelled lingering doubts about the possibility of its verification in reality. In this sense it bears the same stamp of unlikelihood—of being and yet not quite being—of life and death that characterizes all of postexilic Jewish existence. From all that we know about historical processes, social dynamics, and group psychology, Israel's existence is highly improbable (Valery, 1962), but it does exist. The shadow of unlikely existence has darkened the reality of Jewish history over the course of the centuries, and it has not been dispelled by the creation of the state (Neusner, 1973). This is the case even though a great deal of the motive force that brought Israel into being was based on the desire to irrefutably establish and normalize Jewish existence.

## The Aspiration for Normalcy

Is the aspiration for normalization of existence desirable, or does a death-tainted existence have an inherent vitality of its own? This question has been and continues to be hotly debated. It is our intention to analyze this debate in light of its larger implications for the general question of group longevity. There are two points of particular interest: 1). The existence of the death taint is openly acknowledged by opposing sides of the question—especially by those who argue for measures to abolish it; and 2). the issue is a matter of public discussion. This situation constitutes a most unusually clear illustration of a group struggling with the vitalizing potential of death and its possible contribution to corporate existence and group survival. One can see in the debate the monumental struggle of a group to make the best of a grim and tragic reality. The relevance of the debate has been heightened by the particular circumstances in which the State of Israel was established. If ever group life was manifestly vitalized by death, it was in this case.

As Walter Laqueur has indicated: "The war in Europe was over, the world had been liberated from Nazi terror and oppression, peace had returned. For the Jewish People it was the peace of the graveyard. Yet paradoxically, at the very time when the 'objective' Jewish question had all but disappeared, the issue of a Jewish State became more topical than ever before. . . . The victors in the war had an uneasy conscience as the stark tragedy of the Jewish People unfolded before their eyes. It was only now that the question was asked whether enough had been done to help them and what could be done for the survivors" (Laqueur, 1972). The possibility of using the graveyard as the means to launch a more vital existence had already been under discussion by the Jewish people for a long time, even before World War II. Indeed, one can find traces of such a thrust in the thought and action of the Jewish people as far back as one has historical records of them. This possibility was conditioned by historical experience and mythic paradigms that sought to tap the vitalizing power of death.

## The Living Dead

One of the salient images, used by the somewhat emancipated Jews of the eighteenth and nineteenth centuries to indicate their own unlikely existence, was that of the *living dead*. They saw in this uncanny and ambiguous condition the starting point for the revitalization movements to which they were partial. In their own condemnatory and critical attitude toward it they bear eloquent, albeit reluctant, witness to the powerful grip it held over their consciousness.

As Pinsker, that prescient spokesman of the new Jewish national rebirth, wrote in 1882:

> Thus the world saw in this people [the Jews], the frightening form of the dead walking among the living. This ghostlike apparition of a people without unity or organization, without land or other bond of union, no longer alive, and yet moving among the living—This eerie form scarcely paralleled in history, unlike anything that preceded or followed it, could not fail to make a strange and peculiar impression upon the imagination of the nations. And if the fear of ghosts is something inborn, and has a certain justification in the psychic life of humanity, is it any wonder that it asserted itself powerfully at the sight of this dead yet living nation? Fear of the Jewish ghost has been handed down and strengthened for generations and centuries. It led to a prejudice which in its turn, in connection with other forces . . . paved the way for Judeophobia.

Pinsker developed a theory of anti-Semitism based on the notion that "for the living, the Jew is a dead man." The way to deal with the moribund condition is to "devote all of our remaining moral force to reestablish ourselves as a living nation so that we may finally assume a more fitting and dignified role." Pinsker, like many of the protonationalist figures of the late nineteenth century, acknowledged the aptness of the image of the living dead Jew. That some of the protonationalists wanted to transcend this eerie condition does not take away from the extraordinary reality that the description seemed appropriate to them. In their zeal to infuse a less eccentric and, in their eyes, a more bountiful life force into the Jewish people, they gave short shrift to a rather extraordinary life force in its own right, that of the death taint. For if there is one characteristic of the Jewish people that seems constant in its 4,000-year history, it is that it is forever being perceived as moribund and, consequently, continually the subject of a premature obituary. The British Museum possesses a monument from the thirteenth century B. C. E. on which it is written, "Israel is desolated, its seed is no more." Some desolation, some seed! Indeed, if the living dead manage to survive with such a spectacular longevity, perhaps this status bears some looking into. Especially by anyone seeking to understand group survival.

The notion of the living dead Jews seems to be composed of two paradoxical and, at times, contradictory ideas. One of these seems to be that the Jews are tainted with death because they have lived too long.

The other is that the Jews are tainted with death because they lack an indispensably vital part for living. According to the first of these ideas, the Jews are a freakish anomaly of *endurance*, in the other they are a compositional *monstrosity of requisite form* for life. According to this second idea, the Jews are without a necessary precondition for life, yet according to the first idea, they are abnormally lively and vital without it. The anomalous death taint implies both functional and structural defects. The fact that these two notions contradict each other seems to have bothered no one. For how is it possible to live at all, not to speak of an extraordinarily protracted life, if life is defined as the possession of certain vital parts—and they do not exist? Their mutually contradictory implications did not prevent these notions from reinforcing and supplementing each other in practice. In one sense, the Jews are the living dead because they have lived too long anyhow; in the other they are the living dead, and not fully alive, because they have a mortal defect.

### The Influence of Christian Theology

There are two other attitudes that appear to have reinforced these two primary ones. They were held by Christian theologians, for the most part, but that did not prevent Jews from accepting their basic truth and finding more suitable reasons to support it. Indeed, it is an open question just how much the Jewish explanations of Judeophobia are influenced by Christian theology. First, the Jews were stigmatized not only because they did not acknowledge the proferred savior of the world but, even worse than that, they allegedly crucified him. To be responsible for the death of a god is to provoke forces that are mysteriously threatening to one's own future existence. In a sense, killing God is murdering life. The mortal punishment to oneself may be temporarily postponed, but its advent is regarded as a certainty. Second, the living Jews were witnesses to recurring murderous attempts to annihilate them. They were mistreated victims whose continued existence reminded those capable of empathy that they were always the potential targets of murderous intent. The image of the living dead Jew—murdered in the past, and potential murder victims of the future—colored the perception of the Jews even by sympathetic outsiders.

Furthermore, the notion of the living dead became a social stigma with all the force and power that accrues to its successful imputation. The death-taint stigma as applied to the Jewish people was different from the ordinary sense in which every living being is marked for ultimate death. It is not in this natural, constitutive sense that Jews were marked with the taint. It was, rather, in the sense in which some people are marked and singled out for an immoderate, indelible, particularly unseemly taint. These people are the living who in many ways are more dead than alive. They are symbolically dead by virtue of having *sentenced identities.* Among individuals they can be convicted murderers who have been sentenced to death and awaiting execution, or sufferers of fatal diseases who have been diagnosed and pronounced incurable. These sentenced identities seem calamitously spoiled and atrociously injured. Among groups, they can be uprooted, displaced tribes of natives, phased-out organizations, or conquered nationalities and ethnic groups that have been assigned to extirpation, decimation, or annihilation.

In the case of individuals the death taint is (as Lifton, 1973, and Cassell, 1972, have pointed out) a relationship between the self and the body that is an "injured one," in which "the self remains shackled to a body seen as somehow already dead, or permanently injured in some inexplicable way." It is "a relationship seen as fundamentally incompatible with life, between two independent, indispensable parts of existence," one of which is irrevocably defective. On rare occasions a sentenced identity can be transformed into a *reprieved identity* if the sentence is annulled or found to have been inappropriately pronounced, but that is rare. In that infrequent case the injury is somehow repaired and the defective part of the existence is remedied. But for the most part sentences are executed, and most sentenced identities expire. Until they do, however, their bearers suffer the taint of their ultimate (somehow future yet present) mortal end.

### Sentence-Deferring Identities

There is another kind of identity other than the sentenced or reprieved; it is the sentenced identity in which the mortal sentence seems never to be executed. These are *sentence-deferring identities.* These identities have the taint of death upon them already, but their fatal sentence, instead of being executed, is instead continually and unaccountably deferred. The possessors of these identities exist in a kind of dubiously protected limbo. Theirs is the remarkable but unenviable power of life. Such is the case of the Jewish people, at least as viewed frequently by other than Jews, and on occasion by Jews themselves (Yehoshua, 1972).

In this instance the death taint is so indelible that ever-renewed efforts at revitalization are themselves unaccountably characterized by it. The very thing that could disprove the existence of the taint—a renewed or more natural form of life—is itself regarded as unnatural. In regard to the Jews, one of the main reasons for the persistence of the taint, no matter what action is taken, is that throughout much of history the collective life of the Jew has been regarded as obscene. By obscene is meant an offense to modesty, decency, involving the overstepping of some limit of propriety. In some historical periods the more archaic meaning of the term has been appropriate: lewd, abominable, disgusting, or repulsive. In a certain sense it would be as if one of Lifton's Hiroshima victims, the *hibakusha* ("the explosion-affected person, those who permanently encounter death"), had his defect genetically transferred to his death-tainted progeny, and they never died out. Who would be interested in discovering the secret of their group longevity and emulating their lives? Their longevity, rather than being a meritorious achievement, would instead, no doubt, be regarded as a somewhat obscene form of protracted and merciless doom.

A convincing proof of the reality of the imputed death taint among Jews is demonstrated by the fact that they are rarely given credit for heroic endurance. Considering the fascination that longevity generally elicits, this is very strange, for if there was indeed anyone called Methuselah, and he did actually live 969 years, he most likely spent most of his time answering questions about how he managed to live so long. At least after his 120th birthday. This is probably so because there is to be found in most cultures an idea of what constitutes a reasonable life span versus an extraordinary one. When the limits of that reasonable span are exceeded, it is usually the subject of intense and frequently excessive interest. Witness the many expeditions by physicians and physical anthropologists to Andean villages, Pakistani settlements, or Caucasian farms to locate and examine the extraordinarily long-lived And the interest evinced is usually not only scientifically motivated: It appears to have the quality at times almost of hero worship. It is as if an uncommon endurance marked with perceptible signs of continued vitality is intrinsically heroic. Its very existence is an encouraging testament to the possibility of successfully doing battle with inevitable decay, decomposition, and death.

But the Jewish people are not the recipients of any such adulation, for there is another side to the issue. A person hoary with age, who spectacularly surpasses a reasonable life expectancy, is not only venerable, he can be, and frequently is, ridiculous. An uncommon old age is viewed frequently not only as incredible, but also as an incredible absurdity, a bit preposterous. Time has been borrowed from death's domain for an unnaturally prolonged and persistent duration. What should be defunct is freakishly vital, and what should be deceased is queerly vigorous. It is because of this that an unnatural endurance can itself become an indication and omen of the death taint. Keeping death at bay is not only a heroic feat, but if it is done too persistently and immodestly it can be obscene. It is not only death that has a pornographic potential but so, too, does an uncommon vitality. And so it is that there is no automatic moral grandeur that is associated with endurance, if such endurance is tainted with death.

### Resolving Ambivalence

The predisposition to value the particular kind of life that is prolonged resolves the ambivalence toward an uncommon vitality. In the case of the abnormally long-lived Jewish people there is frequently no such positive predisposition. It has always seemed strange that the Jewish people are rarely (except by themselves) given credit for existing so long. Remarkably long as far as nations, religions, and civilizations are concerned (Elazar, 1969). The great civilization have, with rare exceptions, rarely continued to exist for longer than a millennium, and most of them a good deal less. In the case of the Jewish people we have a group that has an unbroken connection with its own cultural past for many centuries, a connection relatively unadulterated by extrinsic foreign influences. It is one of the very few extant civilizations in which the cultural forms developed millennia ago and those existing today are easily recognizable as being substantially the same—whether language, values, norms, customs, literature, or myth. Where are the paeans that are invoked to sing artful praise for this heroic achievement of endurance? Who is trying to emulate the Jewish experience? On the contrary, in the eyes of many, this ability to endure is a questionable virtue.

It is not only because of the immodest relationship with time that Jews have frequently been regarded as having "outlived life," but also because they have existed for much of their history without one of the alleged requisites for national life—a land. Their own land. It is the lack of a land of their own for much of Jewish history that made the Jewish people archetypal wanderers whose dismal journeys and imperiled settlements forever underlined their vulnerability (Roshwald, 1973). But strangely enough, that very vulnerability seemed to emphasize their bizarre talents for survival. For how could a nation so lacking the ecological prerequisites for life be so long-lived? It was difficult to conceive of a people continually existing without a land of their own—it was as if there was a kind of congenital structural morbidity that was rooted in this strange group's corporate being that refused to buckle and crumple.

### Jewish People and Jewish Land

How did the Jewish people manage to live without this vital part of group life for so long? In a sense, the normal death of the Jewish people by losing its land was prevented by its abnormal birth. From its very beginnings the Jewish people had an unusual relationship to its land. Even when the land was inhabited by the Jews, the relationship was ambiguous. Its attachment was not simply based on the usual fact of being born and reared on it. It was a special type of connection.

In the biblical account of the corporate birth of the Jewish people, be it the covenant of Abraham or the revelation at Sinai, the context of birth is alien, the promise is home. In other words, home is not a taken-for-granted reality where being *starts*, rather, according to the mythic account, it is a promised goal to be attained, where being may be *enhanced*. Attaining the title to the Promised Land is perpetually achieved and constantly legitimated—achieved through obstinate striving and legitimated through virtuous action. It is a project to *enhance* an imperfect existence rather than a taken-for-granted *given* of reality. Home is not where you come from, according to this view, but where you are going. Even if you are there already. The Promised Land is an intrinsically unfulfillable promise—that is, if fulfilling a promise is seen as a once-and-for-all-time matter. The most convincing proof that it is an unfulfillable promise is that the promised goal remained relevant even when the Jews were living in the land. Part of the reason for that relevance was the tenuous hold on the land, since there always were powerful enemies seeking to dislodge them from it. There was never a period when Jewish settlement in the land could be taken for granted. If it wasn't radically threatened by enemies from without, it was threatened from within. Consequently, there was hardly a period in Jewish history when a leader could justifiably claim that the promise to the land was unambiguously fulfilled. For this reason the Jewish people can be accurately described as a group of perpetual homecomers. The Jewish religion as "a religion on wheels," as Isaiah Berlin has characterized it, was already that way at its inception. One of the first corporate acts of group commitment for the Jews was a willingness to travel *toward* the land. And the movement does not stop with death. One of the eschatological visions of the final days has the bones of the Jewish dead rolling under the ground toward the Promised Land. It is not only the living that are mobile, but also the dead. They are homecomers all. Jewish bones, especially the ones not already brought to the Promised Land, are mobile bones, according to the mythic vision. Thus, one has from the very beginning a group of people with a double relationship to land, able to cohere as a group without it, but defining their most deeply sacred vocation as a legitimate striving to achieve it. And once achieved, however tenuously, it must be enhanced and perfected constantly, otherwise there will be dire results.

What dire results?

Death.

It has always seemed safer to the Jew to die in the Promised Land, or be buried there, than to live there. For there is always the grim and not unlikely possibility that in life one will be consumed by the very Promised Land that is supposed to supplement an imperfect existence. The land was not only an elusive and desirable quest, it was also an inherently dangerous one. It was hard to say whether the Jew was safer with or without it. For the actual settlement of the land was defined as conditional, and contingent, for the most part, on proper conduct.

The settlement of the land was and is forever being constrained by the fact that it is a holy land above all else. It is filled with both benevolent and malevolent powers, like most things holy. These powers could be activated by behavior that was not in accord with the revealed divine will. It did not belong to the Jewish people alone; it was held in trust by them but dependent upon God's promise. It was theirs as long as they were God's. They had their part of the bargain to keep. So long as they were faithful to their mission, their connection with the land could persist. Should they be unfaithful, then the land would spew forth its decimated survivors from it. They would be purged from it, amid death and plunder. For like themselves the land was set aside for a purpose. It was to be the scene of great and extraordinary happenings. This, too, was the meaning of a holy land. Should the Jewish people fulfill their divinely appointed purpose, the land would be the scene of their elevation and apotheosis. Should they betray that purpose, then the very land would consume them. And so, while the land was infinitely desirable, it was also mortally dangerous. As if to underline this, one finds in the biblical narratives the constant connection between land and death (Brichto, 1968). The first title to the land was originally for the express purpose of burial. It was Abraham's desire to bury Sarah; that was the first overt act of the Jewish people to take steps to acquire the land.

The land is not only a place to live, it is to a significant degree a place to achieve a desirable entombment by being buried well. But it was a desirable entombment that was not easily had. Those desiring to find a resting place were constantly being confronted by the prophetic warning that improper conduct would result in the undignified death of large numbers of the people, and the expulsion of the remainder from the land. It constituted the prototypical admonition to the Jews of the need for single-minded loyalty to their national religious vocation.

At times these death warnings and threats of expulsion became actual. It was the actual destruction of a large part of the people in 722 B.C.E. by the Assyrians, and the decimation of the population and expulsion in 586 B.C.E. by the Babylonians, that gave added credence to the prophetic threat. The memory of these two great premonitory exiles, the Assyrian and the Babylonian, served to strengthen the credibility of the prophetic threat that a break between the people and the Land was possible. But in addition, these cultural memories served as prelusive forewarnings of the great exile to come. By the year 70 c.e., when the great dispersion started, embedded in Jewish consciousness was a memory of a number of mass killings and exiles that ended, for the most part, with the resettlement of the land. These previous premonitory exiles had provided the people with an opportunity to develop the means to deal with exile and mass death as a *conceivable* part of their national life. It was as if almost from the beginning of its history this group prepared itself for a most deprived existence. These historical precedents and the particular structure of group consciousness that developed in response to them made it possible, in very large measure, for the Jews to exist for two millennia without a land. The ability to compensate for its loss and to avoid demoralization is certainly to be regarded as an extraordinary instance of collective élan.

## Fear and Creativity

In spite of the anomalous death taint and corresponding functional and structural defects, the Jewish people, throughout its history, has been extraordinarily creative and alive. Everything written thus far hardly prepares one for an appreciation of these achievements. How is it that a people so dead can be so alive? Living on borrowed time, without the necessary means for a proper group life, has proved to be a most surmountable hindrance. Indeed, it is questionable whether it was a hindrance at all.

Rawidowicz, in a brilliant, polemical, and largely ignored essay, has argued, I think convincingly, that it was precisely the imminence of collective death that activated and energized latent creative collective impulses:

> Yet making all allowances for the general motives in this dread of the end, it has nowhere been at home so incessantly, with such acuteness and intensity as in the House of Israel. The world may be constantly dying but no nation was ever so incessantly dying . . . as Israel. . . . I am often tempted to think that this fear of cessation in Israel was fundamentally a kind of protective individual and collective emotion. Israel has indulged so much in the fear of its end, that its constant vision of the end helped it to overcome every crisis, to emerge from every threatened end as a living unit, though much wounded and reduced. In anticipating the end it become its master. Thus no catastrophe would even take this end-fearing people by surprise so as to knock it off its balance, still less to obliterate it—as if Israel's incessant preparation for the end made this end absolutely impossible. . . . As

far as historical reality is concerned we are confronted here with a phenomenon which has almost no parallel in mankind's story: a nation that has been disappearing constantly for the last 2000 years, exterminated in dozens of lands, all over the globe, reduced to half or one-third of its population by tyrants ancient and modern, and yet re-equips itself for a new start, a second and third advance—always fearing the end, never afraid to make a new beginning, to snatch triumph from the jaws of defeat, whenever and wherever possible. There is no nation more dying than Israel, yet none better equipped to resist disaster. . . . [Rawidowicz, 1948]

In contrast to Pinsker's description of the Jewish people as one tainted with death, pleading for a normal existence, we find in Rawidowicz's description a different emphasis. It is not that death has invaded Jewish existence. It is not that the Jews are constituted by a peculiar morbidity. On the contrary, what is characteristic of the group is its extraordinary *fear* of death. It is an inordinate fear that leads to anticipatory preventive measures of a most peculiar intensity that serve to prevent the end from ever coming. It is this fear, and the anticipatory measures it triggers, that is the real defense against disaster.

What is stressed in Rawidowicz's analysis is the appropriateness of preparations for death-dealing onslaught, while in Pinsker's treatment this is of no import. What is important, to Pinsker, is the *discarding of the tainted status*. What is primary is the need for a normal, more whole and complete existence. A living death can only be remedied by a full life. For Rawidowicz, a full life devoid of this inordinate death fear constitutes the greatest peril for continued survival. For if group death has been defeated time and again by anticipation—morose, perhaps, but nonetheless based on proven realities—who is to say what would happen to the group without it? To relate this position to a known parable: The Jewish people have cried: "Wolf, wolf," but they have done so *tirelessly*, believing it most every time, making necessary precautions, and then have had the experience of having the wolf come with devastating frequency. Rawidowicz believes in the positive value of the 1) warning, 2) the collective belief in the warning, 3) the taking of precautions against the threat, and 4) the assumption of the inexorable continuation of threatening realities. For him, living as an ever-dying people is the surest guarantee for survival; that which provides security and quietude is itself the ultimate threat. Not so for Pinsker. The contamination of the death taint prevents a proper existence; it is a kind of curse, a fate to be deplored and, if possible, remedied completely. It is the aspiration for a new life, not the fear of death, that is to be the primary motive force that energizes.

What we have revealed in these two attitudes is not simply an incidental polemic on the way in which reality was grasped by the Jewish people. Instead, we see in them the modern manifestation of a basic, centuries-old, dichotomous response of a long-lived culture to its difficult situation. Of the two, it is the second, that described by Rawidowicz, that appears to us as the more dominant life response of the Jewish people to its reality. But the first, the aspiration for a new birth, was, nonetheless, preserved in messianic aspirations and embedded in the corporate imagination. To live a half-life yes, but refusing to give up the dream of the full one. This aspiration for the full life frequently made the half-life bearable. But it was the ability to lead the half-life that made possible cultural and historical continuity. What this may indicate is that for a culture to exist it may have to develop anticipatory institutions and attitudes to survive and flourish in morbid conditions. Evidently this is difficult for a culture to do, as Benjamin Nelson has indicated:

> Civilizations do not end with a bang or a whimper. Civilizations generally die laughing. The more closely great societies approach the point of checkmate, the deeper the indulgence of great numbers in their favorite games. In fact, the worse the situation the more hectic the abandonment. It is when all is fun and joy, on the go-go, when the dancers in the charades are on the edge of ecstasy and frenzy, that the hoped for oblivion prevails. At this juncture, treasured elements of the legacy of civilizations slip unnoticed out of focus. [Nelson, 1973]

### Life as Crisis

While Nelson's description may be apt for most civilizations, it is not true for the Jews. It was precisely their ability to anticipate the "point of checkmate" and allow for another move—just one more—and another and another that characterized them most completely. It was the refusal to allow a forgetful and reality-denying ecstasy that was the most typical of Jewish responses to disaster. Life itself was viewed as a context of real and potential disaster—and the main task was to prepare for it. Prepare for it: by adopting a pervasive philosophy of trust that God would never let the end come within historical time; by not making one's survival dependent on things that could be taken away; by developing a theodicy of defeat that justified any misfortune; by building one's basic institutions so that dispersal would not compromise them; by preserving the maximum of autonomy over one's own communal affairs; by having symbolic escape valves to express aggression against one's oppressors and thereby resisting premature, adventitious, and self-defeating uprisings; by prolonging the crisis mentality, through the enactment at regular intervals of an elaborate social drama of religious ritual that had as its major theme ultimate return to the land; by encouraging near-universal literacy so that these lessons could be rehearsed by the individual in his own private study; by assiduously protecting boundaries of membership, so that no matter how dispersed, it was always clear who was and who was not a member of the group; by staging very frequent gatherings of members, daily and weekly, so that the group had a reality for all to see; by regarding oneself as superior to one's oppressors, no matter how powerful and intellectually impressive they were; by remembering one's past glory and making the memory contemporarily relevant; by believing in the group's ultimate vindication; by being devoted to continuity of the tradition but having social mechanisms to interpret and decide extraordinary events; by regulating as much of the intimate life of one's members as possible; by developing a repertoire of strategies to handle various kinds of disasters; by finding protectors whose self-esteem and self-interest is served and enhanced by the very existence of the half-life; by regarding endurance and continuity in time, rather than power and influence, as the real test of culture; and by appealing to the conscience of even those who have killed one's members, to help one continue living. These are only some of the means that were used to preserve this remarkably enduring yet fragile group existence.

The question for the Jewish people was never "to be or not to be," but most frequently it was how to be while not quite being. It was preparation for, accommodation to, and temporary acceptance of, that state of not quite being that contributed to its extraordinary longevity.

The question that has concerned us is how a culture relates to the possibility of its own demise. The usual question that is asked is how cultures relate to the death of their members. This has not been within the focus of our concerns, though it is an interesting question. The Jewish people was concerned with the larger question, from the very first moments of its collective being. We have tried to indicate that this fact contributed to its prolonged existence. I believe this to constitute the fundamental meaning of the sacrifice of Isaac story, in which a father, the promised progenitor of a people, is assured a fruitful posterity, and at the same instant commanded to destroy the agent of its realization (Isaac). His willingness to endanger the manifest guarantor of the promise (his only son) and live an endangered half-life—in which he has only his failing flesh to rely on—proves his worthiness. We have in this treatment purposely not dealt with the Jewish belief in immortality, resurrection, and martyrdom or with other death theories in Judaism since they are relatively well documented and, above all, are related to other types of questions. Nor have we attempted to deal with the complex social and religious factors and circumstances that helped to structure various kinds of responses to the belief in the ever-dying

Jewish people. We have attempted to make plausible the more general thesis that the extraordinary longevity of group life is dependent upon, and intimately connected with, a willingness to live a diminished existence—at least in the case of the Jewish people.

## References

Brichto, H. C. "Kin Cult, Land and Afterlife—A Biblical Complex." *Hebrew Union College Annual,* Spring (1968).

Cassell, E. J. "Being and Becoming Dead." *Social Research* 29, no. 1, Spring (1972): 537.

Demske, J. *Being, Man and Death.* The University Press of Kentucky, 1970.

Elazar, D. J. "The Reconstitution of Jewish Communities in the Post War Period." *Jewish Journal of Sociology* 11, no. 2, Dec. (1969): 187.

Heidegger, M. *Being and Time.* Translated by J. Macquarrie and E. Robinson. New York: Harper and Row, 1962.

Laqueur, W. *A History of Zionism.* London: Weidenfeld and Nicolson, 1972, 561.

Lifton, R. J. "On Death and Death Symbolism: The Hiroshima Disaster." In *The Phenomenon of Death.* Edited by E. Wyschograd. New York: Harper and Row, 1973.

Nelson, B. "The Games of Life and the Dances of Death." Ibid.

Neusner, J. "Now We're All Jews Again." *Response,* no. 20, Winter (1973–4): 151–55.

Pinsker, L. "Auto-Emancipation, 1882." In *The Zionist Idea.* Edited by A. Hertzberg. New York: Harper and Row, 1966.

Rawidowicz, S. "Am-Holeh Vamet" (Hebrew). *Metzudah* 5–45 (1948).

Roshwald, M. "The Idea of the Promised Land." *Diogenes,* no. 82, Summer (1973): 45–69.

Valery, P. "The Crises of Mind." In *History and Politics.* New York: Pantheon, 1962.

Yehoshua, A. B. Public address at Conference Commemorating the Death of Lt. David Uzan, May 1972, Haifa University, Haifa, Israel. Cf. his comments in "Let Us Not Betray Zionism." In *Unease in Zion,* edited by E. B. Ezer. New York: Quadrangle, 1974.

# PART III

# Religion vs. Secularism in a Jewish State

6

# Judaism and the Jewish State

## ISAIAH LEIBOWITZ

Thinking Israelis today confront two related questions: What can we contribute to the solution of world problems, and what can we contribute to the solution of the problems of the Jewish people? There is no need for the Jewish people, with an organized government in Israel, to take up values, slogans, or teachings that have already been formulated by others, and hand them back again to the very same world that is their source. We must concern ourselves only with what we have to offer. This directs our attention to our past.

To my mind, we ought not discuss Judaism from the standpoint of ideas, because ideas are public property and anyone can read anything into them. As long as the disputants are permitted to define Judaism according to the promptings of their hearts, their personal inclinations, and their intellectual or emotional preferences, making Judaism a completely subjective concept, the discussion amounts to no more than an exercise in semantics. We must distinguish between Judaism as an empiric-historic phenomenon, on the one hand, and ideologies about Judaism, on the other. Our discussion has nothing to do with the various interpretations—theocentric, anthropocentric, or ethnocentric—that students of Jewish history have attributed to it, nor with the various evaluations of the creations, achievements, and chronicles of the Jewish people; rather it has to do with these creations, achievements, and chronicles themselves. We must understand the term "Judaism" in an objective, empiric-historic sense: the actual embodiment of Jewish reality through the centuries. That is to say, Jewish reality in its entirety and not in some particular period, not fragmentary revelations, episodic, accidental, personal, and ephemeral.

In fact, in what was Judaism actually embodied? What was the permanent foundation on which it was built? What gave it continuity and identity through the centuries? Judaism is nothing but the religion of Israel as actually embodied in the Torah and in the commandments, whose systematic codification is the halakhah. All of the different, changing ideas and evaluations in Judaism were only superstructure.

## The Essence of Judaism

Others have already emphasized the central significance of religion in Jewish history and its significance to the problems of our generation. But before we can argue about what must and should be taken from the sources of Judaism and from the history of the people of Israel, we must first be clear about objective facts and ask a question, the answer to which is empirical and not ideological; namely: What is the essence of Judaism? The answer to this question does not depend on the values, beliefs, and opinions of the questioner or the one who answers the question, and it is not influenced by them. The answer is that Judaism is embodied in the religion of Israel.

Before we ask what obligation the individual Jew owes to his heritage, we must first put a purely factual, and not a normative, question: What can be extracted from this Jewish heritage? I wish to state as emphatically as I can that the answer to this question imposes no obligation whatsoever. Reality implies and gives rise to reality alone and involves no obligation, and a factual judgment does not bind us to a normative one. I am not discussing here what the Jew must or should do. I am merely stating the fact that those things that a Jew can extract from Jewish history, from the 3,000-year-old phenomenon called Israel, in all its manifestations and vicissitudes, are nothing but religious values.

Religious values have taken a definite form in Judaism: a way of life of the Torah and the commandments, whose formulated expression is the halakhah. It is not possible to erect Judaism on a biblical basis, or on ethics, or on messianism. There are those who offer, as a substitute for Judaism, bibliolatry—the Bible itself, not the Bible within the framework of active Judaism and with the meaning given it by Judaism, but the Bible as a document of elevated ethical values and as a basis for secular, human-anthropocentric and Jewish-ethnocentric education. Jewishly, this approach is a distortion and, from the human point of view, an absurdity. Bibliolatry is not Judaism. It is a strange and highly paradoxical mixture of atheism and Christianity. It derives from atheism in that it deprives the Bible of its religious meaning, and from Christianity in that the latter has always clung to the Bible, using it to attack Judaism.

From this point of view we cannot claim to have contributed anything to world culture. There has never been such a thing as Jewish philosophy, but only philosophies coming from without. Some of them even contradict each other, and are either adapted by Judaism to its needs or rejected. There has never been such a thing as Jewish ethics. The religious faith embodied in the Torah and in the commandments does not suffer ethical categories, does not recognize human conscience or man's volitional intention cognitively perceived (the ethics of Socrates, Stoicism, and Spinoza) or felt as an obligation (Kantian ethics). It recognizes only the worship of God by man; it does not recognize the obligations of man to man, but only those of man to God. As a result, there have never been specific Jewish political or social ideas, specific Jewish artistic or aesthetic values, or a Jewish science. The only specifically unique Jewish creation that has appeared actively in history is halakhah, that is, the attempt to organize the rules of human life against a background of law, the aim of which is the service of God. The world did not accept this approach from us, but rejected it clearly and emphatically. At the time when this Jewish thought was gaining considerable influence, the world launched a successful counterattack. The counterattack was Christianity.

Let us imagine that the Jewish people, with all that it originated and created, had never existed; it is doubtful whether, in such a case, anything in the makeup of the world would be different from what it is. We cannot contribute anything of our own to the solution of problems that confront the world today because our peculiar approach to the world and man is that of the Torah and the commandments alone, which the world has not and is not likely to accept. Anything else that we may have to say is nothing but a paraphrase of what others have said in a more original form. The non-Jewish world does not need us to preach to them the philosophy of Jefferson and Lincoln—they preach that themselves. They do not have to learn liberalism from us, nor humanism, nor the rights of man. It is they who proclaimed the rights of man, and it is they who preach them. There is no point in our talking about being "a light to the gentiles."

Of the Jews of the diaspora, most—we might even say all—live in a gentile world, not only in a materialistic but also in a psychological and intellectual sense, and they are immersed in these world problems that are, in reality, non-Jewish. Hence, the Law will not go forth from Zion. What Zion is likely to produce it cannot produce at this moment, and if it could, the product would be unsuitable for a Jewry that has decided to live in a gentile world.

### Jewish Law

From neither the prophetic vision nor the messianic mission can we Israelis draw spiritual nourishment, for these do not constitute the link between us and Judaism as it actually existed in history. From the standpoint of historical reality, the people of Israel did not live by the Bible but by the Oral Law. A large part of mankind accepted the Bible but did not thereby become Jews. That is, the Bible is not the constitutive ingredient of Judaism; the Bible alone did not create Judaism. The factors that constitute Judaism—again, I state this not as an evaluation but as historical fact—are the halakhah and the prayer book. This alone is the heritage of Jews, and he who accepts them becomes a Jew and is absorbed in the Jewish people. It is the halakhah that made holy scripture out of twenty-four books that are, in part, second-rate literature and third-class history and philosophy, devoid of humanistic, ethical values. It is not the Bible that made Judaism, but Judaism, as revealed in the Oral Law, that made the Bible. Only through the halakhah did the twenty-four books of the Bible receive their holy imprint. Concerning the messianic ideal and the variants this ideal passed through in tradition, Maimonides, the greatest religious thinker produced by Judaism, says: "Man should not busy himself with legends nor spend too much time on the excesses of Midrash, and not make them basic, for they lead neither to awe nor love." Judaism, it is true, produced the messianic vision, but it is not dependent on it. For Judaism in its essence is nothing but the gray prose of the order of man's existence in his daily life, in his time and place, for the purpose of serving God; it is not the poetry of the vision of the end of days, which is merely religious folklore involving no obligations whatever.

When we deprive Jewish history of its authentic content and meaning—its religious content—we are creating a new people without historical continuity, even though it may continue to use historical slogans and labels. This I also state as an objective fact, without passing judgment. We do not have to go far to find a historical precedent. Two hours' flying time from here is a land that bears the fairest name in human history—at least in the world between India and the Atlantic—a land called Hellas. (Many of us feel that the name Israel is a still fairer name, but this has not been so in the history of mankind, in which the name "Jew" is a term of reproach.) Even today there is a land that bears the name of Hellas. But what has this Hellas to do with that other, fair Hellas? It surely occupies the same territory; its inhabitants may even share some of the biological traits of the old Greeks, for they were not physically exterminated but only absorbed by other nations; they speak a language that resembles classical Greek, and use the same alphabet; they continue to use names such as Themistocles, Pericles, Sophocles.

There are prospects for the existence of a State of Israel whose ties to Israel will be like those of modern Greece to historical Greece. It would occupy the same territory; the people within it would have inherited some of the biological traits of the Jews of old; it would speak a language more similar to that of Israel than modern Greek is to ancient Greek; it would use the same writing as that in which the Oral Law, and perhaps even the Torah itself, were written; and its sons would be called by the names of Abraham, Moses, and David. Just as the Greeks are proud that Hellenism was cultivated by their fathers, so would we be proud of that Judaism cultivated by our fathers. Such an Israel is possible, but the state that *has* been established is becoming a Mediterranean state that is severing its ties with the historic Jewish people.

The repudiation of the actual content of Judaism, the work of the Torah and commandments, vitiates their use as a pedagogical tool. There are those who march under the banner of prophetic Jewish ethics. But Judaism is embodied in religion, and this very fact does not permit the existence of a category of Jewish ethics. Religious faith, which is incorporated in the Torah and the commandments, does not suffer ethical categories. It does not recognize human conscience; it is no accident that the world "conscience" is not to be found in biblical Hebrew. And it is no accident that none of the prophets of Israel ever addressed himself to the human conscience. Human conscience becomes a central, focal point only when man does not recognize God. Ethics as a supreme value is an atheistic category that stems from the view of man as the end of existence and the center of creation. The atheist Kant was a great ethicist, since for him man was God.

The prophets placed man against God, and never against man. The people of Israel never struggled and never suffered for ethical values, and never marched in the forefront of ethical consciousness. We have no right to interpret our fathers differently from the way in which they interpreted themselves. Furthermore, it is doubtful whether ethics can be qualified according to human groupings, whether there can be such a thing as Jewish ethics. It is possible that ethics is not subject to qualification by any adjective derived from human collectivities, or from any intellectual current or world view, either.

It is an empirical fact that Judaism is in reality embodied in the Torah and in the commandments and hence cannot be an ethical system. There are only two senses in which ethics can be understood. Ethics is either a volitional effort of man in conformity with his understanding of the truth of existence (the ethics of Socrates, the Stoics, Spinoza) or the volitional effort of man in accordance with his feeling of obligation over reality (the ethics of Kant). But in the prayer of the *Shema* that I and many Jews repeat: "And thou shalt not turn aside to follow after thy heart and after thine eyes" (Num. 15:39). "Not to follow after thy heart" refutes Kant, and "not to follow after thine eyes" refutes Socrates.

A way of life can be derived from Judaism. The historical reality, and the revelations of the tens of generations that have preceded us, testify to the fact that it can be done. The religious way of life drawn from Judaism can be appraised differently from the ethical point of view, and on this matter there will be no agreement among us. But it is not possible to derive from Judaism guidance for a secular way of life. If we empty Judaism of its religious significance we cannot derive ethics from it, for Judaism negates ethics.

The air is filled with slogans of prophetic-ethical vision—the messianic mission, the redemption of humanity through Jewish ideals—but since these concepts have been deprived of their religious meaning, the result must inevitably be cynicism and nihilism. I do not deny that it is possible to educate without religion—but not from Jewish sources. There have been and are societies, advanced from many points of view, not founded on religious principles and not embodying religious content, but rather based on secular values of their own. The attempt to teach secular ethics from sources of Israel must necessarily lead to Kfar Kassim. We should forget about these pyrotechnics of being "a light to the gentiles" and look at ourselves a little more closely. It is fitting that in a discussion of the essential nature, tasks, and obligations of Israel, mention should be made of Kfar Kassim. Thus we may pause and examine more closely the nature and essence of our existence as it is in actuality, and not as it is seen in the light of the messianic mission, which is, after all, a cheap thing, entailing no obligation.

### Judaism and the Jewish State

Official representatives of Orthodoxy, rabbis and leaders of the religious community, stress the religious significance of the political events of our day. I deny it. God did not reveal Himself in nature or in history, but in the Torah. You cannot put a halo around any political-historical event, even the establishment of the State of Israel. Judaism has a number of interpretations of the concept of the messianic mission, ranging from folklore fancy to the conception of Maimonides, but in every Jewish conception of messianism, without exception, the redemption of Israel is linked to the perfection of the world or of man, at least of man in Israel. The State of Israel was established not only without this perfection but, unlike the Hasmonaean kingdom in its day, without a basis in, or impulse from, the Torah. Whether we define ourselves as Orthodox or not, we have established a state as patriotic Jews, and Jewish patriotism, like any other patriotism, is a normal human phenomenon without any implications of holiness. There is no holiness except in the fulfillment of the Torah: "And thou shalt be holy to thy God." We have no right, therefore, to see the establishment of Israel as reflecting on the messianic mission, in any possible sense of the idea. We do not know whether this state is the first flowering of our redemption and whether it arose through divine providence: We do know that it is an achievement of Jews who grew weary of exile and of foreign rule, and that we did what we could, in the light of our understanding and on our own responsibility, not from an impulse derived from the Torah or its teachings.

Arguing for religion based on its usefulness and advantage for man in general, and for the people of Israel and the state in particular, is a kind of desecration of religion. It makes religion an instrument for the satisfaction of human interests, and it makes faith a mercenary love. He who conceives of himself and the events of his life and the destiny of his generation as dependent on providence, and sees the finger of God in all things, is pitiful from the standpoint of religion itself. The problem—and the task of religion—is to live the life of Torah and faith, a life of awe and love, in a generation "of the eclipse of God" as is ours, in which we, with the strength of our hands and in the light of our understanding and responsibility, succeeded in establishing ourselves as a national entity. It is for this reason that I support the separation of religion and state, so as not to make the religion of Israel an instrument in the service of the state; so that religion not become a bureaucracy in a government office.

Between this state, which embodies secular values, and the religion of Israel, there is a need for a clear confrontation. Such a confrontation is not possible as long as religion tries to be a function of the state. Every attempt to take stock of ourselves and to find a way to the world of values obligates us to rise above this two-sided falsification, which is symbolically embodied in the "Rock of Israel," in the Proclamation of Independence. The "Rock of Israel" in the prayer following the *Shema*—the "Rock of Israel" of King David and of the prophet Isaiah—transcends Israel, human values, and all human categories. The "Rock of Israel" of the Proclamation resides in Israel, is Israel itself, is the national genius of the people of Israel. The insertion of the "Rock of Israel" in the secular document of our Proclamation was nothing but a conspiracy—the bribe that the secular community paid to the religious community, which the latter, in turn, did not hesitate to accept. Against this background one can have no confrontation between the world of religious values and the world of national, secular values; and no real struggle between them is possible.

The fateful, transcendent spiritual struggle—which alone can yield us values, and from which alone we can derive normative laws for our position as Jews—is possible only through a clear confrontation between this state of ours, which at the moment is secular, and religion, which demands an altogether different quality of political organization of the people of Israel. Religious institutions established by the secular state; the religious seal affixed to secular functions; positive and negative religious commands included as exceptions in the total array of secular laws, as a result of an understanding among themselves; a secular authority that forces an arbitrary selection of religious manifestations on the community, not for the sake of heaven but for political expediency; and a religion that enjoys the help granted by secular power—all these things are travesties of reality, perversions of social and religious truth, and the source of intellectual and spiritual corruption. The state and secular society must speak their piece without hiding behind the skirt of religion; then we will see whether they have anything to say as a Jewish state and as a Jewish community. And religion must say its piece without hiding behind administrative skirts; then we will see whether it is the Law of Life. Only from such a confrontation can vital cultural values grow out of Jewish sources and flourish for us and our sons and daughters, and for the diaspora as well.

To solve the fateful problems of the triangle—the Jewish people, the state of Jews, Judaism—two formidable obstacles that prevent the conjunction of these three factors must first be removed. The first of these is the artificial administrative connection between the secular state and religion, which makes a genuine link between them impossible. The second is fund-raising drives, which do not unite but separate the state from the soul of the people in the diaspora. Every serious attempt to create a conscious, true spiritual relationship between this state and the Jewish people, in order to rescue diaspora Judaism from vanishing through assimilation and to rescue the state by making it a state for the entire Jewish people—every such attempt founders on the factual rock that the Jews of the diaspora pay a ransom, in the form of gifts of money, which absolves them from fulfilling their obligations to Judaism and to themselves as Jews; at the same time, by receiving money from others, the Jews in Israel, and the state itself, find it possible to free themselves from the task of creating a political and social rule that has the dignity of independent existence. It is clear that as long as the Israeli community is dependent on others for the satisfaction of its needs it will not be induced to make the effort required to change this.

Until Israel frees itself from basing its existence on the spiritual enjoyment and gratification that it confers on other Jews who are neither interested in, nor see any need for, personal participation in its fate, it will not be able to be a source of spiritual or ethical influence, not to speak of religious influence. And until the Jews of the diaspora are deprived of the very attractive opportunity to fulfill their Jewish obligations by gifts of money to Israel, there is no prospect that a spark of real Jewish feeling may be kindled in the diaspora or that a spiritual or religious Jewish revival may take place there under the influence of the State of Israel.

# 7

# The Case for Secularism

## GERSHON SHAKED

The fathers are idealists, heroes, pioneers, striding forward in the
vanguard of the nation, showing the way, what must be done, enthusiastic zealots, dreamers and visionaries, an exemplary elite . . . tara-
ta-ta-ta fiery-feverish, showering sparks . . . bearing a new world . . .
and the sons are speculators!

ha! profiteers . . . totally speculators! . . .

this is the archetype and the prototype, the end of all miracles, that
is the dream, this is its interpretation! Nu, and my sons—whose sons
are they?

Haim Hazaz, 1938

## I

"Exilic culture, the culture of romantic grief and of passive hope, is
doomed to extinction. What shall we do until the dawn of our new
culture, until a culture of creativity and enterprise emerges in the full
light of day? No longer do ghetto strengths, the powers of preservation
and of cowering under protective wings, offer succor. Shall we find
enough new strength both for the effort of a gigantic creative leap and
for sustaining the national soul during the period of transition? Or,
heaven forfend, are we the victims of an abysmal tragedy: to suffer labor
pains but without the strength to give birth." These words were written
in Russia in 1919 by Moshe Glickson, summarizing a past that had but
recently been annihilated, yet expressing doubts regarding the future. In
his belief that ghetto culture was doomed, Glickson shared the views of
many men of his time. When Y. H. Brenner wrote his essay about
Mendele Mokher Sepharim's works, he claimed that Mendele had described a culture that richly deserved destruction—a destruction that, in

any case, awaited it. In Brenner's uncompromising polemic, "settle-ments of Jewish workers in Eretz Israel" was the only answer to the processes at work among European Jewry. He also prophesied a new secular culture as an outgrowth of the cultural-economic revolution that would take place among the Jews (without, however, spelling out the nature of that cultural phenomenon). In contradistinction to Ahad Ha'am, Glickson did not hazard a cultural forecast in his article. Nor did he describe the characteristics of the "cultural center" of the future, but expressed the hope that a culture of constructive development would not resemble the doomed culture of the past. Perhaps Glickson's words do transcend the descriptive and the analytical, for they are certainly an expression of a deep-seated but unarticulated aspiration. Zionist culture was born of the aspiration to have done with the culture of the ghetto, just as many Zionists wanted to take leave of Western culture. In fact, some ideologists claimed that the Jews in Israel would have to adapt themselves to the Middle Eastern culture regnant in the area. All the elements imported from abroad would have to be transformed and adapted to the new life-style, and only such elements that could survive the tension created on impact with the indigenous culture would leave their impress on it.

## II

This subject bears emphasis from another standpoint. Zionism sought to emancipate itself not only from the ghetto but also from the "decline of the West." *Altneuland*, Herzl's liberal European vision, did not appeal to the majority of the *olim*, whose aspirations were directed toward another reality and another society and who hoped that Israel would provide a place of refuge from the cultural decadence of Europe. They aspired to a kind of cultural "October Revolution" that would transform the Jewish way of life and elevate the national spirit of a society fleeing the ghettos of the declining West.

Many of the short stories and poems of the period are imbued with this spirit, and they all speak in praise of the "blessings of the soil" and in contempt of the urban culture that the young pioneers had aban-doned. Although *halutziut* (pioneering) did hold an adversary position vis-à-vis "ghetto culture," the main thrust of its opposition was directed at the culture of the metropolis. It perceived itself as a process opposed to the accelerated urbanization that was then sweeping Europe. A typical example of a work expressing these new norms, which were charac-teristic of the antiurban and anti-Western yearnings of the pioneering society, is Avraham's Shlonski's poem "Metropolis" (although the formal characteristics of his poetry are actually those of an urban, modernistic poet).

*Metropolis*

*Yet again I go a guiltless man*

*Sentenced to carry his soul to a far off crater*
*To see the sons of Abbadon*
*Step-children both to Satan and to God.*

*Here are they—sons of Moloch*
*and sons of Kemosh*
*To which granary shall they carry murder's crop?*
*Phosphorescence of rotting wood instead of* tephilin
*Do I see shining on every forehead.*

*Beautifully faithless city! Then as today.*
*Looking like a mushroom sprouting, black like a phylactery*
*I am so confused in vanity of jubilation*
*Among metropolis' sparks cold as polar glow.*

*Then as today I am among allurements.*
*Seen and unseeing, a headless spokesman.*
*Wandering hurled thus your portraits, brothers,*
*I bound upon my right arm as an amulet.*

*I loved you, my brothers, among stabbing cacti*
*Trampled under hamsin's claws and boulders' aridity.*
*In revolt and in reconciliation we'll submit our necks:*
*Blessed is he whose yoke weighs down upon us*
*Amen.*
*Selah.*

This declarative poem by Shlonski contrasts the "beautifully faithless city" with the "stabbing cacti." That polarity is also found, in various configurations, in the poetry of Uri Zvi Greenberg, Y. Lamdan and Shin Shalom, as well as among most of that generation's storytellers. Sometimes they did not juxtapose these polar opposites, but in blessing the earth they left it to the reader's discernment to discover what they were rejecting. The "stabbing cacti" held more than a *halutzik* Zionist connotation. They indicate a world outlook influenced by the *narodniki* (populists) of Russia and the transformation their thoughts underwent in A. D. Gordon's philosophy. But the existential experience was also a romantic one à la Chateaubriand. While Israel was perceived as being a place of refuge from Western civilization, it was also the return to it, like the Western man's return to nature, return in the name of rebirth.

### III

The pioneers who wanted to recreate or renew culture in Israel faced a forlorn hope. They rejected two basic factors that molded contemporary Jewish history: both the basic tenets of the traditional culture and, simultaneously (and this is a point that requires emphasis), the opposite tendency, which sought acculturation into the modern urban environment.

The *talush* (torn off, in limbo; Shimon Halkin's term for the Jew who was culturally and socially detached) was a product of the polar tension that also characterized the "heroes" of Jewish culture in the nineteenth century. Those who left the ghetto and vainly sought to assimilate into Western society fell between two stools. But these "detached ones" transformed their very distress into a source of inspiration, laying the foundations for a new Zionist culture upon the dialectic of their twofold rejection (of the ghetto and the West).

They rejected the West either because Western culture proved inhospitable, or because, upon closer observation, they discovered that Chemosh and Gomorrah (Sodom's twin sister) were no nicer than ghetto culture. Perhaps the existential source of their search for another culture lies in this double disenchantment. The longings for "Another Genesis" and for the "Gilboa" that characterize Shlonski's poetry arose from the abyss that had opened up before the "detached ones." Having chosen the Zionist solution, they were confronted with the question of what its cultural expression would be. How would they paint self-portraits as artists now that they had seemingly left the fruitful tension that had informed their world while still in exile?

Their position between Judaism and assimilation, between the culture of the ghetto and that of the West, had determined their fate. Many notable literary and cultural achievements had resulted, both when the resolution of the tension tended toward the West (as in the assimilationist works of Freud, Schnitzler, Isak Babel) and when its orientation still ostensibly tended in the direction of the ghetto (as in the works of Hebrew and Yiddish authors). This tension disappeared or was muted when some of them came to Eretz Israel. Indeed, Jews emigrated to Palestine as an act of aliyah to Eretz Yisrael one of whose aims was precisely to find release from that tension and to begin "Another Genesis." They realized full well that their ascent—aliyah—involved trading a cultural decline for a social gain: *reculer pour mieux sauter*—a deliberate withdrawal as a prerequisite of advancement. Israel held out no promise of a cultural rose garden, and could not compete a priori with either ghetto or Western culture. Granted, it could provide them with something not available to them in exile, but it also deprived both the group and the individual of some of the cultural wealth available in the West.

In 1924, Jacob Rabinowitz wrote about the development of Hebrew literature, clearly intending that his observations should be understood to subsume the totality of modern culture in Israel:

> Literature will be different here, which is to say that it will not be Jewish in the conventional sense, but rather humanistic, comprising many genres and shades. Even its Jewishness will be different—as befits a Judaism adapting itself to the life here and deriving from it. There will be negative manifestations as well, so that here and there will be shrinking and retreat. The base will broaden, the back will ache. Neither exultation nor embitterment are called for. One must merely observe and understand.

These words are an accurate reflection of the outlook that characterized the leading group made up of such people as A. D. Gordon, Gershon Hanokh, David Horowitz, and others who wrote about literature and culture. They generally held that the ordinary was preferable to pretension or unbridled ambition. They all joined the two-edged rejection of both the West and the ghetto. But in practice, Western culture and literature continued to serve as a model even when this ran against the theory to which many subscribed.

The majority of those who contributed to *halutzik* [pioneering] culture did aspire to that other, new beginning, but they drew inspiration from many different sources. They tried to give artistic realization to the web of cultural tensions that was forming in the new space they occupied, and they were, of course, influenced by the many traditions they brought with them. Some of the novel elements that informed secular Israeli culture were a love of the soil and of labor, inherited from the Russian *narodniki*, coupled with the strange dream of integration with the "Orient." They certainly did not create a culture ex nihilo. They took the European "something" and the Jewish "substance" with them to their new living space, and these essences were in constant tension with the new circumstances of their lives and with their determination to sever themselves from the "old things" Along with Rabinowitz, they knew that there was a price to be paid for the new start; they would be bereft of the West and of the ghetto's culture at once.

The young pioneers who congregated at Beitaniya during the twenties represented the best of European intelligentsia. They had come to Palestine to strike roots and to be rebuilt themselves in the process of building the land. They testify that this achievement exacted a toll. Something had to be sacrificed. Occasionally they, too, remembered the "onions and the leeks," the cultural fleshpots of Warsaw, Vienna, and Paris: "I retied my spiritual bonds to Europe, antiquated Europe, disreputable, excommunicated Europe. How great it is and how beautiful, how I long for it! For it is the breath in our nostrils and the marrow of our bones!" Thus wrote one of the members of the commune in 1922 in their journal, "Our Commune." He is followed in that same publication by another, who wrote: "Can you honestly forgo the thousands of cultural possibilities, giving up the burning impressions of a European metropolis, the whole wide world churning with unknown wonders—and all that for the sake of realizing our ideas in this land?" The response of Beitaniya's *halutzim* to these vexing questions and aspirations, to their longing in the East for the horizons of the West,[1] was ultimately that there was some existential significance to the new life they were creating that no European palace could possibly afford them.

What, ultimately, did these youngsters, who had relinquished both cultures, hope for? Repeatedly they ask themselves what would characterize the "inferior" culture that would evolve here. Could it compensate them, if only slightly, for what they had lost? Would the new socioeconomic structure, their experiences of newfound independence, or even the future political asylum be able to indemnify them for cultural deprivation? Would they be able to withstand the pain of "two homelands," the one they abandoned and the one being created? The principal compensation was in the experience of cultural pioneering. They felt that they were laying the foundations for a secular Jewish culture. They believed that they were the vanguard of a cultural renaissance. They were the principal proponents of the process of secularization: With their help, religious culture could become the basis for a reconstructed secular Jewish culture. In my opinion, whoever does not regard this as either novel or remarkable (as, for instance, Barukh Kurzweil) does not comprehend the great change that the *yishuv* (prestate Jewish society in Palestine) carried out in the cultural sphere from the early years of this century up to the forties.

There is little point in rehearsing well-known accomplishments that are today taken for granted—foremost among them, the creation of a language, spoken Hebrew. The conversion of an ancient written tongue from a sacred to a literary idiom, thence to a spoken language again, and from a spoken, contemporary language once more into the language of modern writing is an amazing cultural phenomenon. The language itself bears witness to the network of tensions that developed in social and cultural life. The vocabulary, syntax, and structure of "our Hebrew" were formed under the influence of Yiddish, the written and spoken language of the Ashkenazic diaspora. However, a new pronunciation also emerged, with the *milra* (accent on the latter syllable) of Jews from the Orient and with the introduction of an Arabic vocabulary.

Both these sources were affected by the vocabulary of European languages and their syntax. This unusual combination of European syntax with Oriental phonetics as it appears in spoken and written Hebrew testifies to integration and ingathering of exiles. Further, this testimony is far more credible than today's efforts at the artificial resuscitation of ethnic folklore. The first, more credible, authentic examples of cultural integration cited above took place in a variety of sectors in the evolving Israeli culture. Some still-popular songs and folk dances of that period are a strange mixture of dances and tunes brought from Poland, Russia, and Romania (*krakoviak*, polka, hora) and dances and tunes that were current among the Jews of Yemen. Some of the folk dances that were "invented" by Gurit Kadmon and Sarah HaLevi Tannai are experiments in "phonetic" combinations that attempt to synthesize East and West and create a local culture, a kind of mixture fraught with cultural tensions. Another example of this admixture was the fruitful collaboration between songwriter Nahum Nardi and Brakha Tzefira and Esther Gamlieli: an Eastern European composer striving to construct a musical style that would be compatible with the Oriental world.

This cultural "alchemy" was attempted on the plane of "high" culture too: in Nahum Gutman's drawings, the music of Ben-Haim and others, as well as in the poetry of Ratosch. Even the culture of clothes fashion undertook to find a "mediating language" between the Russian *rubashka* shirt and the Arabic *keffiya* headdress. In all the so-called marginal areas of culture there were interesting attempts at fashioning the new out of a novel configuration of extant materials, among them the ideals of the Russian *narodniki*, the ideal of simplicity, Eastern European music and dance, the cultural patterns of Yemenite Jewry, and "bedouin" ideals—real or imagined. This admixture became the new culture of the youth movements. They served as a seedbed in which new "languages" were absorbed much more readily than in other sectors. Consequently, the new configurations became the accepted norm, because the youth movements were considered to be the elite of Israeli society,[2] and their adoption of the new cultural configurations made them into binding models, compelling, au courant. "Israeli" (synthetic) culture was the hallmark of the leaders and trendsetters who attempted to employ it to promote the absorption of new immigrants. Whoever sought acculturation had to accept the youth movements' rules of the game, and whoever eschewed these values perforce was barred from membership in the fashion-conscious group, and relegated to the sidelines. Marginal youth in the 1920s, 1930s, and 1940s continued on a course of pseudo-Western assimilation, preferring the Central European cafés on Tel Aviv's beach to the clubhouses of the youth movement, where the new Israeli youth rites were in vogue.

The attempts at integrating disparate cultural components were sometimes quite ludicrous. The Ohel theater staged a Russian play entitled *Jacob and Rachel*, translated into Hebrew by Shlonski. The actors donned bedouin costumes and mimicked Yemenite Hebrew accents, which had, however, a strong undertone of Russian phonetics. Basically, all these experiments were a search after new forms of expression. Whoever claims that this reflects a neo-Canaanite spirit, which is to say a yearning to strike roots in the new Middle Eastern landscape while severing the roots in the past, simply does not know what he is saying. Genuine "Canaanites" did not seek to create new configurations by confronting the old ingredients of Jewish culture. On the contrary, they wanted to rid themselves of tensions through the simple expedient of massive infusions of local color, which would replace the old tensions with a new culture. But authentic Israeli culture is the product of cultural tensions, rather than an escape from them. The genuine product resulted from sincere efforts to create something "Israeli" in a melting pot, blending a new ideal from the preexisting components (Eastern European Jewish and Middle Eastern) and casting it in its own mold. The leadership elite's ideal was to remove their *galut* finery and clothe themselves in the textile of the "homeland." Consequently, people took leave of their old names, preferring to be called Sadan rather than Shtock, or Agnon rather than Czazkes, Ratosch rather than Halperin, Zehavi not Goldberg, Mazor not Mizrahi. To change one's name was a symbolic act signifying the adoption of a new identity, "assimilation" to something else—leaving the culture of both the ghetto and the West behind.

## V

Refashioning a secular culture in Israel had some deeper cultural aspects, too. Bialik's idea of "Assembly"[3] is one of the most profound and most important experiments in a secularizing nationalization of the religious tradition. In effect, his contribution to the concept of renewal was more far-reaching than Ahad Ha'am's. His ideological essays spoke in the name of secular ideas whose roots extended back to religious society, e.g., the idea of absolute justice. Bialik and Revnitzki's *Book of the Aggadah* transmitted their old cultural tradition in modern dress both to young people and to adults, including budding authors such as Moshe Shamir. This work remains a prime example of a religious tradition that has been secularized and thus transformed into a primary secular cultural vehicle.

The late Professor Schirmamn, in his anthology of medieval Spanish and Provençal poetry, and Professor Tishbi, in his *Teachings of the Zohar,* continued the task of compiling the Jewish tradition in the direction taken by Bialik. His legends and Midrashic material did not originally appear in the form that they took in *Sefer Ha'Aggadah.* Originally the stories were interwoven with discussions of the *halakhah* or with interpretations of Scripture. They were part of a tradition of debate concerning religious laws and commandments, or of homiletics accompanying public prayer and ritual. Bialik removed them from their original environment and reorganized them entirely on secular principles: historically and morally, from Adam to the destruction of the Second Temple, and from man's proper relations to his fellow man to man's proper relations to his family. The religious tradition is sorted out and reorganized in accordance with the needs of secular man, who is cut off from the halakhah and who no longer heeds sermons. From a secular point of view, the views on life expressed in the Aggadah are a tradition of the practical wisdom and common sense of a national group that, in the past, had been principally a religious group. That practical wisdom in its new form (like other elements of Jewish culture) became part of secular culture, and the modern Israeli does not feel obliged to take upon himself the yoke of the commandments or the yoke of communal life. The secular community took shape as a result of those transformations of the halakhah and the Midrash, and later on, of the poetry of the Middle Ages and the *Teachings of the Zohar.*

The basic ideological and practical tendencies of the idea behind these compilations were brilliantly expressed by one of the spiritual fathers of the reconstructed Israeli culture, Berl Katznelson. His remarks on the confrontation between the present and the tradition have become the theoretical foundations of many cultural enterprises, and they are among the most commonly quoted and accepted principles inherited from the years when the new Israeli culture was coming into being:

An innovative and creative generation does not cast the legacy of past generations upon the dungheap. It examines, probes, rejects, and accepts. At times it seizes upon an existing tradition and adds to it, and sometimes it digs about in the kitchen midden and uncovers something long forgotten, scrapes off the rust, and brings an ancient tradition to life, if it can nourish the soul of the generation of seekers. [1934]

## VI

This is not the place to speak at length of the influence of the Bible on the new national, secular life. The Bible has become the cornerstone of Israeli education, and in the secular schools it has undergone a thoroughgoing secular transformation. The educational values of the Bible were not necessarily religious. The historical, archaeological, and national approaches to the Bible have created a Bible for the secular reader whose meanings are different from those that the Bible had in the culture of the ghetto. A similar transformation has taken place with regard to history. (One may agree with the Zionist historiography of Dinur or not, but its influence upon popular historical thought in Israel is undeniable.) The emphasis of historical study has been changed because of the tendency to deprecate the ghetto and the culture of the ghetto and to emphasize the periods of independence, the pre- and postghetto culture. The secular transformation of the religious tradition is also evident in the changes in meaning that took place in the development of Israeli holidays from "Jewish" holidays. Holidays that are essentially religious in nature, such as Rosh Hashanna and Yom Kippur, still occupy the central place in the religious tradition. However, the Israeli tradition took holidays that had been marginal in the historical tradition and placed them in the center of community life: Tu BiShvat and the Festival of First Fruits (Shavuot) were interpreted as celebrations of nature and the earth, and they took a central place on the stage of a ritual consciousness that even inspired ceremonies and dances suitable to these reconstructed holidays. These new rituals did have some connection with the past, but their major link was with the present of the Jewish National Fund, not with the treasury of the Temple of the Lord. Moreover, Hanukkah and Pesach began to occupy a central place in the consciousness and actions of secular Israelis, who gave a secular interpretation to these two religious festivals. It was no longer the miracle of the jar of oil, but rather the war of the Maccabees that seemed meaningful at Hanukkah. The saying that in every generation a man must see himself as if he had personally left Egypt received a thoroughly Zionist significance.

*Were these transformations negative?* I would say no! They established a worthy link between the Jewish life of the past (which had lost its meaning) and Jewish life in the present. They wished to restore the glory of the time before the antiquated culture of the ghetto. They did not entirely reject the culture of the ghetto, but they attempted to transplant and renew it in the Land of Israel. We are therefore considering a sincere effort to adapt the tradition to new, pioneering and antiurban (which explains the agricultural festivals) ideals, and to link it to new cultural elements that had developed in Israel (the new songs, the dances, the costumes)—the dances and songs of the sowers, and of the reapers. The Song of Songs became an Israeli love song, a song of courtship. The songs of Hanukkah took on national significance, and the ceremonies of Pesach were given a new form. All this emerged from the secular transformations we have discussed. They were supported by the school system from kindergartens to the youth movements, and by the social elite of the settlement movements, who created a new Israeli with his own vision of the world.

*Have masterpieces been created in literature, dance, music, and the plastic arts?* As Rabinowitz wrote, "There will be negative manifestations as well, so that here and there will be shrinking and retreat. The base will broaden, and the back will ache." Works were created whose essential power lies in the attempt to become involved in the new domain (like those of Yizhar), and other works were written whose strength is in the expression of doubt that the Jews will be able to sink roots in the new land (Hazaz). The best literary works do not simplify the processes of integration but point at gaps and vacuums, asking questions, raising problems. Thus, literature is aware of the new problem, but the power of the emerging new cultural life, the creation of new cultural idioms, surpassed the finished products in which they were embedded. In any case, many of the works of literature, music, and the plastic arts show that a sincere effort has been made to create a new reality—in time and in space. In his decision to make a new choice, the modern Israeli was no different from his forefathers, who also made changes, and whose relation to the tradition changed from generation to generation, because every generation chose to reinterpret the past, a past whose vital power depended in large measure upon the new selections that were constantly being made. That selection was not only positive, but negative as well. The source of its search for some new possibility is in a revolutionary experience: "Level the old world to its foundations! Build a new world on those foundations." To abandon and demolish in order to build and be rebuilt, says Zionism, thus unwittingly following in the footsteps of Nietzsche and Berdichevski.

*What had happened to the Zionist cultural revolution?* Where is it disappearing? Why are its creators ashamed of their creation? Why have Zionists lost self-confidence and begun to return as penitents to the culture of the ghetto, or to "descend"[4] to Western culture? The social and economic developments typical of achievement-oriented Western societies, on the one hand, and the opposite trend (which is no less typical of Iran than of Israel), which claims that the only proper response to the generation of Western urban culture is religious revival, seem to be taking over our lives. Being Israeli no longer seems attractive; it seems much more desirable to go back and become a "Western" man again, or to give oneself over to piety. Not only have social processes changed, social norms have, too. An anti-Israeli worldview is taking shape in our Israel; in order to mold a new Israeli society a successful attempt is being made to destroy the infrastructure that had been laid down.

There are many reasons for these developments, most of which are social. The "Israel" of the *yishuv* had been a country that absorbed immigrants. While still in the diaspora those immigrants had been trained for their aliyah, so they brought with them the ideals of a new society and a new culture. When those who had been absorbed became themselves the absorbers, they created a "culture of absorption" and set the norms for the groups being absorbed. The mass immigration of the 1950s was too swift for the absorbers to digest the newcomers. Moreover, urbanization and economic changes in Israel transformed the absorbing society from a pioneering to a Western society. Not only did the absorbing society fail to make its mark on the character of the new immigrants, that veteran society lost its own cultural character. A society of *olim*, who had once adopted new social norms and made enormous efforts to establish a modern kind of Judaism and an authentic form of Israeli-ism, once again became a society of immigrants. A great part of those immigrants, even those who were actually born in Israel, are no longer characterized by an Israeli identity. Everyone of any discernment maintains that Israeli-ism has gone bankrupt, which is why some people have returned to Western culture, body and soul—they are in the East, but their hearts are in the Far West. And those who are dissatisfied with Western culture find their way back to the Holy One Blessed be He, or they seek similar solutions from the far-off Indies. Once again the West has become an economic and social ideal, and it goes without saying that it is also a cultural idea. Even if someone does not reach the ultimate conclusion to emigrate to the West, he does import the West to Israel, both in writing and in speech—he is in the East, but his culture is Western.

Israeli-ism feels increasingly ashamed of itself, having no self-confidence to resist Western styles of dress, music, or manners (including Eastern European mannerisms). Simplicity and straightforward human relations are no longer the norm (although they had been central to the anti-Western and antighetto principles of the new Israeli society). They have now been replaced by elaborate ceremonies that are foreign to this area and to the condition of Israel, imported from Poland in cellophane wrappers. "Israeli parties" around the campfire have become cocktail parties held in the backyards of colonels and generals (reserves!). Israeli songs have become the nostalgic melodies of old men who long for the past, men whose old age is shamed by their youth. In this hour of truth (which is not that of nostalgia), we all caper to the dances of the West, and we hum the latest hit tune. Instead of melodies we have Eurovision,

and instead of folk-dancing, we will soon be dancing the last tango of Tel
Aviv. The miserable inner conclusion drawn from the loss of Israeli
identity is simply *yerida*. By emigrating, a person who has accepted
European and American mores as a desirable social norm can put his
longings for a distant land into practice. The emigrant returns to the
very longings that haunted the members of the Beitaniya group. However, those early settlers had struggled hard against their Western urges
in an attempt to produce a new Israeli culture.

In that longing for the West lies the abandonment of the tension
between Judaism and the West, and between Judaism and the local
culture. Whoever leaves for the West abandons one of the two poles of
his culture, and leaves behind his "Israeli tension." He attempts to step
out of the Israeli transformation of the Jewish condition and return to the
earlier state of affairs. This constitutes a return (or an attempt at return)
to assimilation, while the converse of assimilation (Orthodox Judaism)
offers another escape, since the individual is no longer torn apart in an
effort to provide creative energy.

## VII

Ultimately that return is simply a return to the ghetto. Rabbi Shakh
said correctly, from the point of view of orthodox piety, that the Jewish
people, in that it is Jewish, does not need Eretz Israel at all. The culture
of the ghetto does not require the Old-New Land. The Jews in Eretz
Israel tried to transform the culture of the ghetto and to give it new,
secular meaning. The culture of "compilation" is the opposite of the
culture of the ghetto. When return to orthodox piety is authentic, it leads
to the culture of the halakhah and traditional biblical interpretation, to a
religious world that has no need for the modern economic and social
world. The culture of the ghetto is that of the "Kolel." It brings back the
*yeshiva bachurim* whose Torah is their occupation, and whose occupation
is Torah, and a society whose Torah is its flour, and for whom without
Torah there is no flour.[5] The culture of the ghetto in Israel regards the
secular Jewish society around it as if it were gentile, institutions to be
exploited halakhically in order to make a living from the Torah, and to
make a living for "Torah."

## VIII

Israeli society is undergoing another regressive change. One component of the process of knitting a new culture of Israeli-ism was the
attempt at a complex and fascinating mixture of Eastern and Western
folklore, Eastern and Western language. As noted, that mixture was

successful in several areas. One response of Israeli society and its institutions to the disintegration of the "Israeli image" and the loss of "Israeli norms" has been the encouragement of ethnic groups and ethnic folklore (a field that now supports many Ashkenazim). Apparently, the new intention is not to foster social integration, but rather pluralism. Much is said in the name of spurious cultural pluralism, rather than in the name of cultural unity. The Israeli ideal had always been the ingathering of the exiles, changing a dispersed band of exiles into a nation, and certainly not encouraging disintegration and splintering. If the *Maimuna* festival is meant to be a general Israeli holiday, all the better. However, if it is meant to maintain ethnic divisions, not to bring us forward toward an Israeli identity but to distance us from that goal, it simply recreates the culture of the ghetto. Even if that ghetto is in North Africa, it is still simply a ghetto.

## IX

Western culture and ghetto culture in themselves are red herrings. They make Israelis emigrate to New York or send them back to Kabtsiel and Casablanca. Original Israeli culture took what it could from Warsaw and from San'ah, from the diaspora and from the Land of Israel, from the tradition in many guises, and from modernity, which requires a new selection of traditional material. However, that culture aspired to combine its sources, to live with tension, so that tension would produce a new, independent identity. It was aware that that identity might be more limited or even inferior to the sum of identities from which it sprang, but it hoped that at least the identity would be different. In fact, Jews in the diaspora imitated that new Israeli culture. In the Ramah camps run by the Conservative movement in the United States, the campers sang Israeli songs and danced Israeli dances, and they even tried to imitate that directness in manners that will be identified with Israel.

Israeli society has become a spiritual center, although not exactly because it rebuilt the collapsing *succah* of the Rabbi of Satmer,[6] but because it created a new center to be imitated (and not as Ahad Ha'am saw it); but if Israelis imitate the life-style of the youth who attend Camp Ramah (at home, that is, away from the camp), then whom will those youngsters in America imitate?

## X

The struggle for an Israeli identity, no matter how synthetic (in both senses of the word), is a struggle for a certain norm, for a handhold, a point of departure for a society that has lost its European and Jewish identity. When such norms do develop, they sometimes have a tendency to mold people in their image, to demand apparent uniformity. Therefore the Israeli society of the *yishuv* was collective in its thinking and exigent in its demands upon behavior. Some people rebelled against the power of Israeli identity as a norm imposed on pure, independent individuality; the rebels were able to revolt against that identity as long as there was an Israeli image with which it was possible to contend; but once that norm was lost, the baby and the bathwater were both thrown out, leaving an empty tub. The lonely Israeli can no longer discover his Israeli loneliness, because that very Israeli-ism from which he sought to escape has disappeared. What remains is a people whose image is blurred, sitting in the East but whose heart yearns for Western shores, which lives a secular life but is gnawed by guilt feelings because of a lost *yiddishkeit* that it is largely incapable of defining.

Let me emphasize that I do not wallow in nostalgia for an Israeli produced on an assembly line according to some historical specification. Israel needs religious Israelis, Sepharadic Israelis, and Ashkenazi Israelis. The "Western" Israeli may dwell in peace with the "Jewish" Israeli, as long as they share an identity. Nothing is more important to a society as rich in human resources as ours than human and cultural pluralism, on the condition that there is a common ground, a common point of departure. However, fragmentation is increasing and people are losing their grip on the unity of the society. Israelis are becoming hyphenated (Sepharadic-, religious-, or Ashkenazic- Israelis), rather than unified. The single term Israeli is becoming progressively rarer.

The *yordim* and those who have returned to orthodox piety have taken over—the former while sitting on their packed luggage, the latter in their yarmulkas or knitted *kipot*. And I wish to say something once again in favor of that common Israeli ground that has been lost, and that we must seek anew. Israeli secularism has merit. It is neither inferior nor base. Only Israeli secularism can create an original culture of its own here. Without Israeli-ism it is hard to be Israeli.

### Notes

1. An ironic reversal of the famous line by Judah Halevy, "I am at the end of the West but my heart is in the East."

2. See Rena Shapira, "From Blue Shirt to White Collar," *Forum:* 38, p. 127–140.

3. *Kinus* (assembling), an idea he propounded in 1913 at the meeting of the Federation for Hebrew Language and Culture in Vienna. There he opposed David Frishman's call for a completely contemporary Hebrew literature. Later he consolidated his thinking on the

need to extract the best of ancient Jewish tradition, and published it in an article entitled "Youthfulness or Childishness" ("Tz'ierut O Yaldut") in *Hashiloah*, No. 29.

4. An intended pun on *yeridah*, the opposite of *aliya*.

5. Another ironic reference, this time to the *Ethics of the Fathers*, 3:21.

6. An ironic reference to the line from Amos 9:11.

PART IV

# Not Quite Milk and Honey: The Quality of Israeli Life

# 8

# The Exodus from Israel

## B. Z. SOBEL

### The New Exodus

By now it has become commonplace: long lines at the United States Embassy at Tel Aviv vying for both the hard-to-get immigrant visas or for the easier (but still difficult-to-obtain) tourist visas, which can—as often as not—be finagled into a green card and, ultimately, permanence in America. An advertisement in the Israeli press placed by a South African firm asking for fifty technicians is answered by some 1,500 job seekers. News reports about Israeli "wetbacks" wading the Rio Grande from Mexico into the United States, or sneaking across the Canadian border into Alaska and then flying on to Los Angeles on a domestic flight, are not uncommon. Much less common, but certainly shocking, are the occasional tales of Israeli "boat people." Young Israelis jet to the Bahamas and then rent fishing boats for the trip to Miami, stepping ashore at the first convenient marina. Israeli neighborhoods spring up in the world's major cities, such as Amsterdam, London, Munich, Frankfurt, Johannesburg, and, of course, New York, Los Angeles, and Montreal. Fictive marriages are performed with citizens of various countries in order for Israelis to get permanent-residence or citizen status. Israeli doctors staff, at times, full departments in foreign cities. Israeli engineers achieve prominence in various industries. Israelis drive cabs, wait tables, bake bread and, in some cases, engage in considerably less savory occupations. The tales also feature Israeli artists and musicians, kibbutznikim, and moshavnikim, from East and West, native and immigrant, religious and secular, educated and uneducated, army veterans and shirkers, rabid nationalists and peaceniks, academics and carpenters—all are represented in the great movement outward.

A mere three and a half decades after the establishment of the State of Israel, following the greatest tragedy to befall the Jewish people in its history, the Third Jewish Commonwealth is challenged by the most prosaic and ironic of threats to its continued survival—a growing lack of will on the part of tens of thousands of its citizens to stay within it. Furthermore, and at a time when almost any Jew in almost any land can, if he chooses, come home and plight his troth with the Jewish people in its own land, a mere 20 percent have so opted.

As the Yiddish adage has it, "Exile is bitter." But if recent immigration and emigration figures and trends for Israel provide any valid indication, then exile is, at worst, bittersweet, and clearly the preferred mode of the vast majority of the world's Jews. Not only has Israel thus far failed to spark any significant voluntary move of Jews to its shores, but something of the reverse seems to be gaining ground, with thousands of Israelis opting for a new exile and an almost innocent—sometimes it appears triumphant—return to the diaspora.

The Israeli government statistician has been quoted to the effect that for the past two years emigrants have outnumbered immigrants to the Jewish state. Immigration figures are (with the possible exception of those of 1953) the lowest in the country's history—about 11,000 were expected last year—while emigration is at around the 20,000 mark. Somber as these figures might be, they can be viewed as even more so when one realizes that while the figures for immigration are more or less correct, those reflecting emigration are probably underreported. While accurate figures are difficult if not impossible to attain with respect to emigration, all sources agree that a minimum of 300,000 Israelis have left since 1948. The above figure is government-supplied; independent estimates range from a low of 400,000 to the frightening and seemingly absurd figure of 700,000. But whatever the true numerical dimensions of the phenomenon, there does exist widespread agreement among observers that the trend is upward and likely to increase.

## Understanding Why They Leave

What has happened that can explain not only the reluctance of Jews in the *galut* to come but also the apparent lack of reluctance of so many already in Israel and a part of Israel to leave? Has A. B. Yehoshua struck a resounding chord of historical and sociological truth when he asserts of the *golah* that "we foisted it upon ourselves. It should be regarded not as an accident or misfortune, but as a deep-reaching national perversion"? Is the phenomenon to be explained, perhaps, along less existential, less cosmic lines? Does the answer bear less relation to "national perversion" than to such here-and-now pragmatic, measurable, easily definable, and totally understandable factors as the constant physical threat to most Israelis, an unpromising economic situation, an absence of

career possibilities, reserve duty, high taxation, and inflexible and ca-
pricious bureaucracy?

Even if the evidence suggests the centrality of all or some of these
pragmatic variables, the serious question posed by Yehoshua retains its
validity. A deep-seated peculiarity or idiosyncrasy that conditionally
determines collective roots and national existence, while perhaps not a
"perversion," is deserving of exploration, and Yehoshua's phrasing becomes both felicitous and controlled. In other words, if thousands of
Israelis are leaving because of a lack or failure of the national enterprise,
if thousands weigh their commodities (moving the balance to the left or
the right, to staying or leaving) based on ephemeral variables, does this
not suggest a most peculiar relatedness to normal national existence?

The thousands who are leaving Israel now are not penniless emigrants, displaced rural peasantry, an exploited proletariate, a frightened,
oppressed minority seeking freedom to live its own life and culture
according to its own rights. The overwhelming proportion of Israelis
leaving the country are at the very least literate, in a significant proportion of cases professionals of one kind or another, and, if not wealthy,
certainly far from the penniless prototype Jewish immigrant of the
somewhat lachrymose and romantic image of the nineteenth century. I
would, with respect to this latter point, venture a guess, and suggest
that at least in the case of the United States, the Israelis currently arriving
represent the most gilded of immigrant groups to reach American shores
in this century.

Unlike the Greek or Italian, the Israeli arrives not from the depressed
Peloponnesus or the grinding poverty of southern Italy, but from all
parts of the country, all walks of life, all economic strata, and with
savings resulting from the sale of an apartment or an automobile in
Israel's overcharged and inflationary economy. Not only are the majority
of emigrating Israelis not escaping personal economic distress of any
objectively serious dimensions, but they are, in addition, leaving a
flourishing country with a high Western standard of living; a place
where at least on the material plane, a certain ease in Zion has been
achieved. Visitors to the country are constantly amazed at the number of
autos clogging Israeli roads; the stylish dress of the women; the plethora
of banks; the stereo shops; the color TVs; the phenomenon of one-half
million Israelis going abroad for summer vacations; and the "villa" sections growing even in development towns such as Ma'alot and Carmiel.
One notes with dismay or satisfaction, depending on one's view, the
vigor demonstrated by the Israeli Stock Exchange; the high level of
personal savings; the existence of diversified and sophisticated port-
folios; and the "instant" millionaires, the source of whose wealth is
everything from admitted commercial and technical wizardry to land

speculation. Opportunity exists, clearly. The goods of this life can be attained in Zion! No Sicily, no Peloponnesus this.

We are faced with something of a dilemma, a conundrum: Israel is a land of "milk and honey," a country with a constantly growing and expanding economy, a fine climate, a free political atmosphere; a country still enjoying the patina of romance engendered by its remarkable rebirth, astounding growth, and breathtaking victories in war; and the only country that both actually and potentially can provide the sustaining valence for the development of rooted Jewish culture. Yet the country, instead of witnessing an inflow of tens of thousands of Jews from the four corners of the earth, is seeing an outflow of tens of thousands *to* the four corners of the earth.

I would suggest the following causative factors for exploration: While Israel is comparatively satisfactory materially, it does not or cannot answer the expectations of many thousands of its citizens who aspire to more. Thus, the prime factor underlying emigration is economic. Further, the quality of life in Israel (and by this I refer to everything from the threat of war to an intrusive bureaucracy) is so lacking when compared with that in other Western lands as to readily loosen ties to the mother country. Or to turn it about, the quality of life in other lands is perceived as so far superior to what is currently available in Israel as to exercise an unparalleled attractivenss. Finally, the persistence of some deep-rooted, seemingly intractable elements in Jewish history and culture persistently work to undermine developments leading to autonomy and an independent national life.

### Economic Factors and More

The economic element, the desire to earn more, buy more, have more, runs like a red thread through the current (and past) emigration wave. Jews have never been marked by undue material abstemiousness (perhaps no people are so noted), and Israel has, since the early 1960s, followed an upwardly curving line of expectations, fueled by a high level of economic development and no little achievement. From a scant twenty years ago when a two-and-one-half-room apartment, one week a year at the seashore, and sufficient food on the table (with some luxuries such as a radio and a refrigerator) represented the norm of expectation and hopes, we have entered the promised land of luxury flats, trips abroad, stock options, fine automobiles, and the like. Needless to say, most Israelis are not rich; most Americans are not rich either, but the revolution in expectations is relatively fresh in Israel, and the resulting growth in appetite, and panic at missing out or being left behind, is palpable. Observers, friendly and otherwise, have taken note of the seemingly rampant materialism in Israel, contrasting this development with the very recent recallable past, when Israel was (rightly or wrongly) held up as an example of puritan, indeed Spartan, egalitarianism.

"Making it" in terms of goods and wealth is not easy in contemporary Israel. The possibilities, realistically as well as mythically, are more evident, and indeed more probable, in foreign parts—especially in places such as the United States, Canada, and South Africa. But how is one to explain the thousands of Israelis who leave with tens of thousands of dollars resulting from the sale of their apartments and cars, only to start up again in a new and, for most, strange environment abroad? A large proportion of those leaving have "made it"—at least in Israeli terms. Does greed among us know no bounds? Are we (or more correctly, are many among us) more committed to money and goods than to Zion? Are Jews a rare breed, readily willing to trade roots for cash? I do not think the evidence available supports the supposition.

In numerous interviews with departing emigrants carried out during the latter part of 1981 and the early months of 1982, I was repeatedly struck by the following observations:

1. Most emigrants say their decision to leave is not affected by a potentially unchanged economic situation. Most, however, say they won't emigrate if their income is likely to drop.
2. Most (at least of those who emigrated formally and officially, as opposed to those who use circuitous routes) own apartments, appliances, automobiles, and have well-paying jobs. My estimate is that disposable property ranges between $40,000 and $50,000 for a significant proportion of emigrants.
3. Failure to put aside enough cash for an apartment or for luxuries motivates only a small minority to emigrate, and is not even extensively resorted to as a legitimating device.
4. Joblessness is not a significant factor, although lack of job satisfaction might be.
5. Emigrants are willing, at least temporarily, to fill any job abroad, though not in Israel—the exception being sanitary workers.

Surely the dream of affluence does play some role among most emigrants. It does! But, if the evidence available to me suggests anything, it is that the matter is infinitely more complex, involving a gnawing dissatisfaction of a more general kind. Government leaders and establishment figures in Israel would prefer to explain the departure of so many thousands as resulting from material lust alone, thus avoiding blame and culpability. How, after all, can we compete with America, they ask.

But I am convinced that it is a kind of floating, almost aimless seeking of an elusive and hard-to-define grail, rather than greed, with which we are dealing here.

Not all Israelis who leave achieve wealth abroad. Most probably do not, and yet they stay abroad and do not and will not return, no matter what blandishments are extended. Why? Do Israelis not feel love for their motherland, their language, the familiar landscapes of their youth and young adulthood? The evidence suggests, if anything, powerful and potent attachments to all of these, and yet they do not come back.

The suggestion has been made (with a dollop of wistfulness) that they are ashamed to come home nonmillionaires, and thus continue to lurk in the fleshpots until a sufficient nest egg is accumulated. Perhaps. I am more persuaded by two additional and unrelated thoughts: The chimera of opportunity is beckoning more readily abroad than at home—even though it tarries—and thus must be waited out; and notwithstanding the elusiveness of success, it is simply easier to live outside of Israel.

### Other Factors

In Israel, one repeatedly hears it said (and not only by those who leave or who are contemplating departure) that life is difficult in the country. One hears this from academics who claim an inability to write at home, from housewives who assert that the day is never done, from workers who suggest that they do nothing but work, leaving little time for leisure or other activities. When pressed for an explanation, one is told it has something to do with a six-day week, the need to work at more than one job to make ends meet, the relative absence of such household machinery as dryers or dishwashers, and so on. On a purely objective plane, these assertions are weakened by the fact that the workday is not particularly long; Israel, in effect, works a five-and-a-half-day week (and perhaps less); religious and national holidays do not lag behind any viewable Western norm; and washing machines, mixers, gas or electric stoves, and vacuum cleaners are widely owned.

There exists, notwithstanding, the perception that the workday never ends, and I would assert that this results from a climate of "nudgerie" that seems to permeate the atmosphere: Shops are not open at hours convenient to the buying public; government and other offices are not efficient or, on the whole, marked by a climate of civility; public discipline is low, and suspicion of one's neighbors' intentions seems somehow pervasive. This last comment becomes palpable on viewing Israelis queued-up, where one notices that not an inch of separation is allowed to intrude between queuers; this is not out of a desire for intimacy but simply for fear than an inch will develop into an opening for line jumping.

I do not know if a relaxed society exists, and I am certainly unconvinced of its desirability, but I *am* certain that Israel is not an exemplar of the type. There is indeed an edginess abroad in the society; tempers flare, and verbal violence is rampant. A large proportion of those interviewed for my study, upon which this chapter is based, have been abroad, or were born or raised abroad, and in almost all cases reference is made to the fact that "people are nicer in *chutz la'aretz*." Strangers wish you a good day as they make change or pass you on the street, whereas at home you can consider yourself fortunate to receive minimally civil treatment.

One woman interviewed, when asked why she was about to take the drastic step of emigration, laughed almost hysterically, and shouted, "Why? Why? Because over there [in the United States] I am a child of God, a child of God. I am treated like a human being wherever I go. I am not shouted at or abused. I am not automatically suspect. Washerwomen in the supermarket don't command me to watch my step. Why?"

Another respondent (an immigrant from the United States who had been in Israel for twelve years) broke down and wept, repeating over and over the word "garbage": "People here are garbage, garbage. They're hateful. I hate this place." When asked to explain, a list of minor cruelties—more lapses of good taste than anything more evil—were adduced.

In the case of respondent after respondent, life in Israel was invidiously compared with life abroad. People are more polite over there, merchants are more honest over there, government is more benign over there; the weather is better, the quality of goods higher, the opportunities wider, and so on. One can justifiably assert that these responses reflect a legitimating device for what is essentially viewed as an illegitimate or questionable act. One must explain one's own side of the matter. I am not deserting the ship: The ship has failed me.

This legitimating factor is present. But I am equally convinced that a preemigration set of perceptions and feelings is present and has played a role in the decision to leave. Thirty-five years after the establishment of the state, there exists a wide and deep pool of dissatisfaction with the nature of what has been wrought. And while tangibles such as high taxes, reserve duty, the threat of war, the high cost of housing, and the absence of civility all play a role, there is, in addition, a more inchoate, less tangible, less apprehendable substratum of dissatisfaction that, in the long run, must be viewed as infinitely more troubling than those factors already alluded to.

## Unease in Zion

There is unease in Zion, and its elements are varied. Life in Israel, for many, presents a sense of being "locked in," of not having an adequate scope of free choice. This ranges from one's body (army service, war), to government (unresponsiveness), to job choice (limited). Israel, to thousands of its citizens, is a blocked society. Israel is not an undeveloped or rural society, and its people are not reflective of an emerging peasantry. But the constraints noted above are those associated with an underdeveloped or even authoritarian structure, while the myths and expectations are different.

For many of the new emigrants, disappointment with Israel seems so pronounced as to raise questions as to whether any normal society would satisfy them. One might posit that a putative theme of the classical Zionist design—normalcy—does not, in fact, represent a deep commitment for many. Not a "city on a hill" but "the city of God" has been sought and found absent or difficult to achieve. We are, it would appear, what we have been; a people composed of reluctant messianists reflecting a continued and debilitating struggle between what is and what can be, between worship of the golden calf and the explosive shout of *Naaseh V'Nishma*, between the temporal, here-and-now relativities of normal existence and an illusive perfectability. In this sense, Israel is an impossible undertaking. It is a conditional homeland where the very nature of the term homeland rejects conditionality. It is, perhaps, as one observer noted, ultimately a question of grammar; it all revolves around "if." "If" Israel is this, that, or the other thing, "if" conditions are good and propitious, "If" we are true, good, and beautiful I will stay. If not, I will go elsewhere.

One must not lose sight of the existence of some more tangible, more historically rooted aspects underpinning the new exile. There exist decided sociological limits to the length of time in which collective enthusiasms or ideal visions can be maintained in a central societal position. While the simple dream of national revival and the excitement of creating a state and society can be sustained for perhaps one generation—if that long—it will not suffice much beyond that. Deep-rootedness and binding ties to place are not (in contrast to our naive expectations) created overnight. When a collective ideal is buffeted by a sense of smashed dreams, broken promises, false leaders, and a moral vacuum, the tenuous and fragile ties that bind unravel. It would appear that thirty-five years of statehood are both too much and not enough: too long for the dream to remain untainted, and too short for expanding and deepening roots.

This is the case for all nations reaching independence at this particular juncture of world history, when communications are dominated by television and the not-unconnected Americanization of the planet. The global-village theme suggests nothing if not interchangeability (why here, rather than there), and the web of expectations is spun in Hollywood and on Madison Avenue.

### Roots

Thus, a constantly recurring emotion emerging in the responses of emigrants is "What difference does it make where I live? I am just as much an Israeli in New York as in Tel Aviv." This interesting conclusion is further supported by the evidence that at least in the case of Israeli emigrants to the United States, a certain critical mass has been achieved. With hundreds of thousands of Israelis living in the United States, a satisfying degree of Israeliness—language, foods, friendships, and family links—has indeed become a movable and interchangeable feast sustaining those already here and beckoning others to follow.

And they will follow! Not because Israel is extraordinary, but rather because it has become, in the consciousness of so many, ordinary and hence lacking in definition. Thus, choosing to live elsewhere is no longer desertion, and certainly not a crime. Earlier emigrants were wont to explain themselves, to justify, to assert the undying reality of the dream, to swear an early return home. This justifying tendency has declined precipitiously, and it is increasingly acceptable to emigrate and leave it at that. Indeed, there are some discomfiting signs that not emigrating, or at least going abroad to live for a period of time, suggests a certain lack of vigor or ambition among the stay-at-homes.

Underpinning this new attitude toward leaving is a growing sense among Israelis of completion or closure in terms of the creative aspects of state building or Zionism. A corollary is the breaking down of a feeling that we must "just hang in" when in fact the state is built, Zionism is realized, and the country is more or less secure. The time seems propitious to tend to one's own garden, to pursue individual paths to fulfillment, and this, it would appear, is for tens of thousands of Israelis most easily achieved in the "world" rather than in Zion.

This seems to reflect a disturbing skein of continuity with the Jewish past. We are, if not rootless (who is to say that roots are so easily defined as to be circumscribed within a land or a society alone), then certainly with thinner ties to the temporal Zion of this earth than we were willing to admit. The small proportion of the Jewish people who returned to Zion can be said to have done so (largely) kicking and screaming, while the departure from Zion is taking place, seemingly, with ease and almost lightly. Lest this be dismissed as idle subjectivity, it should be noted that for significant numbers of Israelis Israel represented a way station, a point of interrupted migration rather than a final goal. Thousands arrived in the early years of the state more as a result of lack of opportunity to go elsewhere than out of passion for the cessation of exile. One might, therefore, see in the new departure a movement toward completion of an essentially interrupted process, rather than an out-of-the-blue response to suddenly changed objective or ideational circumstances. In some cases, it is the emigrant who is himself continuing on. In other instances, it is the children who are completing the process.

### Exile

Do we prefer exile to redemption? We are probably unsure as to which is which, and in any event we seem to need the dispersal as a sort of antidote to the seemingly unbearable intensity of our group existence. We seem to desire marginality in preference to autonomy, other lands in preference to our own.

# 9

# On Zionism and Jewish Happiness

## MICHAEL ROSENAK

The famed German-Jewish philosopher Herman Cohen was not sympathetic to Zionism. He dismissed the enthusiasms and dreams of the Zionists with the curt comment, "These characters want to be happy." For Cohen, whose consuming passion was for the moral perfection of a messianic age, Jewish "happiness" before the advent of a messianic mankind was a moral betrayal. He must have regarded the desire to be happy as suspect (if not contemptible) on two counts.

First, it indicated a desire to be like everyone else; like those who apparently did not suffer from the reality of a blemished world because they were not burdened with moral sensitivity. On this level, being happy meant renouncing the faith in the coming of the Messiah and acquiescing in a morally corrupt social reality. "A nation like all other nations," if achieved, would be an abdication of mission and an admission of cynical despair.

Second, "being happy" may have suggested a naive faith that Jewish life could be rendered simple through Zionism, that the *galut* of alienation and homelessness in the world of godless men and nations could be ended by a political metamorphosis that brought the Messiah by impudently programming his advent. If "being happy" in the first sense meant worldly wise renunciation of hope, in the second it meant illusion, dangerous innocence, false messianism.

Cohen was wrong; Zionism did not make the Jews normal, and it did not make Jewish existence simple. Franz Rosenzweig pointed out, with specific reference to his beloved teacher, that one learns something even from the mistakes of a great man. Why was Cohen wrong, and what shall we learn from his mistake?

### Again at War

Once again we are at war, this time with those who really *are* our enemies because they proclaim that our collective existence precludes theirs. This war is not against Arab states, whose hurt is symbolic, but against Arabs who have no state, experience homelessness, and insist that this is due to us, that they can be happy only if we cease to be a nation. Meanwhile our ill-wishers, in every cultural and political bloc, renew the attack. Vigorously they accuse us of being like everyone else, all too normal "for Jews." By this they intimate that we are paradoxically much worse than anyone else, not normal at all, not really human, demonic.

We recall having heard all this before. And in the face of this terrible onslaught of lies and half-truths, of hypocrisy and jubilant horror, we realize that Zionism has not made it simple for us. Since it has not brought us the messianic age, and since a less-than-universal redemption may be a promising beginning but is short of tranquillity and therefore sometimes looks like a cruel joke, this makes us unhappy, but also angry. And the anger makes the unhappiness bearable. For we know from past experience that our exodus from the house of bondage and annihilation infuriates the world, and that our survival and determination to live occasions no little trepidation. "Behold a people has come out of Auschwitz and they cover the face of the earth," to paraphrase a fearful, always astounded Balak. "Come then, put a curse upon this people for me," latter-day kings of Moab demand of journalists, intellectuals, and men of learning. Like Balaam, they seem to have been endowed with godlike spirit, but that spirit has become misshapen, perverted, desperately wishing only to defame. So, with TV cameras they roam around the camp of Israel, seeking vistas from which the view will evoke a divine—or at least a United Nations—condemnation. And again unhappiness, followed by anger turning to accustomed, bearable unhappiness.

But for us there is a more significant lesson here. Once again we discover something not only about others, but also about ourselves, in this superbly executed campaign characterized by military accomplishments and perhaps new political opportunities. We are amazed at the self-discovery, always new in Israel, that we are not made for amoral contentment, that Zionism has not made everything facile, that we cannot be happy unless we feel ourselves deserving of God's blessing. Cohen was wrong primarily because our lives have not been rendered simple; and though we wish to be happy, we cannot just will happiness into existence, and we dare not pay any price for it. This appears outrageous to the weary and to the doctrinaire, who claim that if happiness is part of the plan for Israel and mankind, and the return to Zion is the beginning of that redemption, then unhappiness is due to heresy or to a flaw in the Zionist vision. But of course Zionism also calls for the courage to live with the complexities and paradoxes of Jewish existence in a not-yet-redeemed world—a dialectic world in which Jews cannot help waiting for the Messiah, in which they are bound to hasten his coming, in which they may legitimately try to achieve both happiness and human dignity. The war has starkly exposed these complexities and paradoxes to view. To face them bespeaks the capacity for courage, idealism, and dignity.

### Our Legitimacy

First, we face the paradox and frustration of being denied legitimacy even after thirty-five years of Jewish sovereignty. It is easy to say that this is because the world has never recognized, and will never recognize, Israel because of its vocation; that the nations hate us because God loves us. It is equally easy to say that "they" hate us because we are obstinate, intractable, the perennial victims who have ironically become brutal oppressors. Both formulas strive for simplicity, desperately wishing to make Jews happy. But Zionism, proclaiming both Jewish messianism (dissatisfaction with this situation) and Jewish normalization, (dignity in every situation) must declare both of them inadequate and untrue. Zionism insists that we do not gain redemption by turning our backs on the nations, nor may we gain admission to their ranks by cursing Israel. (It falls to the Zionist to insist that it isn't at all simple to be happy)!

Our national movement has, ironically, created another that has learned from ours to feel deeply and articulate the love of this land as a national homeland. This national movement is led by men shaped by frustration and moved by hatred, men who scorn the value of life (Arab as well as Jewish), who extol cruelty as a countervalue, who view our values as weaknesses and our historic desire for compromise as falsehood. The PLO has caught a national consciousness from Zionism, and there are some who say that we are in danger of catching their all-too-normal hatreds and frustrations, leading ultimately to the glory of none and to the death of all. And yet, how be moral with those who deny any extension of moral reciprocity to Jews? How be honest with deceitful and violent men? How be humane toward fanatics in a historical situation in which some 2,000 years after the fall of Jerusalem Jews, too, are restored to space without suicide? It is not simple.

A second complexity and paradox is aroused by war as such. When Jews boast of their victories and call this "a wonderful time," they sound outlandish. Exultation at victory that rings true in a Margaret Thatcher (and others like her who deplore our violence), when expressed by Jews, evokes sad if not contemptuous smiles among us. The simple solution, that of much of the medieval tradition, which partially nourished modern Zionism, would have restored us to our land and simultaneously brought the Messiah to mankind. There would have been no Zahal (Israel Defense Forces), but only ploughshares; no United Nations resolutions against Israel, but a mankind ascending in unison to Jerusalem to acknowledge the universal King. But this is not what happened. Our renaissance is cruelly linked to conflict and destruction and, in the midst of destruction, there is still (and especially) the demand for decency; in killing, there is the annoying imperative to retain the image of man. It is excruciatingly difficult, it is absurd, it is often simply impossible, and it raises, again and again, the question whether one can live with the tension.

No wonder that in this war in which we were not (yet) frontally attacked, but only threatened with annihilation—routinely defamed in international forums and sporadically shot in international airports—the question would arise (even among us!) whether it is justified to seek out our enemies, concealed in the towns and villages of innocent people whose only sin is their impotence and who, together with the Palestinians, pay for it with far too many lives. No wonder that some should comfort themselves with the belief that the pathetic nation that was the arena of this war was deliriously happy at our conquest. But it was not, of course, that simple. And most Jews, whose Zionism belies Herman Cohen's charge, would echo a young tank commander interviewed on the radio during a lull in the fighting, who said: "We are doing what we have to, we must defend ourselves. But how disgusting war is, how much death and suffering!" Cohen could not have expressed the prayer for the coming of the Messiah more eloquently.

The "simplistic" Zionists thought they would be happy by becoming normal vis-à-vis the nations. But we constantly rediscover that it is not in the cards. The image persists of the mythical Jew who is superhumanly better than everyone else, or inhumanly worse. Among the nations hundreds of thousands may die and be maimed in senseless wars, justified by slogans, and *that* is either good or bad "strategy"; yet when Israel fights it is sinful (a perverse vindication for the "normal" world that always knew that Jews were as presumptuous in their historical powerlessness as they are heretical in their decision not to continue without power). One never quite gets used to it, especially if, as a Zionist, one harbors the hope that we *shall* be happy here and that Israel brings the Kingdom of God closer. One never gets over being flabbergasted when a cease-fire is announced and foreign correspondents (in the case I have in mind, sitting in Metulla waiting to "see the action") curse at being deprived of the death and the atrocities they have come to see. (In the recorded words of one of them: "Damn it, I didn't travel thousands of miles to see a cease-fire.") But the colossal human wickedness, pinpointed in anti-Semitism as revealed here, is not the whole story. Not only the gentiles see us mythically. We too wish to be different, know ourselves to be different, and the shock of sharing "the guilt of historical action" (in Eliezer Berkovitz's phrase) is real and agonizing. We want to be more than normal because we envision a mankind that is different, but we fear that unless we act normally—despite the "mythic" treatment we receive—we will not survive to see divine salvation and human self-transcendence. (In this we differ from the men of Agudat Yisrael who, despite Auschwitz, have no qualms about God's working alone in history. One walks in Mea Shearim and is jostled by black-hatted young men speaking English as well as Hebrew, who can be overheard asking one another: "How are you learning this year, well?" as though *that* were the crucial question this summer. One is angry, yet bemused, at the strangeness of this nation even in its own land, just as one does not know what to do with certain Jews in the diaspora who demand that Israel be better than everyone else, and wash their hands of it if it is less than perfect.)

### Redemption and Normalcy

Yet, how to deserve redemption while acting "normally?" The answer is, of course, that we do not act "normally." Our best surgeons operate on Lebanese children, bar mitzvah boys contribute money for blankets needed for the homeless, and we agonize over every report of civilian casualties. But it isn't that simple either. For Jews, while not demons, are not angels either. We have mass demonstrations in Tel Aviv (unheard of in most democratic countries at war), arguments in every army unit, and outbursts at every family table that, while often simplistic, also remind us that such "good deeds" can only alleviate the tragedy but not stifle conscience or make the absurdity into a *simcha.*

And finally, the ultimate paradox. The messianic enthusiasts on the right tell us that this war is part of the process of redemption; the "normalizing" ones on the left, that it is the road to perdition. The former see the wars of the Lord as comforting, the latter assure us that wars that serve political purposes are evil. Most of us don't quite believe either of them. We fear that this war will lead to more bloodshed, more hatred, more agony, yet we dare to hope that it will engender, finally, a reconciliation. We recall that when Sadat made a war for "political ends," it was not condemned but considered wise statesmanship, and, indeed, that it led to a peace treaty; we remember that humane pacifism often encourages the wicked.

Different parties in Israel predict different political consequences and see diverse challenges, but only the dogmatic and the innocent will refuse to pursue their Zionist visions (sometimes quite disparate) in the wake of this war. And the political battle among us, on this score, will be something to behold.

One of the most powerful images in the Bible, elaborated in Midrash commentary, is that of Jacob wrestling on the borders of Eretz Yisrael with a man identified with his enemy and brother, Esau. It was a battle of life and death, waged throughout a dark night. Jacob was strengthened by his consciousness of being chosen; he was vulnerable becasue of his feelings of unease, for he had stolen the birthright. Mysteriously his conviction that it belonged to him, that God wished him to have it, did not completely reassure him. And yet Jacob's strength, miraculously stored up through many years of exile and deprivation, enabled him to persevere through the night. At dawn, his brother and adversary blessed him, and Jacob understood that, in asserting himself, he had fought God Himself and it was He who was now blessing him.

Zionism is engaged in Jacob's battle. Zionism's belief is that, at dawn, we shall be blessed, and that God will account it a virtue that after having prayed, we wrestled.

But that, too, is only half the story. Moses, who "when the Ark was to set out" would say, "Advance, O Lord, May Your enemies be scattered and may Your foes flee before You," would say after the battle, "Return O Lord, unto the ten thousands of the families of Israel," and the latter verse, in some interpretations reads: "Bestow, O Lord, tranquillity to the tens of thousands of Israel." The battle is fought in the hope that God is in our presence and is leading it. But after the battle is over we paradox-ically pray for His return and that His presence, which has left us, be brought back. Indeed, there have been moments in the later stages of the war when we have felt not only untranquil but very disturbed; when our homecoming reminds us of exile. And so we pray for tranquillity, which has been taken from us, even in a "just" war.

A people which lives with these tensions will never have it simple and will not buy happiness cheaply. Herman Cohen need not have worried. As Jews, we are realistic enough to know when it is night; as Zionists, we fight in the belief that the dawn is approaching and that we have the responsibility to be the first to recognize it lest *galut* becomes self-denial and self-defense becomes senseless killing. And our prayer is that at dawn those who struggled shall embrace. Though it may be slightly absurd, we believe that then the striving will be vindicated and all those who were adversaries will discover, in mutual recognition and for-giveness, that they are brothers. A Jewish state that anticipates less than that is less than what we have prayed for throughout the millennia. Herman Cohen was right about that.

# 10

# A Sermon at Southampton

## HANOCH BARTOV

Fellows! We have no history! Ever since we were exiled from our Land we've been a people without a history. You're excused. Go and play football.

Haim Hazaz, "The Sermon"

A weird thought went through my mind when I heard about that Cohen fellow who played soccer at Southampton on the Day of Atonement, which this year fell on the Sabbath. Perhaps, as in a kind of "sociodrama," he wanted to kick at a particular view of Jewish history that he objected to and did not respect? Perhaps he wanted to use his feet to pass on some revolutionary or philosophical message?

This priestly young man, as far as I have been able to ascertain, is a genuine Israeli product; he is one of us nice, prickly sabras. For that reason he cannot plead ignorance. He could not possibly have avoided Yudkeh, the revolutionary pioneer into whose mouth Hazaz put "The Sermon." At one stage of his Israeli or Zionist education he must have come across some literature teacher, some youth movement leader, some newspaper article, some radio program, something or other, that mentioned Yudkeh. Whatever the case, I reckon that it is ten thousand times more likely that he heard of Yudkeh than are the chances of my winning the big prize on the football pools. And out of Yudkeh's mouth came the most basic principles on which Israeli Zionist education is founded. Yudkeh, as every Israeli high school graduate should know, does not simply "object to Jewish history" in the diaspora; "We have no history at all, since we didn't make our history; the Gentiles made it for us." In a word, "A People that does not live in its own country and does not rule itself has no history." And for a People such as this, which has no history, Yudkeh has only one piece of advice: "Go and play football."

A young Israeli soccer star, Avi Cohen, who was under contract to a British team, suddenly gets up at Southampton, on the Day of Atonement, and does just that. Is it conceivable that this is really a trivial matter, that there is nothing unusual about it at all? That, as Avi explained after the game, "I had no choice but to do what was best for my career and for my team"?

Only gradually, after I had read the report of his "sermon," which was printed in one of the Israeli newspapers, and after I had listened intently to the balanced and amazingly circumspect words of the chairman of the Israeli Football Association, did I come to realize that nothing had happened and that "it was nobody's business." If only you were alive to witness this, Yudkeh!

How wonderful it would be if you could be permitted just one more time to break into some meeting, and to stammer something from the depths of your confused and tumultuous soul about history and about football. And not from your standpoint then, forty years ago, when "The Sermon" was first published, but from the standpoint of present-day Israel in 1981. Perhaps not one sermon but two: one delivered by you and the other delivered by golden-feet, Avi Cohen, on this very topic: History and Football.

We've got things so mixed up that lots of traditional concepts need to be reexamined. I, for one, came face to face with my own astonishment at the public desecration of the Day of Atonement, even though I am not an Orthodox Jew. I regard myself as a secular Jew, not a secular Israeli, but quite definitely a *Jew*. Why, I ask myself, was I so shocked by Avi Cohen's public conduct, which showed that he was not subject to any awesome fear other than the fear of having his contract with Liverpool canceled?

A few years ago, when the "back-to-religion" movement was beginning to gain impetus, I heard someone claim in a discussion on Jewish identity: "Although I did not fear the Almighty, nevertheless on the Sabbath I go to synagogue, I make kiddush," etc. I remember that an ancient tremor went through me: How could a person admit that he had no fear of the Almighty? What kind of return to religion was it that lacked just this one thing: fear of the Almighty? From a truly Orthodox viewpoint, it is worse than outright secularism, I said to myself, because it is purely a matter of keeping up forms. It is not coincidental that our sages, who were very wise men, proposed that our fear of the Almighty should be as great as "our fear of man." At least not less than that. But the thought of a person who does not know what that awesome fear is!

Even for a nonreligious Jews, the Day of Atonement is a hidden link between reverence for the Almighty and respect for that society of which one is a part. I refuse to take it upon myself to analyze, to explain, or to define what constitutes desirable public conduct on the Day of Atonement in Israel, and for the Jewish people, wherever they are; every one of us is entitled to choose whatever interpretation seems best to him.

But in this matter there are elements of awesome fear: both that element of mystery, the absence of which turns man into something monstrous, and also, undoubtedly, reverence for society. There is also a long historical memory for Yom Kippur, which just seven years ago (1973—the Yom Kippur War) was refilled with a mighty fear.

According to one definition, a Jew is whoever regards himself as a Jew; according to another definition, a Jew is anyone whom other people regard as a Jew. Whichever you choose, history has decided that on the Day of Atonement Jews stand up and are counted. They do not go to work; their children do not go to school. Jewish artists do not appear in concert halls; Jewish financiers keep away from the stock exchanges. One of the statistical means, for example, used to determine how many Jews live in the United States is known as "the day of Atonement census," i.e., by subtracting the number of pupils absent from school on that day from the usual daily average, one can work out how many Jews there are.

Our priestly young man used his feet to defy all of this. Does this really have anything to do with religion? Or does it have to do with the fear that not every aspect of Israeli life necessarily enriches Jewish life? Indeed, one feels that those aspects that have to do with money, sport, entertainment, or politics limit and reduce it. And perhaps all of this is not worth bothering about at all. A young fellow with a good boot is busy building his career. What does this have to do with the questions that Yudkeh raised?

We may be able to console ourselves with the fact that, although the media are full of news about football heroes, and although betting on them has become big business in Israel, all of this may have nothing to do with the course of Jewish history, as embodied in the State of Israel.

It is a pity that Yudkeh is not here. Our ears have become accustomed to hearing so many new things. So that he too might rewrite his sermon now, or some Avi Cohen might interrupt a meeting the way Yudkeh did, and begin to shout: "Fellows! We already have a history! You're excused from the rest of Jewish history; go and play football!"

# 11

# Occupying Ourselves with the Pure

## ABBA OREN

*I*

One could summarize thirty-four years of Israeli sovereignty, say for a desk encyclopedia: "They grow more cotton per square acre than any country in the world and their proven firepower is more devastating than that of any army." Not bad! Especially when you consider that for 2,000 years their ancestors had had precious little experience as either farmers or fighters. Another nation has been firmly established—the Jews who have rejoined the family of normalcy.

But the debate over normalcy is as old as Zionism itself. Briefly, the ongoing argument is over the end-goal of Zionism. Is the aim to enable the Jewish people to take up the ideological vocation of *am segulah* (a unique People)? Or is it to permit the Jews the pragmatic option of becoming *kekhol hagoyim* (like all the nations)?

Four score less seven years ago our founding fathers brought forth in Jewish Palestine a renewed national presence, conceived in liberty and dedicated to the proposition that all men are created equal. Tel Aviv and Degania were both founded in 1909 in accordance with ideological blueprints. The first was conceived in liberty as the first all-Jewish city in which every proud at-home Jew could be "a walker in the city" because the garbage men who cleaned up and the policemen who directed the small trickle of traffic were all Jews. The second was a kibbutz dedicated to the proposition not only that all productive and service occupations were to be filled by Jews, but also that the fruits of their labor ought to be divided equally. They regarded themselves as the vanguard of a socially reconstructed, egalitarian, Jewish commonwealth.

How has the ideology fared compared with pragmatism?

Now, seventy-three years later, busloads of Arab workers are daily disgorged in Tel Aviv, their passengers dispersing to perform much of the city's manual labor. Degania has encapsulated itself in a sleepyhollow communal ghetto. True enough, the grandchildren of Degania and the more than 200 kibbutzim founded in its wake are not completely isolated; they are the recruiting grounds for combat pilots, and their communities excel in growing cotton. In these two respects they fill primary needs of the Jewish state.

## II

Jewish excellence has an endemic tendency to isolate itself from the hurly-burly of the "real" world. The Gaon of Vilna and Rabbi Adin Steinsaltz reflect one pole, the premodern; academia and the kibbutz represent the other, postmodern. Most individuals of excellence sense an aloneness that they try to overcome by perceiving of themselves as constituting an elite. And elites believe that they and what they stand for are merely emblematic of what their society stands for—or rather, what their society ought to stand for if society could only be an elite. But by definition, society as a whole cannot be an elite, and here is one of the paradoxes of striving to become an *am segulah* (a holy people and a nation of priests). Most Israelis have worked their way out of the fruitful paradox by opting for the ordinary, for nonelite normalcy.

The reluctant heroes of the Yom Kippur War were nonplussed when journalists descended upon them the minute the soldiers opened the tank turrets and asked them why and in the name of what they had fought so heroically. Bone-weary, blood in their eyes, the stench of death still in their nostrils, their childhood buddies lying wounded or dead in the bowels of the same tank, they looked up in incomprehension. "We were attacked, so we fought back—what's so unusual about that?"

Nothing—provided one aims at normalcy; when attacked, fight back. Everything—everything, if one expected that the aim of Zionism would be a continuing revolution of consciousness-raising, a developing artic-ulation of values. Berl Katznelson's call for articulation cojoined with the deed is a case in point (he once said in jest "the *kneidlach* are more important than the Passover Haggadah, but," he swiftly added, "with-out the Haggadah there would be no Seder").

Our educational elite were alarmed: "What has happened to us? Has Zionism's much sought after normalization of the Jewish people pro-ceeded so rapidly that young Israelis grow up accepting the Zionist revolution as a truism, taking it for granted?

For a number of years I, too, subscribed to this put-down of Israeli youth. Charitably I called them innocents, innocent of ideology. In that sense they seemed to fit Rabbi Assi's dictum. Their selfless devotion to duty had become legendary. This was true of all soldiers and even more true of kibbutz youngster. In time of need their altruism and self-sacrifice seemed to be a modern application of "the innocent occupying themselves with the pure.

*III*

Since the Yom Kippur War I have been doing forty days a year of my army reserve duty lecturing and discussing Zionism with soldiers in Zahal (the Israel Defense Forces). Often I begin discussions with the question: What is Zionism? The answers have tended to vary from group to group over the years. Changes can be explained by swings in the mood of the country and the general zeitgeist. But seldom, if ever, during those years have I heard Zionism defined as an *ideology*. Much more frequently, it is seen by young Israelis as a movement, an organization, an aliyah service or a body of nostalgic, pious truisms. The lowest common denominator tends toward something like this: "Jews were always persecuted, this went on for centuries; but during the Holocaust, persecution turned into genocide, and now we have our sovereign state, which will ensure that it can never happen again." At best, Zionism is (mistakenly) perceived as synonomous with Israeli patriotism. This makes Druze soldiers feel good, giving them an "in" feeling they can share with the majority. But at worst, Zionism is thought of by young Israelis as something not personally relevant to their lives.

It would be as unwise to take their "best case" self-perception at face value (they are much more than mere patriots), as it would be to accept the "worst case" charge: irrelevance. For unlike many of their Jewish overseas peers, contemporary Israelis play an incredibly better game than they talk.

They have bought the mischievous notion that the founding generation was much more idealistic than their own. Because they have been schooled to regard their parents and grandparents as luminaries, they see themselves as children of the shadow. It is as though T. S. Eliot was referring to them when he wrote: "Between the idea and the reality, between the notion and the act falls the shadow."

As my discussion with the soldiers warms up, I tell them that Golda Meir was always a culture hero of mine; more than that, that I loved her. However, it was an unstinting full-blown love, and not an infatuation that suspends the critical faculty. I mention Meir (literally "one who illuminates") even now because five years after her death she continues to plague me, and I use the word plague advisedly. To some extent her single-mindedness was a *makah*, a plague. It was also her great strength and the source of her partisan passion. I often cite the misapplied humanism I heard her espouse at Madison Square Garden when I was on *shlihut*. There, she told a rally of Jewish youth: "We do not hate the Arabs for having killed our sons in war, but rather because they have forced us to kill them."

Golda was a woman of valor, not in the patriarchal smugness found in the last chapter of the Book of Proverbs, but in the sense of her intrepid dedication. People of valor whom one admires and loves deserve the best. The best I and other humanistic Israelis could do was to share with her our deep distress with that heartrending statement of hers about the source of her anti-Arab feeling. There were at least two things wrong with it, we told her. The first was moral superiority, an ethical one-upmanship; like the parent with tears in his eyes who belts his kid, repeating with every blow, "This hurts me more than it does you!" She countered by denying the feelings of superiority we had imputed to her. And then, knowing that some of us had lost sons, brothers, and some of our best friends in Israel's thirty years of war, she turned to us and asked, "And you? You don't hate Arabs?" Drawn up short, we had to admit that we did; not individually nor even collectively or even in the abstract, but angrily, as one hates an excuse. "But you have rich blood in your veins, and you all have personal biographies and a national consciousness, some of you taught history, what do you need excuses for?"

Heedless of the difference in station, age, achievement—in short, almost everything between us—or rather *because* the ideology that united us transcended such differences, we reminded her that while hatred was human, one of the aims of Zionism was to be more than normal. Wearily she said, "So we have finally 'merely' normalized ourselves."

I remember thinking to myself, "Yes, normalization. Just like normal Americanism. Just like Mom and apple pie. Zionism is now normal enough for a Norman Rockwell poster. By her lights we should not look for utopia. According to her, we don't want Walden. Grant Wood pitch-fork-faced farmers are enough, with some rubber plants thrown in for decoration."

The end of that discussion revolved around the question of normalization, pacifism, and ideology. Briefly, we claimed that Israel had been so busy fighting Arabs that we had stopped fighting with each other. The Arabs were intent on destroying us, true enough. They did not want us to have a home in the midst of "their" Middle East. But we were so overwhelmingly concerned with confounding their schemes that we had scarcely paid attention to what kind of a home we were building. Her last sentence remains with me to plague me to this day. "First things first. Meanwhile hate Arabs for forcing us to kill their sons; if we win, there will be time for fighting with Jews."

Mom and apple pie indeed! And meanwhile, pie in the sky. Imagine

God postponing creating the Sabbath until all the evil in the created world had worked itself out in the Garden of Eden. Imagine holding the moral imperative to be our brothers' keepers in abeyance until after Noah and his kin came out of the ark. The biggest question posed by *Bereshit* is where do you begin? No idle question, that.

## IV

This very question was addressed in talmudic times, in the Middle Ages, and is still very much with us in the contemporary period. The Five Books of Moses are meant to guide the behavior of the community of believers. Even the most readable and least commandment-laden of the five, Genesis, is value-laden. But the question of where to begin (why not at the beginning?) stems from the unresolved debate over how best to influence behavior. Do you stress the what or the why? What comes first, pragmatic obedience to a code, or the ideology that gives the code meaning? Moses himself, in the fifth of the Books attributed to him, is of little help here: "Observe them and do them [the commandments]; for this is your wisdom and understanding" (Deut. 4:6).

Rabbi Assi (late third and early fourth century C.E.), a school supervisor appointed by Judah Hanassi III, was convinced that the *what* was more important. He disagreed with the twentieth-century "modernist" approach of Gershom Scholem, who said: "The search for 'reasons' for the commandments of the Torah springs from a tendency to transcend mere obedience to them by investing them with some intrinsic meaning."

Said Rabbi Assi: "Why do children begin their studies from *Torat Kohanim* (Leviticus) and not from *Bereshit* (Genesis)? Because children are pure-hearted and [innocent] and the sacrifices are pure. Let the innocent come and occupy themselves with the pure."

I have always had trouble with Rabbi Assi's pedagogical insights. Nor does the indisputable fact that for 1,600 years Jewish educational practice has customarily followed Assi's curriculum rather than mine convince me at all of its correctness. My trouble is astigmatism. In optics this refers to a defect in the eye that prevents rays from one point of an object from being brought to a single focal point. To posit commandments is to be focused. Demanding focal attention to intrinsic meaning of commandments is to court astigmatism. This astigmatism is a classic condition, a hereditary disease among Zionists, although for the last twenty years or so it has shown signs of abating, as normal vision asserts itself in the level sunlight of sovereignty. Gershom Scholem was a Zionist; so was Berl Katznelson. But during the 1950s and 1960s, "Zionism" was regarded as empty verbiage, and young Israelis put it between quotation marks. Pragmatism became the regnant life-style.

During the last fifteen years a transformation has occurred. Observers of the scene have not all caught up with the change yet. It is assumed that ideology has all but atrophied, and the conventional wisdom holds that only among the young of the ultranationalist, irredentist Orthodox *Gush Emunim* does one still find ideology in its pristine form. Before dealing with the fallacy of this view, it would be well to ask whether ideology "is good for Jews."

V

When Ben-Gurion disbanded the (Labor, kibbutz-oriented) Palmah, led by Yigal Alon, soon after he disbanded the (Revisionist, expansionist-oriented) Etzel, led by Menahem Begin, he sought to disenfranchise ideology. In its place he wanted to establish statism. This was also his motivation in disbanding the three ideologically separate school systems. This, too, motivated his unsuccessful efforts to unite all the ideologically oriented Zionist youth movements in a paramilitary, ROTC-like organization, (the GADNA) and his vain attempt to nationalize the Labor Federation's health insurance plan.

Ben-Gurion knew that Jews were fractious, and feared that supreme loyalty to one overriding idea or another would endanger the fragile fabric of loyalty to the state. An ideologically commited person is not necessarily a lawbreaker, but if he is truly and utterly committed there is always a danger, in principle, that he will heed the promptings of a "higher" law.

When the Gush Emunim loyalists intent on settling Kaddum (the first Jewish settlement established in the West Bank despite government opposition) physically pushed aside soldiers at an army roadblock, they were acting, they said, in obedience to a "higher" law. This was precisely what Ben-Gurion had feared. And when, after his election, in his first, hence highly symbolic, public act, Begin went to visit the settlers of Elon Moreh and declared to them and to the press corps, "There will yet be many Elon Morehs," he vindicated their militancy and ideology.

He did not realize, perhaps, that he thereby also legitimated the (in his words) "trauma" of Yamit. When Begin brought up the Camp David Agreements for ratification by the Knesset, many of his erstwhile followers were convinced that he had betrayed the "higher" law that demanded that we occupy the whole of Israel. Acting on the sense of betrayal, they disregarded the orders of civilian and military authorities to evacuate Yamit. Indeed, the local "Representative of God," Rabbi

Ariel, chief Rabbi of Yamit, called on the soldiers who had been sent to evacuate the settlers to "disregard your officers' commands because they are illegal."

Just how dangerous ideology can be was made manifest in the scandalously belated forcible eviction of the cossacks-of-god from the rooftops of Yamit. The government was embarrassed at having to enforce the law of the land on "committed Zionists." But the absence of ideology can be almost as dangerous.

I was sent by the Education Corps of the army to conduct discussions with the soldiers involved in enforcing the law of the land. It was rumored that select units of combat soldiers had indicated to their officers that they expected difficulties in confronting the adversary. The crack troops knew that the consensus in Israel called for honoring the Camp David Agreements and they were squarely in agreement with the consensus, or even to the left of it. But here they were faced not by foreign enemies but by Jewish squatters, nonpacifist conscientious objectors in the name of the law of heaven. "Gush Emunim has stolen the flag from us." How heartrending was the (mostly secular) soldiers' claim that lacking the ideology of their Orthodox opponents made their task doubly difficult. They turned to me—or, more aptly, they turned on me—with the accusation: "Why didn't secular Jewish educators provide us with a countervailing ideology?" In typical Israeli fashion, even in arguments between secular Jews, they quoted Scriptures: "Where there is no vision, the people cast off restraint" (Prov. 29:18). I replied that they should go back and read the second half of that oft half-quoted verse: "But he that keepeth the law, happy is he."

But now, less than a year later, I am not as sure as I was then, on a number of scores, that ideology is dangerous to democracy. First, the case of the petitions, demonstrations, the hundreds of thousands of fully patriotic Israelis who cry "foul" to the war in Lebanon, exercising their legal right of protest. It indicates that the flag has not been stolen as the irretrievable trophy of the irredentist hawks. But second, in the case of Colonel Eli Geva, ideology has reasserted itself as a call to resist the call of formal duty in the name of a higher truth. For the first time in the history of Israel's wars a highly esteemed senior commander has not only privately questioned the wisdom of the orders he was given, not only expressed his disavowal of the aims of the war in classified documents, but gone public with his anguish at the manslaughter that he feared he would be expected for perform.

He has tussled with the question of whether 'tis nobler on the field of battle to use his immense firepower to inflict the slings and arrows of outrageous fortune against the unfortunate Palestinians and Lebanese held hostage by Arafat, or to take a public stand against a sea of troubles he inflicted on himself and on his military career, and by opposing, end them.

I was wrong on a second score too. I thought he was alone, unique. I had forgotten that the ideology of humanism has been alive and well all along, even if stuttering in its articulation. Fifteen years ago, the most important humanitarian document of modern times appeared in the book *The Seventh Day: Soldiers' Conversations About the Six-Day War.* In it, Aharon, a young soldier from Kibbutz Yifaat, had recounted his feelings during the battle for Jerusalem:

> We were in a covering action as the rest of our gang were advancing inside the Old City . . . we had a bunch of heavy machine guns . . . and on the rise opposite us there was some kind of a fire-fight the whole time . . . they shot at us and we shot back . . . some of our tanks opened up on them and they began to run . . . one of them didn't even remove his uniform like many of the others trying to escape . . . he just ran . . . and our entire fire power was trained on him, and he tried desperately to escape . . . he kept running and at last he got away. So it's hard for me to say that the pangs of conscience I had were because of my kibbutz education, but anyway, I was glad that he escaped.

After these words saw print, Arik Sharon condemned the confusion, muddleheadedness, and anxieties they expressed. "Whoever says 'I fired and missed and then felt relieved' is a traitor." It seems that the battle between humanists and those who call them traitors was drawn in the summer of 1967.

Or was it earlier? Again the question of pragmatism versus ideology, the question of where to begin, clamors for attention. During the revolt against the Romans, Rabbi Akiva, the recognized spiritual leader of the rebellion, was asked what idea subsumed the entire rationale of the Jewish life view. He answered that the greatest principle, on which the whole Torah rested, was "Love thy fellow as thyself" (Lev. 19:18). When his followers asked him to explain who "thy fellow" (some read "thy neighbor") referred to, he replied, *"Kol sh'hu ben-brit"*—anyone who is a Jew. Thereupon his pupil, Ben Azzai, took issue with his revered teacher, and said, "There is a greater principle than that," and he argued that the verse that begins chapter 5 of *Bereshit* took precedence: "This is the book of the generations of Adam [man]. In the day that God created man, in the likeness of God made He him, male and female created He them, and blessed them."

Ideological disputations, educational principles, pragmatism born of war, and restraints on the exercise of power have all been with us for two thousand years.

They may well remain unresolved until the advent of the messianic age, even as they provide the fruitful tension that fuels creative Jewish life. Whether we are innocent or tainted, whether Rabbi Assi is right and Rabbi Akiva is the key to our vital survival and Arik Sharon is the sharp edge of survival's sword, or whether Aharon of Kibbutz Yifaat, Eli Geva, and Ben Azzai are closer to the Jewish vocation, can, however, only be proved in the arena of Jewish sovereignty, in the State of Israel, now thirty-four.

PART  V

# Reflections of American Israelis

12

# At Peace with the Army

## WILLIAM FREEDMAN

*I*

On 18 September 1972 my three years were up. Temporary residency, with all the rights, privileges, and immunities appertaining thereto—and they are more substantial than anyone who hasn't lost them perhaps realizes—was over, and I had earned the richly mixed blessing of Israeli citizenship. On 22 September I received notice from my district's draft board that the local equivalent of Uncle Sam wanted *me* and that I was to report for a physical on 10 October. It was no joke. The vaunted military machine was indeed well oiled—or so it seemed. It might take six months to three years to have a telephone installed, and three weeks to have it fixed; a letter from Haifa to Jerusalem might require anywhere from five days to two weeks to arrive; finding the right man in the right government office to handle any problem at all might be the work of generations. But finding an aging, flat-footed, quasi-pacifistic American immigrant took the army no more than three or four days. No wonder no one knew where anything was or how to get anything done in less than seventeen months. Everyone who did was working for the army—or so we thought. Still, the efficiency was gratifying. For one thing, if the nation had the human resources that permitted only one institution to function effectively, surely it had better be the army. And for another, I'd get an early chance to do my feeble, short-winded but earnest part for my adopted country, something I'd never been asked to do—and toward the end would have refused to do—for my native one.

In the States I'd always managed to stay one step ahead of the military, becoming adept in "how to avoid the draft without really dodging." When college students were exempted, I was at the university. When B.A. candidates became eligible, I was in graduate school. When graduate students lost their exemptions, I got married. When they began to draft childless husbands, I became a father. And if exemptions had been denied to all but Romanian agronomists, I was prepared for four happy years at Bucharest A&M. But Israel was different. I could serve here with as clean a conscience as a guilty *galutnik* (diaspora Jew) was capable of, and I was in for what was almost invariably described by those who'd experienced it as a "rich" experience. A "rich" experience is the standard existential equivalent for the "sweet" girl your mother wanted you to ask out—you wouldn't enjoy it, but you wouldn't forget it either—and I wanted to hear more. Not that it would matter much. Basic training may be a blind date with what we, in our infinite sensitivity and decency, used to call a "dog" or a "beast," but it was not something you refused to show up for, or ditched halfway through the ordeal. Still, it's well to walk open-eyed even into the inevitable, so I sought out veterans of these programs for the aged for information on what to expect and advice on how to deal with it.

Perhaps the most comforting thing about the basic training stint is that travelers of my age (35) and thereabouts return from its bourn in three weeks (and, it turns out, on weekends as well, with special leave for births, weddings, family problems, or bar mitzvahs). Nothing short of Parris Island could be unendurable for such a short span, but I was hardly less curious. The one source who'd open up for me confirmed my suspicions. The real trial was psychological, not physical. There were eighteen-hour days to be coped with, night watches that lengthened them to twenty or twenty-one. And there were imaginary bunkers to be stormed, bellies and elbows to be crawled on. But this sort of thing was manageable. I'd been a weight lifter from age 16 to 33, when creeping senescence and creaking joints took me off the boards, and despite wickedly flatted feet and a gasping short-windedness that made me fearful of forced runs or lengthy hikes, I was confident the body would perform. The problematic organ was the psyche. My source spoke of the surprising regression to infancy he experienced—the virtual shutdown of his adult mind; the role of passivity; the need to obey the orders, often seemingly arbitrary, of a 19-year-old commander (my informant had a 17-year-old daughter and a 15-year-old son); and the rapidly developed hiding response, the withdrawal into the shadows whenever someone in authority came looking for "volunteers." I've always had very special younger-brother problems with authority—I take orders with as much goodwill and resignation as Khaddafi brings to Zionism, a fact that probably explains my career choice as well as anything—and I wasn't at all sure I could endure with the maturity of silence the arbitrary and humiliating barks of a khaki-colored student manqué with stripes. It turned out to be no problem at all. Not because I discovered in myself unsuspected resources of maturity, ego strength, tolerance, and restraint, but because, to my enduring gratitude and delight, I found them in the army.

I passed my physical (which means, I assume, that I had a body)—and equipped with flashlight, hand mirror, soap, toilet paper (that was important), and Tums—prepared for my call-up in June of '73—due to begin, mercifully (intentionally?), on the last day of classes at the university. When we arrived at the base at about 6:00 on a cool and pleasant Sunday evening in late June, our platoon—as unlikely a collection of Schweiks as any army might wish to be spared—was greeted outside the barrack by the base commander, a fleshy, smiling giant of a man (about 6 feet 4 inches and 270 pounds, I'd guess), with more the mien and manner of a Jewish Santa Claus than a lieutenant colonel. He welcomed us, assured us he understood how difficult it was for us to be taken away from our jobs and families, told us that while our training wouldn't be easy, neither, he hoped, would we find it too difficult, and said he hoped that his new policy of every Friday afternoon and Saturday off would ease the pain. He spoke glowingly of the importance of immigration to Israel, parried jokes and comments from the ranks (significantly, we were not lined up to receive him, but had simply swarmed haphazardly around him), and, since about two-thirds of our number were Russians, stumbled good-naturedly through his Russian repertoire. We would make our way together "slowly slowly," but for me it wouldn't take that long. In a situation like this I was a sucker for a smile, so anxious to be disarmed that within three minutes I'd piled my formidable arsenal of defensive weapons at my feet and thrown my psychological arms in the air. Compared with me, the vaunted Italian warrior of a thousand jokes was Audie Murphy run amok. Still, there was an element of hesitation in my surrender. This was a colonel!? Sure, we weren't regular army and this wasn't standard basic, but were these what passed for officer-trainee relations? And if they were even remotely comparable with what the regulars experienced, hadn't I better have another look into the American job market? It's all very sweet and jolly, to be sure, but what I'd learned from twenty years of John Wayne, Jack Webb, and Hank Bauer was that the only way to win a war was by shaving the heads of new recruits, throwing warm oatmeal in their faces, and expressing doubts about the continence of their mothers. Now here was this great mountain of a colonel pretending we were human beings (even those of us with shoulder-length hair and stenciled mazes of mustache and sideburns on our faces). It couldn't last. But the only illusion here was the illusion that it was all illusory. We could keep our hair if we liked, and though we got numbers and dog tags, we kept our names as well.

Don't get me wrong. Basic training, even for us, was no dance of the sugarplum fairies, and this army has its share of crew cut vocal cords, officers who in real life or dream have seen a few too many of those John Wayne and Jack Webb films and watched with goose-bumping awe as old Hammerin' Hank Bauer, that hustlin' exmarine, stretched singles into doubles and bore down on that hapless shortstop with Iwo Jima in his eyes and Guadalcanal in his flashing spikes. Our company captain, for example, a tough Druze who remarked casually and believably that he could collapse a wall of concrete blocks with his bare fist, was gifted with a vocal and expressive range extending roughly from piercing to more so, and a sense of humor reminiscent of Jonathan Edwards. The master sergeant in charge of protocol and discipline, compared with whom the captain was Henny Youngman on a good night, won permanent membership in my own private *spiritus mundi* with a salute such as few men have ever given, received, or borne witness to. He leaped a full foot and a half into the air, nearly shattered his frontal bone with a flying right-hand salute, and landed in a vague flurry of clattering legs and heels. One of the three corporals who, along with a sergeant and second lieutenant, commanded our own platoon had a touch of the old disease himself, and worked unpersuasively, annoyingly, and unsuccessfully to command a respect he despaired of by dealing with us as though we were a troop of aging German shepherds who should long ago have been mercifully destroyed. An army, as a number of the Russians in our outfit repeatedly grumbled, is after all, an army. But all but the few *kvetchiest* of our malcontents could not help but acknowledge that these refugees from the military adding machine were aberrations, that there were relatively few Haldemans or even Deans in the palace guard, and that the palace—such as it was—was, in this sense at least, hardly guarded at all.

The first day of *imunim* (training) established the pattern, as it turned out, for most of the next three weeks. It was not so much a course of instruction or a training program as a battle, and this not between good and evil but simply between wills: perhaps, rather, between will and will-lessness or ineptitude. In this corner, Avishai: 5 feet 11-inches tall, 150 pounds of lean sun-darkened sabra (native-born Israeli), and at 21 gifted with a self-possession, calm, and emotional maturity that rarely allowed his determination to do the near impossible—to make soldiers if not fighters of us—to diminish into a defensive authoritarianism or humorlessness. And in this corner, seventy-five has-beens, including some fifty Russian immigrants (eight of them Georgians) and a motley assortment of North and South Americans, Scots, French, British, Greeks, and Indians. There is no generalizing about the others—the numbers were too small—but the Russians might be divided into three groups of roughly equal size: those who, while far from pleased to find themselves back in a military machine, however benign and however briefly, were determined to do more or less what was asked of them; those who, out of resentment, recalcitrance, defiance, pride, and a variety of less definable or less visible reasons, were determined to do a great deal less; and those, including most of the Georgians, who could not do what was asked of them simply because they couldn't understand the language in which it was asked and to whom, for whatever reasons, no amount of translation was ever likely to be much help.

The Russians—these, at any rate—are a remarkably vital and vocal people. They seem to cherish, feed off, and revel in their language (in the army framework, primarily unprintable language); and almost no instruction or bungled execution passed without a parleyed medley of comments, mockeries, and obscenities, none of which the lieutenant could possibly have understood but most of which he serenely over-looked, smiled at, or asked to have translated. He was 21 years old, deadly serious about a deadly serious business that for all he knew was being obscenely ridiculed. But somehow he knew—and he was right, of course—that the banter and bungling, while perhaps symptomatic of relative indifference, were rarely more sinister than that, never personal and almost always good-natured. And he managed what I could only admire: a delicate combination of earnest dedication to his work and tolerant, even willing, good humor toward those who took it so much less seriously than he and who did it so conspicuously less well. He may have been following a carefully prepared script. Whoever determined policy in such matters must surely know that one does not treat what are euphemistically referred to as "mature" men like 18-year-olds fresh out of high school. They are more likely to be resentful of unexplained orders, defensive and hostile in the face of authority (especially in the hands of men half their age and five times their competence), sensitive to the transparency of idle threats, and unintimidated by the more genuine. All this applied several times over to most of the Russians in our outfit and, by their own admission, to the recent immigrants in general. What we have here is not the typical Russian (whatever that may be), not even the typical Russian Jew, but a careful selection. Those who are here are here because they did not take kindly to restrictions on their freedom, because they had had their fill of arbitrary authority, and because they could not be intimidated by threats or punishment. War-time is one thing. Most had served three years in the Russian army and were in relatively good physical shape; a few were excellent marksmen. If called, they would perform. But by any standards they are a peacetime army's nightmare, and the lieutenant was obliged to call on resources deeper than policy. There was no "defeating" these men, no bending or transforming them (or anyone else in three weeks, for that matter, though many of the rest of us were either more pliable or already bent). But he held them to a standoff, gave us the training we were sent for, kept his head and a great deal of grudging but well-earned respect. He may simply have been following orders, sitting on his own more aggressive instincts and trying to charm us into a cooperation he'd have been happier wringing from us. But I doubt it. The lieutenant was a mensch, and when it was all over I told him so.

Toward the end the teeth ground harder, but the prevailing sense of decency, of humaneness, the maintenance of self-respect and respect for the other was never quite eaten away. The most difficult of us all was an extremely bright, hypersensitive, and proudly stubborn immigrant named Moshe, an accomplished engineer who demanded a recognition of his worth the Israeli job market denied him and who simply could not take orders from anyone:

—"Moshe, put on your work hat."
Moshe doesn't move.
—"Moshe, put on your work hat."
Moshe doesn't move.
—"All right, then, don't put on your work hat; put on your helmet" (much less comfortable in the summer sun).
Moshe puts on his work hat.
—"Moshe, put on your helmet."
—"I have my work hat on."
—"Moshe, I said put on your helmet."
—"What for? I've got my work hat on."
—"All right, Moshe. You can stand up back there behind the others." (The rest of us were sitting on the ground.)
Moshe puts on his helmet.
—"Moshe, I said stand up."
—"But I've put my helmet on, like you said."
—"Moshe, stand up." (The voice is getting angry now.)
Moshe stands up, but after a minute or two he puts his rifle behind him and sits on the barrel.
—"Moshe, hold your rifle in your hands."
Moshe doesn't move.
—"Moshe, hold your rifle in your hands."
Moshe reaches behind him and grabs the barrel in his hands without changing his position.
—"Moshe, I said hold your rifle in your hands."
—"But I'm holding it in my hands. What do you want from me?"

—"Moshe" (very angry now but still controlled), "don't go head-to-head with me; your head will break before mine does."
—"What I've been through, you've never been through. I'm not afraid of you."
—(Almost shouting now, but not quite): "Go back to the barracks and wait for me there."

Moshe's remark was insulting (according to some of us who didn't like the professional heroics of it), unjustified, and, at best, uncalled for. The incident, however, was but a harsh rendition of a more comic and much subtler dance we danced for eighteen days, and in the end it came to much the same thing. The transgression, by normal military standards, was serious and punishable, but Avishai chose to let it go. He and Moshe had gone head-to-head and nothing had been broken. Moshe had put on his work hat, put on his helmet, stood up, and gone back to the barracks—all as he'd been told, if somewhat belatedly. But in the end he had said his piece and gotten off clean. He'd proved, as for some reason he felt he had to, that he wasn't afraid, and he'd gotten away with whatever it was he felt he had to get away with.

Letting him off was perhaps a sign of weakness as well as generosity, but as much as either, I think, a sign of uncertainty. The army didn't seem quite sure what it wanted to give its *miluimniks* (reservists) or what it wanted or had a right to expect in return. Fulfillment of the law of universal service aside, this drafting of the seemingly undraftable has two main purposes: to make some kind of soldiers out of these paunch-bellied figures, and at the same time to aid in the complex and difficult process of absorption—to make these Russians, Americans, Paraguayans, Englishmen, Chileans, and Greeks feel, somehow, a bit more Israeli, more a part of the land because they are required at least to play at defending it. The two purposes, however, are not always compatible—digging trenches doth not inevitably a lover of the soil make—and the army hadn't quite made up its mind how much of each it had a right to hope for and which, in the event of conflict, should take precedence. Judging from the reports of other reservists who served at various times in the same or at other bases, under the same or other commanders, it is clear not only that a great deal depends on who happens to be running your own particular show, but that the general policy is still in fluid search of formulation. Before the Yom Kippur War, however—perhaps because immigration seemed at that point a more serious problem than security—absorption had the upper hand. The search, I'm told by more recent recruits, still goes on. There is no longer any question of the primacy of security over immigration, but whether a fractious middle-aging immigrant can be converted, even by tough discipline and ready punishment, into a reliable securer of our peace remains problematic. Like a number of other pressing postwar questions, it pesists unanswered.

Moshe's escape, like the light sentence dealt three seven-hour deserters in our platoon—they merely lost their Saturday passes—was no doubt owed to this "absorb 'em with kindness" policy. But a comparable sense of consideration seems to pervade the military experience at almost every level, in comparative terms at any rate. Regulars may argue with me here, but only because few are familiar with the maliciousness of the training in other fighting armies. Had any of these four transgressors been regulars, they'd doubtless have been treated far less gently, but I saw few traces of the kind of formality, disciplinarianism or arbitary tyranny one usually associates with the military. There were a number of regular outfits on the base while we were there, and while their training is infinitely more demanding, their treatment is only somewhat rougher. New recruits talk back frequently to officers and noncoms, question, argue, and ignore their non-training-related orders—if only briefly—and get away with it. There's a good deal of shouting and occasional threatening, but the recruit usually backs away before anything comes of it, and his superiors usually allow him plenty of time and space to retreat with pride and identity intact. I entered the army fearful that I lacked the calm, patience, and security to tolerate arbitrary harassment, and learned that, by and large, the higher-ups need more of each than the lower-downs. Fortunately most, if not all, of them have it. No one is "broken" here. The officer relies, by and large, far more on respect than on intimidation for the results he wants, and it usually works. When it doesn't, there is no taste for confrontation, and the persistently defiant often defied with relative impunity. That seemed all right at the time—a small price to pay for keeping the personal peace and avoiding harsh punishment—but now, the October war behind us, I begin to wonder.

## II

A great deal of what I've reported so far in such uncharacteristically glowing terms (these are new responses for me, and they surprise me) is simply humane behavior in a context in which one has learned not to expect it (the glow, I suspect, is largely relief at not having to deal with what I did expect). Individual decency and magnanimity are fine, lovely and important assets, but they can't be relied on to define an army's character. They're matters of personality, of the genetic and environmental draw, and not to be counted on. The difference between my experience and that of some of my friends is probably owed to blind luck. With the exception of one strayed wanderer from the halls of Montezuma, all the officers and noncoms of our platoon were highly civilized beings. My friend, it seems, fell in with the wrong crowd and paid the price.

Decency, it may be said, is prevalent in the Israeli army not because Israelis are inherently more decent than other people, but simply because it has not been institutionalized out of the military experience. It's not regarded as bad form, a sign of weakness, or a dangerous invitation to anarchy or cowardice. What interests me more, however, because ultimately it is more solidly grounded and a more reliable determinant of the character of the military, is what has been either formally or semiformally institutionalized in the Israeli army: accessibility. The higher-ups are accessible to the lower-downs, and it is no mere diversionary ploy. They listen, and when the situation warrants it, prove receptive. All this is no doubt truer for the older reservists than for the regulars, but it describes their experience as well.

Approachability in the army begins, perhaps, with the use of names. It is either a remnant or a myth—and probably a bit of both—that all Israeli soldiers address each other by their first names. The stripeless are told to address the striped as *ham'faked* (commander), and while that rule is quite uniformly respected among regular troops (as saluting is not— one almost never sees it anywhere but at instruction sessions and official ceremonies), we ignored it after the first few days. It was difficult for us to address men fifteen to twenty years our junior as commander, and one by one we dropped it. No one said a word. What we adopted in its place was the system of address the officers and noncoms use among themselves. In a curious inversion of whatever logic one may expect of protocol, officers address their noncoms by their last names, and are called in turn by their first. Thus our sergeant and corporals were Levi, Vitkin, DeKel, and Bar-Am to their lieutenant, and he was Avi to all of them. When we picked up and began to use the same nomenclature, an uncomfortable and unnecessary barrier came down, and while regular recruits rarely cross this line, merely hearing the names passed among the officers and noncoms and witnessing the almost total informality of their interaction cannot but have its effect. Somehow a dressing-down from Kimmelman or Mizrachi is not the same as a reprimand administered by a hairless organism known only as "Yes, Sergeant" or "Sir." And perhaps more important still, the trainee himself retains his name; to his own commanders, who know his name, he is never 270359, scrub, dog, or worse. A Rosen by any other name, perhaps, but not by none at all.

Then, too, there are the interviews and gripe sessions. Two or three days after our arrival we were all sent in for private interviews with our lieutenant. I was still playing war movie then, so I greeted him with the tripartite salute we'd all been taught the day before:

1. Extend right arm ninety degrees from the shoulder;
2. turn palm upward;
3. bend elbow until side of right-hand index finger meets brow above right eye.

The lieutenant politely told me to can it, i.e., cut it down to some rough form of number three and let it go at that. This was my first lesson in what became increasingly obvious thereafter: the schizophrenia of the military and the consequent disparity between regulation and behavior. At some time or other we've all see the same films, read the same histories, and accepted the same rituals and myths. One of the most ingrained of all military assumptions is that no army can function effectively without discipline: probably quite true. Another is that discipline necessarily includes such trappings as formal salutes, heel-clickings, gun-spinnings and specialized terms and tones of deference and address: more doubtful. The IDF (Israeli Defense Forces) policy makers have not escaped art, history, or pop culture, so most of the rules are there, and the Israeli army regulation booklet is probably no shorter than most. The problem is that, with a few stiff exceptions, no one seems quite convinced of proposition two. The British acted on it when they were here; and those Prussians fought like crazy. But somehow our own military history seems to suggest the separability of the two orders of discipline from each other and of fighting effectiveness from at least the latter. The belief, apparently, persists. The war, whatever else it may have put an end to, has not destroyed the army's faith in these distinctions. There's a gnawing and perhaps slightly guilty sense that they probably ought to do it as the textbooks say, but somewhere underneath it all, only a few really believe and act on it. Not only does a discrepancy result between instruction and performance at the Mickey Mouse level of business, but so do radical differences between the various officers, and almost-comic incongruities between the day-to-day casualness and the stiff-jointed, mechanically voiced formality of ceremonial occasions.

The interview with the lieutenant is a forum for mutual acquaintance, a technique for putting the greenie at ease, and a vehicle for the registering of whatever questions or complaints he may have. It can serve no informational function since all the hard information the new recruit is asked for—where he lives, what he does, his marital status, etc.—has already been recorded elsewhere. It's really a kind of benevolent hoax, a formal interview fronting for an informal bull session, and while an officious lieutenant could no doubt turn it into a cool and even unsettling affair, he'd be thwarting its purpose by doing so. Our lieutenant made it a point to tell me that his home was only a kilometer or two from my own, that he had relatives just across the street from me, and that perhaps when this was all over for both of us we'd meet as civilians in Haifa. The old "lecturer in English literature" ploy is no doubt worth at least two softening points in an exchange of this kind, but none were needed. The point of the interview was to find out how I felt, being in the army at this unmilitary age, and to make me feel a little less nervous about it than I probably did. It worked, and if it's managed with the same disarming ease that mine was, it should work for the regulars as well.

In addition to this one-time personal interview with the platoon commander, there are also weekly complaint sessions with the company commander, in our case the wall-breaking captain. Every Tuesday after lunch the entire company is marched out and assembled in a three-quarter rectangle to answer questions about conditions and treatment and to register any complaints they may have. The captain stands on the unoccupied side of the rectangle, pen and pad in hand, and throws out questions, answers others, and records whatever legitimate-sounding grievances he hears.

—"How's the food?"
—"Fine, no complaints."
—"Except the bread. Yesterday it was stale and the loaf on our table was turning green."
(Writes.)
—"How are your commanders treating you?"
—"Fine."
—"Very decent."
—"No, wait a minute. Our commander was supposed to relieve us from guard duty at two this morning, and he didn't show up until three-thirty."
—"What's his name?"
—"Do I have to give his name? I don't . . ."
—"What's his name? If we're going to get anything done here I've got to know his name."
—"Well, it was Yonatan. Platoon Number one."
(Writes).
—"Are you all getting to sleep on time?"
—"Yeah. We get up early as hell and I wouldn't say we get enough sleep. But we get to sleep on time."
—"Anything else? Any complaints? Just make sure they're general and of some importance. Let's not get into petty griping here."

—"The sinks where we wash our mess tins have no drainpipes. All the food particles are allowed to pour directly on the ground. It's against all the most elementary rules of sanitation [that's one of our Russian engineers talking]. There should be a pipe channeling the waste underground."
(Writes).

That's a much-abbreviated and -simplified sample. Standing out there in the midday sun is no unmitigated joy, and there's a lot of shuffling and talking the captain is none too fond of. He lets us know it, once every four minutes or so and with cumulative impatience. Then too, there are a number of private, petty, and often unjustified grievances that go through him like fingernails on a blackboard, and he does not suffer in silence. If anything, the sessions stretch on too long. The captain insists on hearing out every raised hand, and by the end, the ball is in the court of the *nudniks* (carpers). The others gradually lose patience, moan, whine, and finally shout at the last-ditchers to throw in the towel and let us go. But objective self-assessment is not the new recruit's special strength, and on it grinds, down to the last few seconds of the full hour. *Nudniks* and many-sided impatience notwithstanding, the session is at the very least a useful spit valve and a mark of good intentions. But a spit valve is a messy device if it only leads back into another part of the horn, and the most gratifying thing about these sessions is that most legitimate complaints are tended to. Yonatan caught it for showing up an hour and a half late; the bread from there on out was a great deal fresher than it had been; and two days later I noticed a new drainpipe leading out from the massive sink behind the mess hall and disappearing underground.

The base commander is hardly less accessible than the officers who serve him. Not everyone visited him privately, of course, but then hardly anyone really wanted to or had occasion to. All that is needed, it seems, is what our mothers used to call a "mouth" (as in "this one has a mouth on him"—our fathers often called it "lip") and an inclination to open it at somewhat inappropriate times. I have both.

One moring early in the final week of training we were visited out on the shooting range by a major general and his wife, one of those handsome, supremely composed blond wives who seem to have been distributed, rather than married, to generals. He was asking predictably friendly rhetorical questions and getting equally predictable, much too chummy answers.

—"How you getting on here?"
—"Great, great."

—"One hundred percent."
—"Any complaints?"
—"No."
—"None at all."
—"Everything's fine."
—"Getting good training here?"
—"Absolutely."
—"The best."
—"One hundred percent."
—"How do you feel here? Do you feel more like Israelis now that you've been in the army?"
—"Absolutely."
—"One hundred percent."
—"Much more. We feel great."
—"One hundred percent."

Very cute, very chummy, very familiar, a lot of bullshit. But look out. It's Freedman, and wait . . . I'm not sure but . . . wait a minute . . . yes . . . he's opening that mouth and Oh my God, what is he saying?! Suddenly, from somewhere in the last row, there's this voice and it seems to be mine. What it was saying was something like this:

—"I don't know what level we're talking on here, but if you're really serious about wanting to know how we feel about this experience, this isn't really the way to do it. In a framework like this, I'm afraid, you'll only hear what you want to hear, and if you really want to know how we feel and what we think, you should speak to us not out here and all together, but privately and one at a time."
—"I'll speak to him myself," volunteers the colonel. "Where are you from?"

It's only at this point that something begins to brighten in the accumulated density of this mind. It's only now I realize that I've probably, in Cathcart's* terms, added several black marks to the colonel's column. Here he is smiling alongside the general, watching his boys glide smoothly through a performance every civilized being has played a thousand times, following the rules of the game like mature adult players, when up pops this 2-year-old mouth in the back row, whining like a sore loser who's never played a game of social checkers before and flinging the counters off the board. I try for redemption. "I'm from the States. I know: We're all spoiled complainers there [this is redemption?],

---

*The obsessed colonel in Heller's *Catch-22*.

but that's not the point. It's not that I have any major complaints. Not at all [ah, that's better]. It's just that I think if the army is genuinely interested in the effectiveness of its training program and in how the new immigrants respond to it, we should discuss it in a format where we can get into the matter in some depth." Beautiful. "Depth." That's the word here. Who's complaining? Certainly not me. I'm just one of those morbid intellectuals hung up on depth. It didn't seem to matter, though—not because my last remarks had failed to patch things up, but because the colonel's voice and appearance suggested he wasn't really wounded after all. He had said he would speak to me and he simply repeated his offer. We fixed a time for that afternoon.

Most of the members of the platoon began to flash thumbs-up and ringed thumb and forefinger signs, take my hand, and slap my back. Some commented on my bravery, another on my mouth, and another simply asked me why I'd done it. It was a good question. The fact was I really didn't have any very serious complaints, not personally, but two things were bothering me. One, I really didn't like that game we were playing out there, i.e., "I ask you pseudointerrogative questions and you give me the answers we all know I want to hear." It was the game they played "over there," in those "other" armies. This seemed to me different, and I wanted to insist on that difference. And two, I had really begun to care, first about these Russian immigrants I'd come to know quite well over the past two and a half weeks, and no less about this army that had won my child's heart forever simply by not playing drill sergeant with me. I knew the Russians had not been charmed out of their boots (as perhaps I had) by the Israeli military; that they had complaints they were refusing to articulate, allowing a few of the more satisfied to speak for them; and that, in fact, not one of them felt "more Israeli," more fully integrated into his new society, for the experience. Most felt no less so, but a few did, and since I cared both about them and about this country, I wanted to suggest a few changes.

As for courage, that was never an issue. I'm not a particularly courageous person (unless a recurrent inclination for tactless moralizing be taken for bravery), and in retrospect one of the most interesting implications of the incident is that fear and a sense of threat played no part in it. I had come to regard this army as a kind of indulgent teddy bear—a terror out in the woods, perhaps, but a cuddly sort of creature in its own den—and it never occurred to me that to shoot my mouth off was to stick my neck out.

At 1:00, p.m., when I went to see the colonel, I was told he had guests and couldn't receive me. I should come back early that evening; I'd be notified as to the exact time. Aha! The runaround. Don't call us, we'll call you. A familiar touch of the cold civilian bureaucracy, something I was well acquainted with and, for all the disillusioning letdown, could deal with. When 5:00, 6:00, and 7:00 p.m. had come and gone without the call, I was convinced that I'd been suckered; and while I was angry at my own persistent naïveté and disappointed by the broader implications of the ruse, it was, after all, no worse than anyone had a right to expect, and no mortal sin for all that. The army, after all, is the army.

At 8:00 p.m. I was sent for. The base commander's office was large, lined with pictures, banners, and trophies, but ultimately as unpretentious as he was. The furniture was inexpensive and relatively sparse—no rugs, no mahogany, no ebony or alabaster desk sets. I was as pleased to see that as I'd been to note a year and a half before that the Foreign Ministry was a complex of old army barracks, the "Indian Desk" a shabby version of my own. Everyone talked about waste and extravagance in the upper reaches, but if it existed—and it must have—it was kept well hidden. I had buttoned my fly especially for the occasion—no easy task with all those split, too-large and fragmented buttons—and was prepared to salute as well. But the colonel was writing something when I walked in and not looking up, so what would have been my second salute in three weeks passed out of history.

I sat down and waited for the colonel to finish what he was doing and look up. When he did, he began with a question that knew its answer. "You're not happy here, are you?" "Well, of course I'm not exactly happy," I began innocently, warming up to a series of subtle qualifications and an extended discourse on human happiness. But I didn't get far. "We always have trouble with Americans. I don't know why, but they think this is Vietnam, and they hate the military. Show them khaki and they see red." And with that, he took a three-page letter out of a folder he had on his desk and asked me to read it.

It was from an American "Remember the Alamo, *Pueblo,* and *Maine*" veteran of the Tet offensive and a number of missions over Laos, who had moved to Israel and spent several weeks in a course parallel to the one I was in. The purpose of the letter was to advise the colonel that adults of "high intellectual accomplishment"—particularly American—were simply not military material. They would never take an order simply because it was issued. They always wanted to know why, and nothing anyone could do would ever transform them. He was advising the colonel and the Israeli military to give up on the idea of making them soldiers, let alone fighters. The author of the letter wasn't half as stupid as he was contemptuous, but all this was beside the point. I was that adult of "high intellectual accomplishment," of course, and showing me the letter was the colonel's way of saying he had me figured. Twenty minutes had gone and I was about to be dragged off into a discussion of American radicalism that would no doubt consume—however interestingly and congenially—whatever time remained. I had got in to see the colonel, but we were going to chat amicably and part friends, and my salutary advice to the armed forces would be buried with my bones. So I canned my apologetics—my why-I-came distinctions between identification and raging chauvinism, between flags and decals, my feelings about that military and this—and simply reaffirmed that I had come not with complaints but with proposals, that I cared about this place and wanted, if I could, to help it do well what it had in mind to do.

Somehow that seemed to change things. The colonel passed a sheet of blank paper to his personal assistant, a talkative, homey, cigar-smoking captain named Haim, and told him to take down my suggestions. My basic premise was that, given what the general had said, the army had us here for two main reasons: one, to make some kind of soldiers out of us, and two, to make us feel more comfortably at home in Israel by increasing our commitment to it. My feeling was that while the two purposes were not necessarily compatible, neither were they unavoidably contradictory, and in any case, if I had gauged the sentiments of my platoon correctly, neither was being done as effectively as it might be.

That said, I made my specific proposals, and while each one served the colonel as a vehicle for English practice, charming anecdote, and sensible theory, I'll reduce the conversation to its substantive skeleton. We'll lose much of the colonel himself—a very real loss—but it's his stunning, even somewhat unnerving responsiveness that I want to reproduce.

On the matter of absorption and integration, the aim, it seemed to me, was defeated at the outset by the seeming arbitrariness of the entire enterprise. Few if any of us really knew what we were doing in the army. As far as we could make out, we were merely playing out our quite expendable roles in the program of universal service, serving primarily, well, because everyone served; and while we recognized the justness of it, ultimately it was debilitating. The colonel assured me we were expected to perform, in the event of war, some very real and purposeful functions (he was frighteningly right, it turned out), and began to set them out for me.

—"Don't tell me now," I jumped in. "Tell them, all of them."

—"Haim, mark that down. Fix a time for me to talk to the new *olim* [immigrants] and explain what they're doing here. What else?"

—"Well, one of the most difficult things for us to take is the dodge that passes for an explanation: 'You have to do it this way because *kakhah zeh b'atzava* [that's how it is in the army].' " Perhaps one of the principal differences between a 35-year-old and an 18-year-old, I suggested, is that, like the offensive Tet man said, that kind of explanation only sets the former grumbling.

—"Haim, get all the lieutenants down here. I want them to hear this. I want every order explained to these men so they know just why they're doing what we have them doing."

—"[Hey, wait a minute. Don't take me so seriously. I'm only . . .]."

When they arrived, he told them. He also handed them pens and paper and told them to listen to what I had to say. "This is a Jew with a head on him."

—"[Did you hear that, Ma? Not just a mouth. A head. The colonel says I got a head on me]."

—"What else?"

—"Well, one of the Russians in the platoon suggested that if you were serious about making us feel somehow more Israeli through this experience, it might be well to take us on a tour of the area, show us what went on here before and during the Six Day War."

—"Haim, how much would a tour like that cost?"

—"About twenty-five hundred pounds [$600]."

—"Let's see if we can get a budget for it. It may be too late for this outfit, but maybe we can do it for the next. OK, anything else?"

—"Well, assuming you really do have a serious military role in mind for us, I'm not sure [note the new signs of hesitation and qualification. I'm getting nervous now; this guy's actually listening] we're getting enough target practice. For one thing, since the whole company goes out to the range together and since only twelve can take target practice at a given time, we all spend most of our time simply waiting."

—(Picks up the phone). "Get me Amos. Amos, didn't I tell you I don't want all the boys out on the range at one time? Tomorrow morning I want half of them watching the film, the other half taking target practice, and in the afternoon switch them around." (Hangs up). "What else?"

—"As I said, taken all in all, I just don't think we're doing enough shooting. If you calculate the amount of time we actually use our weapons, it comes to little more than thirty or forty minutes. How well can we possibly learn to shoot in so little time?"

—"Don't worry about it. We know what we're doing. You may not realize it, but the amount of practice you're getting is just about right. Still, a little more can't hurt." (Picks up the phone). "Give me Amos again. Amos, I want three thousand more bullets for each platoon. I want them to get in a little extra shooting."

Amos, it seems, was really on the other end of that line. The next day we were divided into movie-watchers and target-practicers and then switched. The night after that the colonel sat us down for a brief but pointed explanation of the army's plans for us (it helped; a number of the soldiers were grateful for it), and when it was over we were marched out for an extra session of target practice (I graciously declined credit for that; that sort of thing wins no friends). It was too late for a tour of the area for us, but I was told the following day that it had been worked into the programs of the new groups just arriving.

What all this reflects, I think, is first of all the very special openness and responsiveness of this particular base commander. He told me, with some pride, that he had had more than 400 visits of this kind in the preceding year. I believe his figure and would justify his pride, but he is only an extreme instance of a common virtue; and what this in turn reflects, along with the persistent personalism and flexibility of the military, is its special concern for new immigrants and its search for a program that will contribute to the extremely complex and not invariably successful national effort to absorb them, integrate them, reconcile them to their new surroundings, and their new surroundings, i.e., the sabras and *vatikim* (older settlers), to them.

How useful were my proposals? I'm not sure. Nor do I know how seriously or for how long they'll be tested. But the army is looking; it's interested and concerned, and it will take whatever sounds sensible from as far down as it may come. There is nothing farther down than a *miluimnik,* and what I had to say was taken seriously, I suspect, not because I lecture at the university, not because this Jew has a head on him, but because I seemed to be talking from inside, speaking in faulty Hebrew for myself and a number of Russians, Argentinians, Americans, and Frenchmen to a sabra colonel who insisted on answering me in English.

At the closing "swearing of allegiance" ceremony, each of us, in full battle dress, responded to his name with a presentation of arms and a loud "I swear" and received a copy of the Bible. And as we stood there under the stars around a massive Star of David formed of windblown candle flames, rifles in one hand, *Tanach* in the other, we heard the colonel's echoing voice:

"You have with you now a Bible and a gun, and I do not distinguish between them."

> And I do not distinguish between them
> And I do not distinguish between them

There was a poem in there somewhere, a frightening one perhaps, but not necessarily. What the colonel meant was that this was not the first time in our history the Jew had found it necessary to defend himself, his tradition, and his Book with arms, and that, sad to say, the Book and its people could not survive without the arms to defend them. But one can look at this lopsided Janus from the other side as well. I heard not one word of anti-Arab vilification or propaganda during my three weeks of training. The enemy was consistently referred to as precisely that: "the enemy." The word *Arab* was almost never used in that context, and even "the enemy" was spoken of not with hatred, not with contempt, but with a respect few on the outside seemed willing to grant him before October. Things are not always so. Other reservists have heard what I was spared, but in the end one can only conclude that the relative humanity of the Israeli soldier (and for all the contrary propaganda, no one seriously doubts it; where would *you* rather be a POW?) Is owed in large part to the milieu in which he's trained. Despite the permanence of threat and the growing pressures, technological and administrative, for more rigid and more standardized discipline, the Israeli army has somehow managed to retain strong measures of the egalitarianism and responsive personalization that marked its beginnings. Perhaps the Book has also had its influence on the gun.

How high a price does a fighting army pay for a relaxation of hierarchical authority and discipline? All this was back in June 1973, and like very nearly everyone else in this country I was too comfortably certain about too many things. The price, I'd have said then, was low enough, if indeed one paid at all. But we've been through a war since then, and there are 3,000 fewer of us here to consider the question, many of them lost in the first few days because some preparations were inadequately made or were never made at all, because some orders were ignored, lightly dismissed, never delivered, or delivered too late. How closely related are the two phenomena, the relatively casual discipline that pervades army life at almost all levels and the blunders committed not during but just before and in nonpreparation for the battle? Distantly if at all, I like to think. Humane interpersonal relations and maximum battle readiness should not be mutually exclusive. Respect for the individual during training and service should not preclude the individual's respect for the likelihood and consequences of threat and combat. One ought to be able to "get away with" something without wanting or troubling to. I was certain of that a few months back. Now I do what we all do here these days: I wonder. I don't know better; I simply wonder.

# 13

# My Discovery of Zionism

## STANLEY MARON

To many people, Zionism means providing refuge for harassed Jews in a time of crisis. The conventional image of the State of Israel as a shelter for otherwise homeless victims of anti-Semitism motivates many American Jews to contribute regularly to the UJA, and in so doing they perpetuate the biblical tradition of redeeming their less fortunate brethren. Possibly this act constitutes their strongest, and perhaps even their only, link with Jewish tradition. American Jews, living in affluence and security, do not see themselves in need of rescue, and therefore the idea of settling in Israel does not come easily to them. The notion that settling in Israel is today an essential part of being a Jew is not part of conventional wisdom.

In my case, the decision to settle in Israel required an extended period of gestation. I had to move a long way in order to get from an assimilationist and anti-Zionist ideological position to a Zionist and anti-assimilationist commitment. What motivated me was a profound personal need to clarify my own identity. Only later did I discover that this issue of identity, and not charity for hapless Jews, is what Zionism is really all about.

At a certain point in my life I became aware that the social mobility that the modern market society provides, in proportions never before realized in human history, is a singularly important freedom. The curious amalgam of Protestant and liberal ideologies that has accompanied the triumphant establishment of the modern market society is based both religiously and scientifically on the assumption that each individual is responsible for his own destiny, and that society should accord him the necessary freedom to pursue his own ends and secure his own interests. Social mobility has become the most widespread expression of that freedom.

At the same time, social mobility is the most destructive social force known to mankind. Traditional society was destroyed by social mobility—not by war, industrialization, or revolution. Japan has shown that an industrialized society can be formed without violent civil war or revolution, and can even be more successful when retaining the traditional foundations of society. Much of what is negative in the modern market societies of Europe and America (massive urbanization, problems of personal communication, instability of family life, for instance) is a direct result of social mobility.

Yet social mobility is regarded as a central freedom in the modern market society, allowing as it does for individual adjustment within the social environment. Many millions of people have availed themselves of this freedom, have changed radically their places of residence as well as the structure and character of their society, without producing a better world. For mobility comes at the price of termination of one's immediate involvement in a specific human and natural environment, with no guarantee of achieving a comparable involvement elsewhere. Frequent mobility results in superficial human relations, though it also may stimulate intensive personal growth and achievement. In general, social mobility is motivated by individual self-interest, in the private pursuit of happiness. A sense of responsibility toward the group is not very strong in those who most avail themselves of social mobility.

Like many others of their generation in the period before the Russian Revolution, my parents utilized social mobility to leave the traditional Jewish community in Eastern Europe and reach the legendary land of America. That was in the years when the Russian government actively encouraged the emigration of Jews from its borders. My parents were drawn along in the powerful current of migration that brought more than a million Russian Jews to America within a relatively short period of time. Together with most of the others, they left a comprehensive and traditional way of life for the purpose of seeking greater physical and economic security in America. They found the desired security, but did not find a comparable substitute for the traditional way of life that they had left behind.

The price demanded for success in achieving economic security was rapid and total assimilation into the American way of life. My parents did their best to learn the language well, to master the rules of the game governing the market economy, and to make themselves as indistinguishable as possible from their American neighbors. For them, settling in America was a rewarding move of personal achievement that left no regrets for the "old country" and all it represented. In terms of physical and economic security, they were much better off than they had been in Russia.

Nevertheless, their assimilation into American society was only superficially successful. A command of the language and integration into the market economy glossed over the fact that their assimilation was very limited. As their son, born and reared in America, I took for granted the personal and material security that they had so prized, but I also inherited from them the alienation that they had managed for the most part to ignore.

This alienation is concerned with the identity of the individual, and with fundamental questions of his existence in this world. As a native-born American, I identified with my social and cultural environment, and yet was bothered by a feeling of transiency and of not having roots connecting me at a deeper level with what was going on around me. With the years, my awareness of the dominant influence of the market in determining social and cultural trends deepened. I was disturbed by the commercialization, object-worship, and institutionalization of society, though not yet able to comprehend adequately the reasons for my dissatisfaction. For that, I had to wait a number of years, until the appearance of the literature of criticism, beginning with Whythe's *The Organization Man*, and culminating in Marcuse's *One-Dimensional Man*.

During those years, I was deeply immersed in the existentialist experience of being "thrown into the world," without any idea of why, or what I was supposed to do. I felt an overwhelming need to attain a sense of meaning in life, and so to have something firm on which to make my stand. I turned to the study of philosophy (in America, Europe, and Asia), only to feel, like Omar Khayy'am, that I went out the same door I came in.

Eventually, I got to Israel. Previously I had rejected my roots in Jewish tradition, and now I felt a need to understand what I had rejected and to make an informed decision. As a first stage, I learned Hebrew. Speaking the language of the Bible gave me an unexpectedly large measure of emotional satisfaction. Also, I felt a rare sense of kinship with all those sharing in the unique endeavor of making Hebrew a language fully capable of coping with all contemporary needs. But this was not enough to offset the negative features of Israeli life, particularly the growing domination of the market economy and the increasing tendency to imitate American society. Not for that had I come to Israel.

After a year in Jerusalem, with the help and encouragement of Amos Oz, I went to Kibbutz Ma'ayan Zvi in order to learn at first hand about the revolutionary attempt to build a communal way of life. Shmuel Bergman guided me to the works of A. D. Gordon, and that helped me immeasurably in understanding the ideological background of the kibbutz. I found in A. D. Gordon a profound and extreme critic of the modern market society, who provided a convincing explanation of the basic bond between the individual Jew and the Jewish people, and called for a creative revival of Jewish national life. These were precisely the issues with which I was trying to cope.

Acceptance of the basic assertion that there exists an entity known as the Jewish people immediately changes the whole picture of assimilation. Formerly, in denying that assertion, I had alienated myself from the Jewish people of which I was a part. By accepting the assertion that there exists a Jewish people, I was able to pose the essential question of whether I chose to build my own life within the context of that entity. My previous failure to do so had alienated me from that larger historical reality to which I naturally belong, and inevitably had caused a crisis of identity. Awareness of that connection brought understanding that the first step in overcoming personal alienation is the return of the individual to Jewish culture and Jewish history.

All of this provided me with a new and more meaningful way of approaching the subject of identity, together with A. D. Gordon's practical instructions for realizing a reintegrated identity through direct participation in the building of Israel. This practical Zionism is one of the pillars of kibbutz ideology, so that living in the kibbutz became much more than what French existentialists call *engagement,* for it is nothing less than a full-scale revolution. "Direct action" is the essence of Practical Zionism, and this may account for the relative neglect of its ideology by practical Zionists in general and kibbutz members in particular. The result has not been favorable, for you cannot carry out a full-scale revolution without clear and continuing ideological guidance. Indeed, practical Zionism's revolution has faltered and produced much confusion among its supporters, with immeasurable damage to the Zionist cause.

A. D. Gordon did develop an important theoretical formulation of his views, but he presented it for the most part by way of scattered articles having to do with specific issues of largely passing interest. As a result, his considerable influence was exerted almost entirely through personal contact, so that his ideas are virtually unknown to, and without influence on, succeeding generations. It should also be mentioned that A. D. Gordon was an anarchist who believed in the importance of direct creativity within the flow of life, and objected to having his views formulated abstractly or made the formal subject of discussion. Shortly before his death, he expressed the wish that what he wrote should be discussed or used only if and insofar as there remained within it living value, "that is to say, neither literary nor publicist value, but only vital value for new life."

To my good fortune, I found the proper complement to A. D. Gordon's practical Zionism and anarchist view of life in Yehezkel Kaufmann's great intellectual achievement, *Golah Venekhar,* which surveys in two large volumes the essential questions of Jewish existence in exile, and of alienation. Although my command of Hebrew was still rather limited, I read both volumes with intensity and a rare sense of spiritual adventure. I found in Kaufmann the answer to many questions that I had carried with me for years. Particularly in the second volume, I discovered the ideological foundation for a Zionism that I could accept wholeheartedly, and that strengthened my commitment to practical Zionism.

Kaufmann demonstrates with clarity and detailed analysis of the sources what catastrophic results for the Jewish people came out of the introduction, in the sixteenth century, of a new conception of law shaped by Protestant-liberal ideology. The chief novelty in the new conception was the notion that each person stands alone before the law as a separate entity, in direct contrast to the traditional Jewish view that the individual is also and always a part of the larger group, and responsibility remains mutual. The group continues to be responsible for the individual, and the individual is irrevocably involved in his obligations to the group, as long as the normal life pattern exists. Liberal constitutional law struck at the traditional foundations of the Jewish community and shattered its basis of mutuality by recognizing the individual as an independent entity, ultimately responsible for himself and concerned with his own ends.

Through Kaufmann, I came to a completely different understanding of liberalism. I came to realize that liberalism did not bring true emancipation to the Jew, but succeeded, where violent persecution had failed, in shattering the continuity and comprehensiveness of Jewish tradition. It brought the majority of Jews to do what force could not compel them to do—to alienate themselves from the Jewish community and the Jewish people, and seek assimilation in other cultures and among other peoples.

The liberal ideology is rooted in the Christian Reformation and in the industrial revolution, both of which have contributed decisively toward the atomization of modern society. However, neither these two developments, nor the emergence of liberalism, can be understood without taking into account the overwhelming influence on them of the expanding market, which made individualism and social mobility the basic characteristics of modern society.

Zionism, as I have come to understand it, aims to return the Jews from destructive modernism to constructive traditionalism. Zionism is not, and cannot be, just an imitation of European nationalism; nor can it be an attempt at national assimilation, an alternative to individual assimilation, in the sense of helping Israel to become "like all the nations." On the contrary, Zionism is dedicated to restoring the alienated Jew to the Jewish people, to Jewish culture, to Jewish history, to Jewish tradition, and to Jewish messianism. What Kaufmann helped me to understand is that Zionism and liberalism are mortal antagonists. Any attempt at playing with the term "liberal Zionism" displays ignorance of what liberalism and Zionism are really about.

Zionism means returning to Jewish national life, based socially on the community. Zionism cannot thrive in a market society based on individualism and social mobility. In this sense, the State of Israel in its present form does not concur with the requirements of Zionism, and shall have to undergo significant changes before it can become a Zionist state with a Zionist social structure.

I have found in the kibbutz the kind of beginning that is needed in order to rebuild Jewish society and ultimately reach a Zionist community. The kibbutz is a revolutionary rejection of modern market society in favor of a return to traditional communal life. Instead of individualism and social mobility, there is sharing and rootedness. In the kibbutz, the family has once again become the center of social life. Despite full integration of advanced technology in the kibbutz, the family continues to grow in size and stature. Today the typical pattern is the broad traditional family of four generations, all living in one large shared home. The Zionist success of the kibbutz, in addition to vital contributions to building and defending the State of Israel, is that it has shown the way in which individual alienated Jews can find roots in Israel and create a traditional community. Obviously, there is still a long way to go before the kibbutz can be fully integrated into Jewish tradition. Contemporary expression of that tradition is only in the process of developing, but already the kibbutz is making its own distinctive contribution. Surely the result will have little resemblance to what characterizes Orthodox patterns in the present, which are to a large extent only petrified modes of bygone times, with all too little relationship to what is really important in Torah.

Orthodox Judaism has not yet adjusted itself to the Zionist era, and to the demands of contemporary Jewish existence. Their interpretation of tradition based primarily on the sanctification of ritual purity, to the neglect of the Ten Commandments and "duties of the heart," is out of tune with reality and will have to be replaced by an interpretation of tradition meaningful to the majority. Most Jews today do not accept the Orthodox interpretation. Zionism is expected to meet the needs of the majority, and in this sense Zionism is opposed to Orthodox Judaism as well as to liberalism. After all, Zionism has opened up a new era, and now must bring forth the creative powers to shape the contents of that new era. That is a challenge in which diaspora Jews must participate.

I believe that the kibbutz is the most authentic expression of Zionism, and the most likely instrument for changing the life of the Jewish people from within in this Zionist era. Like the Zionist movement in general, the kibbutz has emerged from the background of assimilation into European culture, and matured through rejection of that assimilation. Much in European culture has been used as a means for founding and building the kibbutzim, and there is a certain dialectical irony in that process. However, the ultimate goal is settlement in the Land of Israel, and revival of authentic Jewish culture, and so the creative continuation of the oldest living culture in the world, for all Jews.

# 14

# Israel: Dream and Reality

## BERNARD OCH

Twenty years ago, I left the United States and came to live in Israel. Like other American Jews, I came with a dream. It was the standard Zionist belief that after 2,000 years of exile our people would come and build a normal, peaceful Jewish life in a Jewish state.

Today, twenty years later, that dream no longer exists: It was blown apart during the Lebanon war. It was during this period of bloodshed here and isolation abroad that I awoke. I finally realized two basic facts about our people. First, the Jewish people have not come, and will not come, to live in Israel. The vast majority of Jews do not want to live in Israel. Second, peace and security are not to be found in Israel. Living in Israel generally means living with tension, conflict, and bloodshed.

One hundred years ago Zionism appeared on the scene. It turned to the Jewish people and made them a promise. The promise was called "normalcy." Zionism claimed that as long as the Jews remain in exile, they will live an abnormal, unnatural life. For the essence of exile is fear, degradation, and abnormality. The promise of Zionism was that once a Jewish state was established, the Jews would finally be able to live a normal, peaceful life. They would become a nation like all normal nations.

This was what Zionism promised, but it never kept its promise. You can say many things about Israel: that it is a good state or a bad one; that it is basically a socialist state or a capitalist one, etc. But there is one thing I defy anyone to say: that Israel is a normal state; that the life we live in Israel is a normal life.

### Nice Jewish Boys

For an example of normal life in Israel, I would like to introduce my son Eitan. He is 19½ years old and a rather nice person: tall, slim, intelligent, and he even listens to his parents—every now and then.

I recall being an American 19-year-old. How does a normal 19-year-old spend his summer vacation? He may spend it traveling, or perhaps working to earn money for college. But my son Eitan is a soldier: a soldier in the Israeli army. At age 18, my normal son entered the army and volunteered for the Golani Brigade, which is an elite infantry unit of normal young men who have been trained to attack, fight, and kill.

When the war broke out in Lebanon, Eitan's unit was in the front line of attack. They swept up the Lebanese coast, through Tyre, Sidon, and into the airport of Beirut. Eitan was the RPG specialist in his platoon. An RPG is a rocket-propelled grenade, which is carried on a soldier's back. Eitan became an expert in blowing up tanks and armored personnel carriers, at demolishing buildings in which terrorists were hiding.

After four weeks of fighting, Eitan came home on a two-day pass. He ate, he slept, he went to see his friends to find out whether anyone had been wounded. At night we sat down to talk, or try to talk.

I sat there with my normal 19-year-old son, after four weeks of fighting and bloodshed, and I did not know what to say. How do you ask the questions you do not want to ask? How do you hear the answers you do not want to hear? He described the fighting, the destruction, and the fear he felt when shells were exploding around him. He told me how his unit was pinned down under Syrian fire for twelve hours, how he had to enter buildings where armed terrorists were waiting in ambush. He spoke of a friend, a young boy his own age, who was hit just ten feet from him, and who died in his arms.

I listened and I thought to myself: What happens? What happens inside of you when friends are being killed around you; when you yourself are forced to kill? How do you feel when you squeeze the trigger and destroy a human life? I watched my son as he spoke. He looked the same and yet he was different: There was a weariness, a heaviness, about him. He had seen and done things that no 19-year-old should ever have to see or do.

The war in Lebanon was the third war I have experienced in Israel. It was the most difficult war for me. During the Yom Kippur War, I was in the army and Eitan was at home. This time Eitan was in the army and I stayed home. It is hard to fight in any war, but what is unbearable is when you stay at home while your son is out there fighting in the war. You stay at home, you go to work, you go through the motions of living. And you pray. You pray to God that nothing should happen to your son. You feel so powerless, so helpless. And when it's over, you feel so relieved, but at the same time you feel guilty. Someone else has paid the price: Someone else is weeping over his son.

Friends of ours paid this heavy price. Their son, Oded, was killed during the first week of fighting. Oded was an officer in the para-troopers, about to finish his army service. He had planned to study at the university, to become a doctor like his father. He too was a "normal" boy: a quiet, unassuming boy whom we came to know and like as we saw him growing up. He grew up not to become a doctor but a casualty: a broken body lying on the field of battle.

I went to see his parents, to be with them during this time of pain and sorrow. I came into their home, where there were about a dozen people. The room was silent; no one was talking.

What can you say at such a time? What words can you find to express your feelings? The words sound so trite, so artificial, so useless. So you sit in silence. Each one realizing that he himself could be the mourner. He himself could be sitting there mourning the death of his own son.

This is part of what it means to raise a family in Israel, to watch your children grow up, knowing without any doubt that the time will come when your own son will have to fight, when your days will be filled with fear and anxiety. This is the "normal" life we live in Israel today.

### Back in America

The war in Lebanon changed not only my thinking about Israel, but also about the Jewish people. During those weeks, I remembered my childhood—way back when I was a little boy growing up in Roxbury, Massachusetts. My parents were not very learned or educated Jews, but they succeeded in bringing us up with a basic commitment. They taught me that Jews, no matter where they live, are one people: that we all share a common past and a common future, and that the Land of Israel is our home.

A small blue and white box that we called a "pushka" stood on our icebox next to the pantry. Each week my mother put a few pennies or nickels into this box. As I think of it now, I realize that there was something symbolic, profound, and beautiful about that "pushka" and my mother, in her small apartment in Roxbury, saving her pennies to buy land in Palestine for the Jewish people. Each penny taught her two sons an important lesson: that the Jews are one people and they have one home.

My mother died last year. But if I could still speak to her, I'd probably say: "Mother I love you very much, but you were wrong. What you taught me wasn't true—the Jews are *not* one people and Israel is *not* their home!"

### Are We a People?

It took me twenty years and three wars to fully realize this. A people, a real people, lives in the same land, shares the same culture, speaks the same language, feels the same joy, suffers the same pain, and fights the same wars when their homes and lives are threatened. This is what a normal people does; but not the Jewish people. The Jews in Israel and the Jews in America do *not* share the same home, do *not* share the same culture and language, do *not* share the same day-to-day living experiences that together form and fashion and mold a people, and give them a genuine oneness.

Being a people means sharing responsibility. For the past, it was easy for the Jewish people to identify with the Land of Israel. For Israel was only a dream, a prayer, and a hope for the future. But today, for us, Israel is a reality. And sharing responsibility for a reality is something entirely different. A financial contribution, a visit, a demonstration or an outpouring of concern, however genuine, does not constitute sharing responsibility for what is going on in Israel today. And despite the support, the identification, and the concern that American Jewry directs to Israel, we are becoming two separate and distinct communities living worlds apart.

I know that for thousands of years the Jews remained a united people despite the fact they were dispersed throughout the world. But the social, economic, and political conditions that produced a united Jewish community in the past do not exist today. The unique Jewish institutions that flourished within the ghetto walls do not exist today. The educational structure, the traditional family, the legal and judicial system that together molded our people are all relics of the past. Today the Jew in the United States is a fully integrated member of American society and culture.

These factors have brought about a basic change in the attitude of the vast majority of American Jews to the Land of Israel. In the past the Jew, no matter where he lived, never looked upon his country of residence as his home. There was always a distinction between where the Jew lived and where he felt he should be living. There was a difference between what the Jew was doing and what he wanted to be doing. Today this distinction no longer exists. The American Jew feels that America is not only where he is living but also where he should be living. And this is a new phenomenon in Jewish history.

For the first time in our history, the Jewish people have legitimated living outside of Israel. They have transformed this reality into a value; they have transformed what was once a necessity into a virtue. For the first time in our history, a majority of Jews look upon living outside of Israel as a legitimate alternative to living in Israel. This is contrary to what Judaism has been teaching for 2,000 years. This is not why Jews prayed for 2,000 years. This is not why Jews suffered for 2,000 years.

### Back to the Dream

The dream has changed. The Jewish people will *not* arise and come home en masse. And life in Israel will *not*, for the immediate future, be normal, serene, and secure. Yet part of the dream remains: Despite the price, despite the pain, despite *everything*, some Jews—who are now called Israelis—will continue to pit themselves against the harsh realities. And they may still create that reborn Jewish people yet in the making.

# 15

# A Critique of Criticism

## ETAN LEVINE

### Introduction

Long after the acrid smoke of battle clears, long after silent grass grows over fresh-dug graves, long after memorial candles flicker in broken homes, there will be pain in Israel. It will not be only the pain of seeing the obscene specter of vicious anti-Semitism raising its ugly head again throughout Christendom, nor the pain of seeing our increasing isolation and pariah status in the international community, be it in the lands of Islam, the Afro-Asian world, the Soviet bloc, and even Western Europe and the United States. More specifically, more painfully, and more surprisingly, it will be the memory of the American Jewish reaction during one of Israel's most trying hours.

We were pained but hardly surprised when Operation Peace for Galilee, directed against the capital of international terrorism, met with universal vilification rather than appreciation. We were pained and somewhat surprised when aspects of the operation were distorted beyond recognition, and these distortions used viciously to malign the Jewish people generally, and the Jewish state specifically. But we were both pained and stunned to hear, amid this litany of anti-Israel hostility, the voices of criticism from American and European Jews.

### The "We Are One" Claim

In recent years, many American Jews have rhetorically asked, "Don't we have the right to criticize Israel? Considering all that we do for the State of Israel, the support we give it, the identification we have with it, and the manifold claims it makes on us, don't we have the right to criticize Israel?" In a sense, the entire question is gratuitous, though, because criticism is what American Jewry has been engaged in ever since the establishment of the State of Israel: The very fact that six million American Jews opt to live in the United States constitutes an unequivocal criticism. It is a rejection of both the Zionist ideal and the Israeli reality: Somehow our historic mission isn't worthy of being joined.

In a large measure, we in Israel are to blame for the frustrations of American Jewry, because we sold out the Zionist claim. In earlier days we may have been blunt, but we were honest when we addressed American Jewry. We said, in effect, "If you want to be part of Jewish history in the making, then come join us. Be part of the resurrection of our people in its homeland, instead of sitting on the sidelines of history and basking in the vicarious warmth of our passions and our achievements." Not only was this call from Zion unheeded, it was bitterly resented. Because the American Jew, who now clamors for the right to criticize Israel, has never leigitimated the right of Israel to criticize him!

In time, Israeli leaders accepted these "ground rules," and participated in the creation of a myth. It is the myth that is reiterated in sermons, repeated in print, emblazoned on T-shirts and bumper stickers, and proclaimed over and over: We are one. Why can American Jews, at the supposedly most solemn moments of the Jewish year, declaim "Next year in Jerusalem!" without the slightest qualms over having absolutely no intention of fulfilling the declaration? Because we have legitimated their diaspora; by congratulating them on their fund-raising and public relations activities, and by accepting this "contract," we have given de jure recognition to their claim that we are one. And therefore, by definition, their criticism of Israel is self-criticism, and perforce legitimate, and even noble.

The fact that American Jewry refused to put aliyah to Israel on its agenda may be understandable; less understandable is the fact that this affluent Jewish community does nothing to aid those few Americans who do immigrate to Israel. However, least understandable is that we in Israel have prostituted ourselves for the sake of monetary contributions.[1] It is an implicit admission that the Zionist claim is unacceptable. And it is precisely because we "sold cheap" and allowed American Jewry a wholesale, cut-rate identification with our very distant land that they now feel it is their natural right to be critical of "their" Israel.

And we sold out very cheap. Thus, with all due respect to the fund-raising that constitutes their major endeavor, American Jewry contributes less than 3 percent to Israel's annual budget. Not 1 percent, not even .001 percent of American Jews come to settle here; not 1 in 10,000 joins our ranks. More German Christians than American Jews come here as tourists. Still, American Jewry proclaims, "We are one!"

## The Existential Realities

It is virtually axiomatic that when we profess something that is not an authentic, organic part of us, we profess it with increased vehemence and intolerance. "Intolerance is the 'Do Not Touch' sign on something that cannot bear touching. We do not mind having our hair ruffled, but we will not tolerate any familiarity with the toupee which covers our baldness."[2] Thus, American Jewry does not want to listen when we tell them, "We are not one, by any meaningful criterion. You do not share our realities, our triumphs, or our disasters. You do not share our military burden, our societal problems, our cultural challenges, our international situation, or any of the crises facing religion, language, economy, or anything else, for that matter. You live in a totally different environment, which is affluent, secure, and almost irresistible; witness the Russian, Israeli, and other Jews who have flocked to your shores in recent decades. You opt to live a life almost totally divorced from Israel. Whether or not exercising that option brings you fulfillment is your affair; but the reality is that, no matter how you may attempt to becloud or deny it, you are not part of the Israeli adventure.

"And to our mind, the loss is yours, as well as ours. For it is not simply that you did not join us in 1948, when the Jewish people, or a part of it, reconstituted itself in its ancestral home. Nor is it that in the subsequent decades you have not shared with us your massive talents in technology, science, democratic process, humanities, culture, and virtually every area of human endeavor. Rather, or further, it is because even from this distance we can see something that you choose not to see: You are in a crisis, due to the disparity between your dogma and your existential reality. You are, in fact, men and women dissolved into an anonymous mass, without an authentic world, without roots or provenance. 'You have no real faith by which you live, no compelling mission, and no sense of purpose.'[3] And that is why you must repeatedly assure yourselves that we are one. And that is why you must be critical of Israel."

It is a talent of the weak "to persuade themselves that they suffer for something when they suffer from something; that they are showing the way when they are running away; that they see the light when they feel the heat; that they are chosen when they are shunned."[4] And nothing demonstrates this more clearly than does the recent "anguish" of American Jews over Israel.

## The Honesty of the "Anguish"

Over and over again, in the general and the Jewish media, one encounters Jews attesting to their profound "anguish" concerning Israel's actions during Operation Peace for Galilee. Thus, in his "Letter from the President," the head of America's largest rabbinical group tells his colleagues: "As summer now draws to a close, we remember with no small amount of anguish the moral dilemma posed by Operation Peace for Galilee. . . ." His letter includes such gross distortions as "How do we help our people properly evaluate Israel's army at the gates of Beirut threatening to destroy the city if the PLO did not vacate?" and "One of the tragedies of the Middle East conflict has been our inability to view the Arab people in any kind of positive light. . . ."[5] Another American rabbi, writing in the *New York Times,* states that he agrees with Yasir Arafat that "Begin and Sharon are not Jews. The crimes they commit do not conform to Jewish morality or tradition."[6] And yet another rabbi presumes to lecture Israel that "Begin Must Go."[7] These are but three of the myriad expressions of outrage and moral indignation emanating from American Jewish "friends" of Israel. Some may be dismissed as the headline-hunting, knee-jerk criticism of Israel that characterizes certain American Jewish leaders who promulgate the basest anti-Israel canards in the name of morality. Others, however, are worthy of serious attention.[8]

Before proceeding to the substance of American Jewish criticism, one must examine its underlying authenticity. For although this may come as something of a surprise to American Jewry, to many Israelis this "moral anguish" rings false, as though it is a self-indulgent exercise in "the ecstacy of the agony." We have become so accustomed to the verbal protestations of moral agony on the part of many American Jews—relating to virtually every aspect of Israeli life—that we wonder how such professedly moral souls manage to rest so peacefully, so passively, and so acceptingly. They are, after all, citizens of that country which is the world's largest arms merchant; which decimated hundreds of thousands of innocent civilians in massive firebombing, which is the sole country to have used nuclear warfare, and that, too, against civilian populations; which denied entry to Jews fleeing the Holocaust, thereby participating in their liquidation; which supports some of the most despotic, oppressive regimes on earth; which is conceived of, by most of the human race, as a country whose credo is "What's good for General Motors is good for America," and which places a greater value on dollars than on death; which, while claiming to be an honest broker in the Middle East and elsewhere, is no less guilty of causing human misery than the superpower enemy that it uses to justify its machinations; and which justifies its twentieth-century wars, fought thousands of miles from its shores, on the basis of a domino theory, yet castigates us as militaristic, while we live in a tiny sliver of land in which there is no home not in sight either of a hostile border, or of the sea into which our powerful

enemies have sworn—and attempted—to throw us. How curiously se-
lective the moral outrage of American Jewry is.

Some American Jews have attempted to restore sanity and balance, for
". . . in the rush to find scapegoats for the brutal massacre of civilians in
Beirut, it is curious to note that Sharon, Begin and Israel are the only
candidates; no one has called for the punishment of the Christian militia
murderers.

"The world's political and news media ought to recall that nations
often have difficulty in controlling the actions of their own soldiers, as
the U.S. did when Americans, led by a lieutenant, massacred Viet-
namese civilians at My Lai on his orders.

"I do not recall any nation being held responsible for the killing
rampage perpetrated by soldiers of an ally. But, as is often the case, a
different standard is applied when Israel and Jews are involved."[9]

Another American Jew has written that "for years, the nations of the
world have, with hearts of stone, witnessed in silence the internecine
warfare in Lebanon and Syria. The victims were mostly civilians—men,
women and children slaughtered in blind hate."

What awakened the conscience of the world was the massacre in
Beirut, which, in itself, was nothing but a repetition of what had been
tolerated in silence over the past two years.[10]

What, then, motivated the universal outcry of grief and outrage? Was
it the realization of some biblical vision that turned the hearts of nations
from stone to flesh? How one would like to believe so. Does this chorus
speak in terms of peace and goodwill?

Sadly, no, the full fury of excoriation is directed against the government of Israel; the actual perpetrators of the heinous crime are not even
mentioned. Arafat, the authority on warfare against civilians, is listened
to respectfully in his expression of sadness and disbelief about such a
depraved act.

"What we hear is not the voice of a new moral world; it is the unholy
alliance of Israel's enemies."[11]

Most Israelis would concur with these exposés of the world's moral
outrage; and given the track record of American Jewry on many issues,
they would question the honesty of American Jewish "anguish" as well.
But, of course, the motives of an argument do not disqualify its substance; and that is what bears analysis.

### The Philosophy of "Free Speech"

Not even the most latitudinarian of political philosophies justifies the
claim that freedom of expression is an absolute value: that there exists an

unrestricted right of anyone to say anything at any time. And thus there are inevitable restrictions against slander, libel, perjury, incitement to violence, endangering the public weal, misrepresentation, etc. Freedom of speech became a basic concern of Western democracies not because of the subjective pleasure of utterance, but because of the discovery by the classical Greeks that dialectic (as demonstrated by the Socratic dialogues) is a primary method of arriving at truth. In particular, it was recognized as a means of attaining moral and political truth.[12] "The ability to raise searching difficulties on both sides of an issue causes us to detect more easily the truth and error about the various points that arise."[13]

There is a profound difference between dialectics and sophistry. For the purpose of dialectics is to confront ideas with opposing ideas in order that the debate will lead to truth. It is not a trial of strength, but a cooperative endeavor, structured to allow the disputants to emerge with more wisdom. In sophistry, however, the aim is to win one's case; the sophist uses rhetoric, not dialectic. Its concern is with persuasion, not with creative criticism for the purpose of inquiry.

The dividing line between liberty and license is "where freedom of speech is no longer respected as a procedure of the truth and becomes the unrestricted right to exploit the ignorance, and to incite the passions, of the people. Then freedom is such a hallabaloo of sophistry, propaganda, special pleading, lobbying, and salesmanship that it is difficult to remember why freedom of speech is worth the pain and trouble of defending it."[14] And when American Jewish spokesmen, or private individuals, hasten to add their criticism of Israel to that of the non-Jewish world, genuine debate with Israel is lacking, and their freedom of speech is not functioning as it is intended to. It surely will not change Israel's opinions, because "it has lost the principle which regulates it and justifies it—that is to say, dialectic conducted according to logic and the rules of evidence. If there is no effective debate, the unrestricted right to speak will unloose so many propagandists, procurers, and panderers upon the public that sooner or later in self-defense the people will turn to the censors to protect them. An unrestricted and unregulated right to speak cannot be maintained. It will be curtailed for all manner of reasons and pretexts, and to serve all kinds of good, foolish, or sinister ends.

"For in the absence of debate, unrestricted utterance leads to the degradation of opinion. By a kind of Gresham's law the more rational is overcome by the less rational, and the opinions that will prevail will be those with the most passionate will. For that reason the freedom to speak can never be maintained merely by objecting to interference with the liberty of the press, or printing, of broadcasting, of the screen. It can be maintained only by promoting debate."[15]

What, in fact, has been the effect of American Jewish criticism of

Israel? First, it has isolated Israel even further internationally. Thus, "Rarely has an American President had more potential for putting pressure on Israel. Jewish lobbyists are taking issue with Jerusalem as never before."[16] Second, it has elicited a backlash effect, for "the more reports there are of the determination of the U.S. government to unseat Begin and to bring about Sharon's resignation, the more Herut, the Likud and the coalition can be expected to rally around the two men. The American government is certainly entitled to its opinions. It should at least be sophisticated enough to realize that seeking to translate them into overt anti-Israel pressure can only have a boomerang effect."[17] Third, it has created a situation wherein American Jewry is sometimes perceived in Israel not as an ally but as an adversary, aiding and abetting other interests. Thus, it has recently been disclosed that President Ronald Reagan and Secretary of State George Schultz have a very deliberate and sophisticated strategy for forcing Israel's hand into participating in a scenario perceived by Israel as contrary to its own interests. "Pressure, the Americans concluded, would also develop from outside Israel, especially from American Jewish political activists and Israel's other best friends in Washington."[18]

If American Jews (who, of course, brook no interference by Israelis in American politics, elections, or issues) apply pragmatic criteria in determining whether they have the "right" to continue their condemnation of Israel, the answer should be self-evident. For it has served to strengthen the enemies of Israel, has elicited a counter-productive hardening of Israel's attitudes, and has driven deeper the rift within the Jewish people—a people which American Jewry would like to consider one! And in no single issue is this as apparent as in that of the legitimacy of war.

### The Legitimacy of War

The legitimacy of war is traditionally evaluated on two levels: the grounds for the initiation of war *(jus ad bellum)*, and the means by which the war is waged *(jus in bello)*. The literature on the subject is voluminous, because however difficult the fact may be to accept, "wars, lesser military actions, the threat to resort to them, and even more fitful uses of violence and terrorism are the major, albeit not the sole, human mechanism of political and social change."[19] Given the real nature of things, by what intellectual or moral right does a segment of American Jewry invalidate our resorting to war except as a desperate last resort when the enemy has chosen the time, place, and conditions best suited to his aggression? By what right does it use full-page ads in our newspapers and theirs to weaken our resolve, as well as our political stability and international posture, thereby constituting itself as an inadvertent fifth column? Are the grounds for the objection *jus ad bellum* or *jus in bello?*

Concerning *jus ad bellum,* American Jewry knows that for three generations Israel has been engaged in a war not of its making, against Arab nationalism. American Jewry knows that the Jewish people, both in its disaspora and in its homeland, is a nonmilitaristic, peace-loving people, and this despite its recurrent necessity to resort to arms, and despite its prowess when it does so. Should it not be self-evident that Israel is unquestionably within its rights to resort to war to defend itself, and not only when its enemies are already exerting a murderous stranglehold?

One cannot help but question the intellectual as well as the moral underpinnings of American Jewish criticism. They apparently have forgotten that whereas Jewish tradition incorporates a fervent yearning for a messianic age of peace, prematurely assuming the advent of the Messiah is considered hubris and misguided in the extreme.

Many American Jews would challenge this thesis, arguing that Operation Peace for Galilee does not satisfy *jus in bellum;* that in toto or in part it was not defensive. That opinion may be their prerogative, but does it justify their outpourings of public indignation, castigation, and strident criticism? One Israeli has responded in this vein: "Henry Siegman contends that the issue of the Israel government settling 'for the respite and peace the first phase of its operation [Peace for Galilee] brought for residents of the Galilee . . . is a legitimate subject for debate'—implying that this applies also to American Jews.

"In my opinion, it is indeed a legitimate subject for debate—among Israelis, whose homes, lives and sons' lives are at stake and who have to bear the consequences of the government's policy in terms of human sacrifice. American Jews, on the other hand, with all their financial, ideological, political and emotional involvement in Israel's fortunes, do not lay their lives on the line. Their sons did not fight in Beirut, and if Israel had stopped short after 45 kilometers and the PLO had returned to harass Israel as a result, their homes and lives would not have been threatened by katyushas.

"So, if a debate is intended to persuade the Israel government either to pursue or change a certain policy which can have life and death implications one way or another, and is not merely an academic exercise in free speech, then I challenge Henry Siegman's right to participate in this debate—as long as his participation is confined to the debate and not to the consequences of living in Israel."[20]

And moving from the *causus belli* to *jus in bello,* the actual conduct of the war, one wonders whether the American Jewish critic did not know the facts or simply did not care about them. Does he know how many tens of the 37,000 buildings in Beirut were actually hit by bombs? Does he know that overseas television distorted the actual war from start to finish, stooping even to screening old footage of the Lebanese civil war and portraying it as recent damage? Does he know that casualty figures were exaggerated tenfold and oftimes more? Before joining the international anti-Israel diatribe, it is the responsibility of the American Jew to know. And he must also know that the Jewish army incorporates a concept of "the purity of arms," in which violence is used only as a last resort: that in the Jewish army "kosher" applies to weapons, and not only to eating utensils. He must know that many Israelis met their deaths because of these humane, noble principles: endangering themselves rather than cause needless death among the enemy. As to the actual conduct of this operation *(jus in bello)*, the American Jewish critic is guilty of either malice or ignorance. In either event, his credentials as critic are unacceptable.

## Israel's Self-Criticism

It may even be necessary to remind the self-appointed American Jewish guardians of Israel's morality that ever since its inception, the State of Israel has been characterized not only by self-assuredness but by self-criticism as well. In large measure this was a derivative of classical Judaism and its conception of the critical life. Faith was not viewed as an exercise disengaged from reality, nor was skepticism viewed as essentially negative. Rather, faith and skepticism were understood as being man's two fundamental needs. Although their union was often reluctant, faith and self-criticism became the two loci of Judaism. The familiar talmudic dialectic method of question and answer, certainty and doubt, faith and skepticism, criticism and creativity, became the method whereby Judaism was constructed: Through criticism the Jew transcended his own parochialism; through creativity he constructed his civilization.[21]

Whatever is the manifold etiology, even Israel's most vociferous critics admit that it is a model of democracy; that despite the countless threats it faces, both from without and from within, the free expression of ideas is not only protected but also exercised. Never has democracy been so sorely tested, and never has it survived such strains. There is hardly an issue of which a segment of the population is not emphatically critical, and that it does not oppose with all of the means at its disposal.

Operation Peace for Galilee is an example par excellence: Not only did its very inception meet with opposition in the Israeli parliament, but each phase, and each military escalation, met with impassioned objection: in the Israeli media, in parliament, and in all public forums. Thus, the mass rally held in Tel Aviv to protest the war and its aftermath, to depose the government, and to establish the legal inquiry into the entire affair drew 400,000 participants.[22] This was the largest proportion of any populace of any democracy ever to demonstrate against its government.

Not all Israelis agreed with the massive protests against the government, of course. The thrust of their objections is found in a typical letter to the editor of the *Jerusalem Post*, taking issue with the editorial. "Shame of the Nation" (20 September 1982). The writer states, "I believed I was about to read a condemnation of those who demonstrated in different parts of the country to put the blame for the Beirut massacre on the Prime Minister ('Killer Begin'), the Defense Minister, the Chief of Staff and the Israel Army.

"Reading the editorial, however, I found that I was among those who were supposed to be ashamed, who were supposed to 'exorcise the shame that has engulfed' them. Who is the editorial speaking for? I feel horror and anger over what happened in the refugee camp and in Beirut, but not shame—that I reserve for the hypocritical nations of the world and those citizens of Israel who have joined them and perhaps set the tone for the malicious attacks on Israel, its Government, its people and its army.

"Mistakes may have been made in Lebanon but, in the opinion of many, they result from the fallibility of human thinking and planning, and not from culpable intent."[23]

Many Israelis, though critical of Operation Peace for Galilee on several grounds, still refuse to accept the international verdict of heinous guilt. Thus, in a letter to the editor of the *Jerusalem Post*, Monty Rosen writes: "There is no need for the Jewish people to bow their heads in shame because of the events in Beirut. The responsibility lies on the shoulders of the world community.

"The mastermind of the slaughter of our schoolchildren at Ma'alot, the butchering of our civilians on the Tel Aviv highway, the massacre of our athletes at Munich, the planner of the highjacking of civilian aircraft, was received with a standing ovation at UN headquarters and given a hero's welcome. He was given an audience by the Pope, terrorism was legitimated and the terrorists were given a license to kill. Now the world stands aghast; it is apparent the license was given only to kill Jews.

"Arafat sheds crocodile tears, but he sowed the winds of terrorism and now his people have reaped the whirlwind."[24]

The international divisions in Israel are so strong that a Christian Embassy official in Jerusalem was moved to advise that, "by blaming themselves, Israelis make it harder for their friends to defend them." And a Christian resident of Jerusalem has written, "For me, the most painful of many painful developments in the past two weeks has been the spectacle of Israel's leaders cutting one another to pieces before an audience that includes not merely Israel, but the whole world. Have these leaders faced the fact that the restored State of Israel is in danger of foundering on the same kind of internal divisions and jealousies that precipitated the destruction of the Second Temple?"[25]

Even Israelis abroad castigated their government's policies. One Jewish writer, reacting to the interview of an Israeli member of Knesset on the BBC, was moved to write: "The BBC is openly anti-Israel. It has conducted an incessant campaign of distortions, half-truths and misrepresentations on radio and television. To witness an Israeli politician join in the chorus is repugnant, debasing and dishonorable to all those who have given their lives, to the maimed and to the bereaved.

"For Israelis to join their enemies in denouncing their legitimate government at such a critical time is tantamount to self-destruction."[26]

In the same spirit, an Israeli writes, "I am shocked by a phenomenon I am witnessing daily, and not an initial isolated reaction: the spirit of mob-lynching displayed by all the nations in their unjustified condemnation of Israel for something she did not do, and stopped as soon as she could. This is not a mob of individuals who are caught up in the heat of a sudden impulse, but includes responsible government officials, many of whom claim to be our friends." The writer continues, "What is even worse in this collapse of morality is the fact that many of the victims of the lynch spirit have joined the enemies of Israel in a treasonable attack on their own country."[27]

What unites the polar positions on this issue, as well as on all of the many issues yet to be resolved, is that they are self-critical arguments within Zionism: Regardless of the outcome, it is those in Israel who will have to live with the consequences of the decisions.[28] Thus, Israelis are told that "as an American Jew who has always sustained Israel's right to exist [sic], I want to express my grief and horror for what Israeli leaders have allowed to happen in Beirut. . . . For the first time I am ashamed to be a Jew. And I believe that if the population of Israel does not rebel . . . it will be tragic for us all."[29] What is missing is the price that the writer will pay, in the event of error. Given the massive self-criticism within Israel, castigation from without is gratuitous, at best.

## The Consequences of Criticism

Many Israelis, of all shades of opinions, resent American Jewish criticism. It is not only because of the fact that, facing the concerted antagonism and hostility of the world, and the inevitable self-doubts that our pariah status engenders, criticism, castigations, and shaming is virtually the very last thing we either expect or need from American Jewry. Nor is it even the fact that much of American Jewish criticism is no more than demagogic name-calling, nonempathic, and irresponsibly uninformed. Rather, it is the inescapable fact that it is the Israeli, not the American Jew, who must live with the consequences.

American Jews would not agree, of course, because, in fact, they too have a stake in Israel. Not only do they provide it with a measure of support, but they also identify with, and are identified with, the Jewish state. They are caught in intellectual-emotional binds, whether because of the reactions of non-Jews, because of their own sense of guilt, or because of their relationship to a state that is theirs yet not theirs. And so, American Jews, who by and large are keen, analytical, and balanced in other situations, find themselves intellectually paralyzed regarding Israel. And predictably they tend to be extreme: running the gamut from uncritical approval and adulation to antagonism and perpetual criticism.

While empathizing with this concomitant of diaspora living, the Israeli Jew must say, in effect, "Sorry, but we cannot help you in your discomfort; we cannot pursue policies that we perceive as suicidal, in order to ameliorate your unpleasant situation. And to expect it of us, and to attempt to force us to do so, is really beneath contempt! For if you are wrong, it is we who will pay the price. You were not vitally involved in our decisions concerning the Six Day War, the Entebbe raid, or the other actions that you chose to perceive as spectacular triumphs; you were not vitally involved in our decisions concerning the Yom Kippur War, Operation Peace for Galilee or other actions that you chose to see as disasters. By your own decision, this is not your 'turf.' "

American Jewish tourists may be deeply moved as they stand in the Tel Hai cemetery, where our fallen lie and where there is etched in stone the verse "In blood and fire did Judah fall, in blood and fire will Judah rise." But with all due deference to the emotions elicited, the Israeli reminds the American Jew, "It is not your blood; it is not your fire. It is our precious sons who come home in boxes; we bury our dead. You have declined our invitation to join us in the struggle for a Jewish state. What we ask of you is merely that you tread softly over the graves; be ever so careful before you besmirch the ideals for which they died, the country for which they gave their lives, or the actions by which they met their deaths. For if not, then you are guiltier of obscenity than any desecrater of Jewish cemeteries, and you and the swastika-dauber make common cause."

### Israeli Expectations

The aftermath of Operation Peace for Galilee is a time of soul-searching in Israel, and along with other fundamental issues there is the question of our expectations: of ourselves and of all Jews who genuinely feel that we are one. Somehow we have to bridge the rift between Israel and American Jewry. This rift has saddened us, particularly those of us who hail from the United States, Canada, and other Western countries. Unlike during earlier wars, when overseas Jews with friends or relatives in Israel deluged them with telegrams, telephone calls, and letters, this time there has been reported "Sounds of Silence" in which more than half of the "Anglo-Saxons" polled had not heard from friends or relatives during the conflict.[30] Apparently the distress, confusion, and disagreement of our relatives and friends over the war transcended their concern for our well-being. One overseas Jew later explained: "This time, things are reversed. In the short term Israel is not militarily threatened, and we are distant from Israeli casualties. However, we are surrounded by sharp disagreements over the moral and political issues." And one British Jew communicated that "the barbaric actions of your Israelis have undermined the situation of English Jews, and we are certain to suffer from an anti-Semitic backlash."[31] The war in Lebanon has patently weakened (or exposed the weakness of) Jewish unity. And the fibers of Jewish unity must not be allowed to disintegrate further; otherwise, all of us will pay the manifold costs of the consequences.

American Jewry must understand that our national policies cannot be constructed on the basis of their moral indignation. Their hostility will not deter us from what we perceive to be our indispensable needs; Israel will not compromise its physical security and perhaps its very existence in order to win points with American Jewry. No matter what the issue may be, as a matter of principle Israel, as any nation, cannot abdicate its right and responsibility to determine what is crucial, what cannot be compromised and cannot be tolerated. If, indeed, a friend is someone who knows all about you but likes you anyway, then American Jewry must allow us, right or wrong though we may be, to determine our course of action. Admittedly, we Israelis fail to meet the idealistic standards established for us by many American Jews; in truth, we fail to meet the standards that we expect of ourselves. But by no stretch of the imagination, by no criteria, do we deserve the exaggerated, strident accusations emanating from members of diaspora Jewry. Accepting our differences of opinion will perforce involve certain frustrations for American Jewry, including, perhaps, the disapproval of the non-Jews to whom it looks for approval. But at least the conscience of American Jewry will be clean. In any case, that is the bottom-line expectation of Israel; that is the price for there being any meaning to the idea that we are one.

In considering Israeli expectations, we cannot ignore the expectations of those who fell and those who were bereaved by Operation Peace for Galilee. One father of a fallen soldier has said:

"For a short while, this year as in former years, the nation will remember its war dead. There will be memorial gatherings, speeches, a bugle call, moments of silence. Having done our duty, we will then resume our existence with a clear conscience.

"But the wounds of war never heal. The young boy who fell in action will never return. The young soldier who lost his sight remains in darkness forever. The warrior with amputated legs will never run again. Bereaved parents will never again embrace their lost sons.

"What makes young boys give up their lives? What makes them defend their country to the last drop of their blood? Do they cherish and value their homeland so much; so much that they are willing to die for it? Does the eventual danger of national annihilation make them so disciplined that they are willing to fight to death?

"Whatever the answers to these questions, the fact remains that they do so, to bequeath us life, to safeguard the continuity of our existence. Can we accept their sacrifice as just another free gift?

"Life is not evenhanded. Fate is often unjust. We who keep the candle of memory flickering for our fallen sons must do it with a pang in our hearts. We deserve no special rights for this. Yet, one single privilege should be granted to us: to demand of ourselves and others that their lives and acts be in the spirit of those who have handed down this heritage."[32]

To the extent that American Jews join us in fulfilling the expectations implicit in our relationship—to that extent, and only to that extent, We Are One!

### Notes

1. What is more revealing than the fact that Israeli leaders, when visiting abroad, characteristically meet with American Jewish contributors, rather than with those groups of men and women, boys and girls, preparing to come to Israel and link their personal destiny to ours?

2. Eric Hoffer, *The Passionate State of Mind* (New York, 1955), 43.

3. Karl Jaspers, *The Origin and Goal of History* (London, 1953), 1, 271.

4. Hoffer, *The Passionate State of Mind*, 36.

5. These rewritings of history are found in Arnold M. Goodman, "Letter from the President," *Rabbinical Assembly Newsletter*, 1 September 1982. Appended to this letter is, of all things, a fund-raising appeal signed by the prime minister of the State of Israel (Jerusalem, 8 August 1982).

6. Robert E. Goldburg, *New York Times, International Edition*, 26 September 1982, 6.

7. Arthur Hertzberg, *New York Times*, 7 September 1982, 7. The author is now best known for the alacrity with which he springs into print to castigate us.

8. Thus, in her sensitive rebuttal of Arthur Goldburg's citation of the U.S. Constitution and Declaration of Independence, asking, "Is Israel to be held to a higher standard than these great documents?" Roberta M. Roos replies, "The answer is 'yes' and 'no,' depending

upon who you are. . . . From the community of nations and from the Gentiles, the answer must be 'no.' Israel has the same right which any other country has, to do what is necessary to protect itself. But from the community of Jews, of whom Mr. Goldburg is a member, the answer must be 'yes.' We must hold ourselves to a higher standard. We recognize this when, in our daily prayers, we praise the Creator, 'who has not made us like other nations of the universe.' " Her letter concludes, "I have little patience with non-Jews who chastise Israel for behaving immorally when it acts as other nations do, but I have even less patience with Jews who excuse our moral failings by equating us with non-Jews" (*Jerusalem Post*, 10 September 1982, 16).

9. Leon M. Fox, *New York Times*, 26 September 1982, 1E6. In a similar vein, Jack Ziv-El writes, "Israel is in the position of the watchman who allegedly failed to perform his duty properly for whatever reason. Israel is not the thief who took advantage of it. The media, particularly abroad, keep using the word 'responsible' in connection with the atrocities committed in Beirut, thereby blurring the distinction between the watchman and the criminal, resulting in our enemies having a field day.

"Israel is technically accountable and answerable and the people involved in our government must pay the price for gullibility and poor performance of duty. The moral responsibility, however, falls on those who murdered now, and the PLO who did the same to their enemies" (*Jerusalem Post*, 1 October 1982, 8).

As a case in point, the BBC coverage is described by Burton Caine in the same issue: "Since arriving in Israel on June 25 as a visiting professor of law from the United States, I have listened to the BBC daily. I would agree that, generally, the reporting conforms to high standards for accuracy and objectivity. But when it comes to Israel, a different personality emerges. Often, I have listened to the very end of a prolonged anti-Israel canard just to make certain that I have not missed some introductory disclaimer such as 'This is the PLO allegation.'

"It seems that the BBC views its mission as a campaigner for Arab causes out of some misguided sense of balance. That is, without a counterweight, the news would favour Israel. Otherwise, the BBC stance is inexplicable. I certainly affirm the BBC's right to freedom of expression. As a professor of American Constitutional Law, I could do no less. In my view there is no requirement that the BBC be fair, objective, or truthful, and its claim to such attributes is provincial, smug, or even narcissistic" (p. 16).

10. Since the establishment of the State of Israel, there have been thirty successful revolutions and forty unsuccessful ones in the Arab world, as well as innumerable assassinations (for example, Anwar Sadat and Bashir Jemayel). The huge inter-Arab butcheries included the civil war in Yemen that claimed more than 200,000 lives, due, in measure, to the use by the Egyptians of poison gas against their brethren. The list of atrocities and mass murders within the Arab world in recent decades is simply too lengthy to catalog here. For a recent list, see Y. Ben Gad, "A Way of Death," *Jerusalem Post*, 28 September 1982, 5.

11. Alfred Dessau, *New York Times*, 26 September 1982, 1E6.

12. Walter Lippmann, *The Public Philosophy* (New York, 1955), 871.

13. Aristotle, *Topics*, Book 1, ch. 1, 101. 3ff.

14. Lippmann, *The Public Philosophy*, 100f.

15. Ibid., See also J. S. Mill, *On Liberty* (London, 1946), 28f., Leo Strauss, *Natural Right and History* (Chicago, 1963), 5.

16. Hedrick Smith, "Beirut Killings", *New York Times*, 26 September 1982, 1E2.

17. Y. Goell, *Jerusalem Post*, 24 September 1982, 15.

18. Wolf Blitzer, "A Deft Use of Power," *Jerusalem Post*, 10 September 1982, 6.

19. Cf. Y. Goell, "Legitimacy of War," *Jerusalem Post*, 14 July 1982, 10. The author continues, "Certainly the effects of diplomacy, legislation and of consciously directed formal

education, to mention only some alternatives, pale into insignificance when compared with the use of violence as a mechanism for such change. Perhaps the only other instrument that equals violence for sheer effectiveness is the persistent propogation [*sic*] of ideas—primarily by demagogic means speaking to the gut emotions rather than to the intellect—coupled with a resort to violence at the right moment. . . . Before writing off the effectiveness of bellicose actions, one should consider recent world history and Israel's experience. . . ."

20. E. Shimoni, "The Right to Debate," *Jerusalem Post*, 24 September 1982, 16. This in response to H. Siegman, "American Consensus," *Jerusalem Post*, 14 September 1982.

21. Cf. Fred Denbeaux, *The Art of Christian Doubt* (New York, 1960), 30f. One might add that to this day Judaism exists without a binding credo.

22. This estimate was provided by Tel Aviv Chief of Police Turgeman, as well as by media reporters on the scene.

23. M. Feingold, "Whose Shame?" *Jerusalem Post*, 24 September 1982, 16.

24. *Jerusalem Post*, 16 October 1982, 16.

25. Ibid., 1 October 1981, 16.

26. G. Joseph, *Jerusalem Post*, 10 October, 1981, 16.

27. I. R. Korotkin, *Jerusalem Post*, 10 October, 1981, 16.

28. Cf. Shlomo Avineri, "Struggle for Zionism's Soul", *Jerusalem Post*, 23 September 1982, 8, for application to the issue of the "occupied territories."

29. E. F. Gross, *Jerusalem Post*, 23 September, 1982, 10.

30. Nechemia Meyers, "Sounds of Silence," *Jerusalem Post*, 27 September 1982, 5.

31. Ibid., also referring to the many experiences of Israelis recently abroad in Europe.

32. Abba Shel Gabi, "Yom Kippur Thoughts," *Jerusalem Post*, 24 September 1982, 15. See also Etan Levine, "The Reconstruction of Jewish Space," *Reconstructionist* 46 (December 1980): 7–14.

# PART VI

# The Israeli Argument
# with the Diaspora

# 16

# My Expectations of American Jewry

## GOLDA MEIR

In attempting to convey my expectations of American Jewry, I will begin by sharing the contents of a letter I recently received. The woman who wrote it described the first performance of the Israeli delegation to the Moscow Youth Festival. She did not dwell on the artistic standards of the performance. She began with the words: "He cried." When I first saw that opening sentence, I thought she was referring to some Russian Jew who had been deeply moved by the performance—and I myself have seen Russian Jews weeping. But this time it was a young, stalwart sabra she was describing; a second-generation Israeli kibbutz member who knows no Yiddish and certainly no Russian, and who had probably never before been out of the country. According to the theories we have heard here, this young man should have had a very narrow Jewish outlook and been concerned not at all with Jews in the *galut* but only with the small country of Israel or even only with his own small kibbutz. Yet it was this boy who was moved to tears on seeing his brethren in Russia, with whom, supposedly, he had nothing in common—neither language, nor past experiences, nor suffering.

Were I to state in one sentence what it is that we want and expect of you, is that your children, too, shall be moved to tears on meeting Jews in a *galut* like that of Russia. That is all. Present-day Jewish youth, outside of Israel, is not capable of that. Our children are neither more handsome nor more precocious nor more wise than yours; they have no more remarkable abilities than yours, but they have one great quality: They are free and healthy, normal and independent Jewish children. They know what it is to build and to fight, to struggle for their own existence. They have seen their comrades die for them and for their own land. They are not the only Jewish youth who have died in war, but they alone have fallen on Jewish soil.

If our youth were raised in an atmosphere in which it did not matter whether Jews lived in Israel or in the diaspora, that boy would not have wept that evening in Moscow. He wept because, in his own simple way and in the atmosphere he had breathed since his childhood, there is something that rebels against life in the *galut*.

We must be quite frank. I confess that when I visit my hometown in America and see my old friends and comrades doing well, their children older than mine, their grandchildren older than mine who live in the desert—I confess I pity them when I think of the difference between the ways my grandchildren and theirs are reared.

We have nothing against Jews in the *galut*. It is against the *galut itself* that we protest. And I do not understand the state of affairs in which we are not allowed to say what we feel because someone might misunderstand us and believe that we are interested only in the small and narrow confines of our own land.

### This is Zionism!

I also fail to understand when people say that there is danger for Israel if we continue hammering into the minds and hearts of Jews in the diaspora that they must come hither. If we tell our fellow Zionists what we experienced during the scores of years until we reached our present stage, if we say to them that Zionism means not only to work for Eretz Yisrael, we are told that by this emphasis we make our world so narrow and our culture so shortsighted that we may—heaven forbid—become Levantine. In my opinion, anyone who takes that view denies the very principle of Zionism.

We have always believed, and I personally have thought, that the foundation of Zionism is more than geographical independence. I have always believed that Zionism means Jewish emancipation in every sense, including the spiritual and cultural, so that a Jew who creates cultural values may do so as a free man. It may be an assumption on my part, but I believe that there is no Jew in the *galut* creating as a free man and as a free Jew. Only a Jew is Israel can do so. If a Jew lives in Israel and creates as a free Jew and as a free man, writes about various problems in the world, about Jewish life and non-Jewish life, about science, art, and literature, his writing will not be less universal than that of a Jew who lives in the *galut*—in every *galut*, even in the best of them— for there he must, willingly or unwillingly, consciously or unconsciously, adapt himself to his surroundings. Then he is not free.

In these discussions ways and means have been sought to make possible double loyalty and to prove that it is not dangerous to the countries of which diaspora Jews are citizens. But is double loyalty a danger only to those countries? Is it not a danger also for Jews? Is it not a danger to Judaism if a Jew must feel loyalty to two sovereign ideals? Must we only see to it that Americans who believe that double loyalty is not good for America should feel comfortable? Is it comfortable for Jews?

I must confess that sometimes I am led to believe that my Zionism may be imperfect, for I fail to understand what we have often heard during the past ten years—that the State of Israel is not the final goal of Zionism. Sometimes this is said by people who previously urged a definition of the final goal of Zionism. If you maintain that the State of Israel cannot be regarded as the final goal of Zionism so long as there are not millions of Jews living there, I agree. But what exactly is meant by the statement "The state is not the final aim of Zionism?" What did we understand by the "final aim of Zionism" before the state emerged, when we had to devise devious ways and means of bringing Jews over to Eretz Yisrael and had to adapt ourselves to the reality in which we lived? Zionism wanted Jews to gain independence in their own land, have their own language, and create all the social and cultural ideas that have been enumerated. It would certainly be foolish to say that Zionism means that once we are a people of close to two million in Israel the aim is achieved. There are many Jews and many Zionists in the lands of the diaspora who would like to talk us into believing that we must be satisfied with that. We disagree. At least, we urge you, do not claim, and do not bring up a young generation in the diaspora with the idea, that though the State of Israel is a good thing in itself, it is not Zionism. What then is Zionism?

I should like to ask you something. Jews in all generations strove for Eretz Yisrael. It is immaterial how we define that urge, whether religious or not. But that urge for Eretz Yisrael was one of the fundamentals—the main power—that kept us alive and maintained us in the world. Jews wanted Eretz Yisrael, and so they prayed to God and mourned and lamented and fasted on Tisha b'Ab. And that desire of theirs had an extraordinary influence and was a decisive factor in Jewish life. But was Eretz Yisrael created thereby? Did Eretz Yisrael become a tangible fact through that? Wherein lay Herzl's great achievement? It was in the fact that he gathered Jews together and told them that their yearning and urge for Eretz Yisrael must not remain only a dream, something for which one must weep and pray, but that it was something that could be accomplished—if they actually wanted to accomplish it. And so the Zionist movement came into being. And the Zionist movement in its own fashion aspired and worked for the creation of a Jewish state and Jewish independence. The Zionist movement said that if we wanted our state, it could be achieved. These Jews achieved the state.

Now I should like to ask you: How is a Zionist who does not personally go to Israel to build the state more important than a Jew who is not a Zionist, who on Tisha b'Ab sat on the ground and wept with all his heart and mourned the destruction of the Temple, as though it had happened only yesterday? I do not underrate such weeping and mourning. But how is a modern political Zionist, who does not go to Israel to help build the country with his own hands, how is he more important for the state than those Jews who shed tears on Tisha b'Ab? Why are we not allowed to say that after the emergence of the state a Zionist is only he who packs his bags and comes to Israel? What else can a Zionist aspire to?

It is suggested that we should be partners. I am the last to underestimate the tears of sorrow or the tears of joy of the Jews in America, and I have seen both. They wept at moments of great danger for Israel, and they wept at moments of great joy for Israel. They wept from afar, and I shall be the last to think lightly of it, because I know that they wept from the bottom of their hearts. But I cannot be satisfied with that, despite the great value I attach to it. My dear friends, there is a great difference that we dare not underestimate, the difference between the family that lives here and whose son or daughter went out to fight in Sinai, and a good, sincere Zionist family living in New York or in Buenos Aires or in Johannesburg that looked on from afar. Yes, their hearts beat warmly, I am convinced of that, and in their own fashion they prayed to God for our success; but there is a difference. One cannot do away with it. One must not try.

### Two Great Tasks

I was also under the impression that after the rise of the Jewish state we would have to undertake two tasks and that we would have to try with all our energy and understanding to find ways to reach all Jews, so as not to leave any of them out. Possibly the two tasks may be welded into one. They are to build up and consolidate the Jewish state, and to preserve and guard every Jewish young man and woman, every child in the diaspora so long as they have not come here; the goal is not to create all types of theories saying that it matters little if they remain there. One must constantly demand that they come here, but in the first place one must guard against the great danger that we may not be able to understand each other. The spoken language is immaterial, for at times one fails to understand one's fellow even when the same language is spoken. I have always thought that since the emergence of the Jewish state there are no Jews, apart from the American Council for Judaism and the Communists, whose hearts do not beat for Israel. But that is not enough.

We speak of the free world. The free world is also free to assimilate, and the danger is by no means small. I have always been of the opinion, and I still am, that as far as the Jewish state is concerned, work should not be vested in organizations, though certainly they have had great importance in Jewish life and for the state. Jews, Jewish communities as such, Jewish groups without special tendencies, must now be concerned with two things: to build up and strengthen Israel and to work toward aliyah. We lament every day that passes without Jewish life, without Jewish education, without the Hebrew language, without preparation for work in Israel. Not one day, not one hour must be wasted in that respect. One must not acquiesce in the idea that the diaspora will be permanent.

Whoever talks himself into the belief that the Jewish people in the diaspora can exist as it would in Israel, and that it has a lasting chance of survival there, is deeply mistaken. One must not make peace with assimilation. Assimilation means being cut off from the Jewish people. Whoever becomes assimilated no longer exists for us. Nor must one make peace with the idea of mixed marriages. The children of mixed marriages are not full Jews. It depends on the Christian mother or on the Christian father and whether she or he is large-hearted or broad-minded enough to allow the children to go to a synagogue. The compromise is often to go neither to a church nor a synagogue, or to go to the church. At any rate, it is not one of Judaism or of Hebrew or of Israelism. Don't give me instances of things turning out otherwise; I, too, know of Christian women being devoted and wonderful Hadassah workers. They are exceptions, and they simply prove the general rule. Half-Jewish children are not wholly Jewish children, and a mixed family atmosphere is not a Jewish home. One must not acquiesce in such conditions. Their effects in the diaspora are obvious.

### Zionism Does Not Compromise

Zionism never made any compromises. No, not even over the Uganda question. Zionism had the courage even to oppose Herzl and to say: "No Uganda, no compromise!" Would you want us to compromise? And are you offended by our not wishing to accept a situation in which only a small section of the Jewish people, only 14 percent or 16 percent, will live in Israel, while the majority of Jews will remain in the *galut* and will, from afar, either take pride in us or criticize us? It matters little and it is all the same which of the two attitudes they take. They will be far away, in either case. Admittedly, they will feel with us and help us to build up the country, but only from afar.

Obviously, as long as the debate continues between you and us; as long as we make demands and you express no opposition to them (I don't want to believe that you are opposed to aliyah); as long as we make demands and say that aliyah in itself is a good thing but that we should not demand it, and have no claims upon you—as long as that is the state of things, you will not in your heart of hearts be able to believe that the Jewish people now residing in the lands of the diaspora, in the free countries, will continue to remain a Jewish people. Whether you acquiesce in assimilation or not, it is a fact that Jews are drifting away. No, it is not we who are pushing anyone off the wagon. They keep falling of their own accord; they slide off; many of them do not even want to make an attempt to get on.

We want the Zionist movement to be the force that harnesses all Jews, that brings them to Israel and, as long as they remain in *galut*, gives them a meaningful Jewish life with a knowledge of Hebrew and a deep Israeli atmosphere in the home and in the upbringing of their children. And if there is talk of a university, it should be the University of Jerusalem, and not any other. And if there is talk of a summer camp, it should be a summer camp in Israel, and not any other.

You say that this is double loyalty, that it means creating a Jewish ghetto in free America. Yes, I should like to see in free America what you call a ghetto—Jewish children brought up in Jewish homes with one goal and one desire and thought: to be in Israel. I am not so foolish as to think that can be done overnight. We have not yet reached the stage where we can discuss this with Jewish fathers and mothers. First of all we must discuss it among ourselves, and realize that this approach is essential.

And another thing that I believe is that every Sunday school in American is a blessing for us. Rather than that children should grow up ignorant of anything Jewish, it is better that they should meet every Sunday for a few hours and that they should be told something about Judaism, even in English. It is better than nothing. But that is not a Jewish education. It is not Hebrew, and it gives nothing of the Israeli spirit. It is not sufficient.

### Being True Partners

I know how fully to appreciate the love that Jews bear for Israel; but if we Israelis were to come to you and express confidence in our strength and belief that "the Jewish state will in all circumstances be in a position to fend for itself," I would say the confidence is quite mistaken. With only a certain percentage of Jews in the world here, with only the present Jewish strength in Israel, it is impossible in the world in which we live, in the constant danger by which we are surrounded, to guarantee the state's security. It surely cannot be done by singing songs of praise. Please do not misunderstand me, but every time I hear anyone in

New York or in Chicago or in Los Angeles singing Israeli songs, "Hey Daroma," "Aravah," or other songs, my heart leaps up and I am delighted. But by singing songs about the Negev in Los Angeles or in Texas, the Negev will not be built up. Songs about the Negev sung in New York or in Boston are wonderful only if they serve as instruments and a path for the youth to go to the Negev. Otherwise, Jews will remain living in America and will continue to sing about the Negev for a few years longer, but the Negev will remain in its desolation.

I agree with those who claim—possibly it's not logical or rational—that Jews will come from Russia to Eretz Yisrael. I simply do not have the strength to tell myself that these three and a half million Jews will be cut off forever from us. When they will come I do not know. It may be tomorrow, it may be in ten years' time, I cannot say. But Jews in the free world, Jews who are devoted to Israel, Jews who must be brought up in devotion to Israel, cannot and must not continue to remain afar; they must feel with us, and be partners with us: yes, partners, but not long-distance partners. That cannot be. One is a partner and the other is a sleeping partner, and Jews in the diaspora invest not only money but also love and dreams and yearning and pride in Israel. Yes, that is all very well. But from afar it is not possible to irrigate the Negev. And Israel's existence depends on whether or not the Negev remains a desert and on whether or not the Galilee remains a region of barren and rocky hills. It depends on whether Jewish youth who must defend Israel, when need arises, are here. I cannot separate the security and the existence of Israel from the presence of Jews in Galilee. One cannot exist without the other, they are inseparable, knit together, and they must be together.

Israel was built not for the chosen few who came here originally from Eastern Europe, not only for those who are forced to come here, and not only for those who cannot come because they are not allowed out of other countries; Israel has been built for all Jews, and Israeli Jews will not give Jews in the diaspora peace until large masses of them come here.

I believe you, and every one of us believes you, when you say you envy us. This must mean that something is being created here that is lacking in America. Why, then, should you take it amiss when we say that you should see to it that your children and grandchildren should not be in a position to envy us but should come here and be with us and share the happiness of our children?

I know that Jews will continue to live in the diaspora for many years to come and that we must be concerned with their life there. Jewish leaders in the diaspora are often told that they must not leave for Israel, because their contribution in the diaspora is more important. There can be no greater lack of realism. The more people taken out of the diaspora community, the richer the community becomes. This is paradoxical but true. A Jewish community from which there is no aliyah becomes spiritually impoverished. Did the prewar aliyah from Poland and Lithuania make those Jews poorer?

No real bond can exist between Israel and the Jews of the free countries without a great immigration to Israel.

# 17

# Toward Radical Redefinition

## A. B. YEHOSHUA

In numerous articles I have tried to establish the urgent need to stress normalcy as a value and to conduct an intramural Jewish struggle against the concept of chosenness. We must see ourselves as an integral part of humanity, neither superior nor inferior. We must adopt this position as an unequivocal value, without evasions or sophisticated interpretations. Declaring that we are better has three adverse effects: It causes people to suspect us; it imposes upon us criteria that we ourselves cannot live up to; and it causes us, consequently, frustration and self-recrimination. The State of Israel has a basic right to exist, even if it has organized crime, corruption, and social injustice. We wish to improve the quality of our existence, not because we have to prove our moral superiority, nor to justify our existence to someone, but simply because we want to improve ourselves. Once and for all we must get rid of the slave mentality, which turned an inferiority complex into a sense of mission, superiority, and elitism. The more conscious we are of the negative instincts that underlie our sense of superiority, the more chance we have of uprooting it.

Secular Zionists always sensed that the religious question was one of the most dangerous traps lying in wait for them, so they always preferred to bind the sleeping tiger in the fetters of political coalition agreements. The status quo is, however, a highly explosive concept. The potential for conflict is frightening because the emotions pent up on both the secular and religious sides are immensely powerful. These disputes have to be smoothed over and shored up in agreements, for the slightest breach in the dam could lead to a deluge. Perhaps in the early days of statehood there was a misguided notion that the days of religion were numbered, that its effect could be blunted by means of agreements and the status quo, and by the legitimacy with which the secular system endowed it; subsequently, religion would become institutionalized and gradually lose its vitality until it died a quiet death. Or, alternately, perhaps it was felt that it would be better to erect a network of agreements precisely because a religious revival was in the offing and it threatened to be so uncontrollable as to sweep away the entire system. Whatever the reason, the purpose of the status quo was in one way or another to suspend the struggle between religion and state. The status quo in Israel was intended to replace the *golah* experience as the salient factor that had muted the eternal conflict in the total Jewish system of life. The difficult security situation always served as a convenient excuse for preserving the status quo. However, there were always an unspoken assumption among Israelis that when peace came, the wars of the Jews would break out over the religious question. Historically, the most violent clashes between the citizen and the authorities, or between rival groups of citizens, were always over religious questions.

I have no wish at present to go into the complex questions aroused by the conflict between religion and state. I shall only say that this conflict always induces an escape to the *golah*. If we really want to eliminate the *golah* as a feasible possibility—at least for the Jews now living in Israel— we must consider changing the religion from within. What is needed is religious reform. Some of the basic values of the religion must be questioned, the national horizon of the religion must be made more flexible, and, above all, new and separate sources of authority must be created inside the religion. We are in need of some new and genuine religious reformers. We need a Jewish Luther. These reformers could come from the margins of Orthodoxy movements, which, for their part, will have to undergo a process of "Israelization." To put it bluntly, religion is too important to be left to the religious. Secular Jews, or those who are known as secular, must become involved in religious affairs, not as romantic penitents, but as daring reformers.

It is astonishing to see what a cool reception the secular element in Israel's leadership gave movements of religious reform, and how totally insignificant was the help it extended to them. There were two particular reasons for this: First, the subject was highly sensitive for the religious parties, they were ready to make concessions on many issues, provided their exclusive authority in the field of religion went unchallenged. Second, the American coloration of these movements appeared artificial and lacking in authenticity to Israel's leaders, who grew up on notions of authenticity delimited by the Eastern European Jewish experience. Had Ben-Gurion at the height of his power, intellectual influence, and enormous authority gone to pray on Yom Kippur in an Israeli-style Reform synagogue instead of shutting himself up in his house for the day to pore over Spinoza or Aristotle, he would have endowed reformist thought with a decisive measure of legitimacy. In addition, reformist thought would have undergone a radical process of Israelization. It is only now that some time has elapsed—since Begin came to power—that one of the profound differences has emerged between the present administration and the previous one: that is, namely, the inner attitude toward religion. The leaders of the Labor movement had been much more secular than the average Israeli of today.

There can be no realistic hope for a normalization of the Jewish people without a radical approach to the religious questions. If we want to see any significant change in the next 100 years, we shall have to start rethinking the religious question right now. A total war against religion would be meaningless, because the Jewish people has a profound collective psychological need for religion, although this impulse is governed by a cyclical pattern of ebb and flow. The only reform that secular Jews want is the kind that will make things easier by granting them freedom *from* religion. This way of thinking is basically misguided. The problem is not to make the commandments less burdensome, but to expose them to the complexity of life and to fulfill them while changing them. It is astounding to see to what extent the Jewish religion has managed to resist change and to survive without changing its essence even in Eretz Yisrael under Jewish sovereignty. Since Jewish Orthodoxy is not capable of changing and does not want to change, change will come only through the creation of additional centers of authority.

In summary, in order to get right to the source of the *golah* virus within us, there is a need for profound thought, involvement, and courage on our part. Brenner once said: "That is the question. In order that our character may be changed as far as possible, we must have an environment of our own. Yet in order that we may create that environment with our own hands—our character has to change completely." We already possess the environment. We do not wish to change our character merely for the sake of changing it, but in the clear context of the unending war against the *golah* potential lurking inside each one of us.

### A Program for the Future

A number of practical conclusions emerge as courses for action in the immediate future. If Israel's prime minister were to appear at the opening conference of the bond drive in the United States and, instead of speaking once again about Israel, the territories, and relations with the United States, he were to announce ceremonially that this year the state of Israel refused to accept money from the *golah* out of anger over the fact that only the money immigrates to Israel, not the Jews; if Israel's prime minister or her senior representatives were, by a dramatic and demonstrative act, to condemn the *golah* for the absence of aliyah and were to announce that the money was being sent back to the *golah* for the sole purpose of boosting aliyah; if the State of Israel were to stop sending teachers, educators, and communitty emissaries to a Jewish community that does not fulfill even minimal aliyah quotas, perhaps some impression would be made, and perhaps the question of the *golah* would be placed at the center of things. I do not claim that millions or even hundreds of thousands would come, but even if only a few extra thousands came, it would be sufficient. That in itself would constitute a revolution.

At present, approximately 2,000 American Jews per year immigrate to Israel. Even if the number increased to 20,000, not even .005 percent of American Jewry would be represented. But from the point of view of Zionist fervor, it would be a drastic change. On the one hand, such an aliyah would put a stop to the catastrophe of Jews leaving Israel; on the other, and additional 100,000 Jews would be bound in the *golah* to Israel through family connections and friendships. From a scientific and cultural point of view, it would be most important. But can it be done? One can at least begin intending to do it. One can try to believe that it is possible.

Recently, Israel has become a too-familiar presence in the *golah*, especially in the United States. Paradoxically, it is no longer necessary to immigrate to Israel to live in Israel, and it is possible to acquire scraps of significant Israeli reality in the *golah* itself. The aura of distance and mystery surrounding Israel has become blurred, if it has not vanished altogether. The media contributed to this, but they are not the only ones to blame. The constant deepening of relations between the *golah* and Israel has obscured the dividing line between them. Perhaps it was thought that in this way people's hearts would be prepared for aliyah, but the reverse is true. What has been created is a legitimate reality of substitutes for aliyah—of quasi aliyah. We must at all costs reestablish a certain feeling of alienation between the *golah* and Israel—a controlled disengagement, as it were.

A not inconsiderable group of Jews abroad has forged a network of very intimate relations with the leadership of the State of Israel. This group is party to more of Israel's state secrets than are parallel groups of Israelis. At the cost of a 5 percent contribution to the national budget, the *golah* has become a recognized intermediary in our relations with foreign governments—a service we rightly chose to do without in the early years of statehood. The mutual dependence of Israel and the *golah* has greatly increased. Spiritually the *golah* needs Israel. Our political conflicts, our economic problems, and, in a certain sense, Israeli culture provide the spiritual nourishment for Jewish identity in the *golah*. These have replaced the Talmud, the Kabbalah, and the Responsa. Hence the *golah* will not abandon Israel the moment it initiates an ideological conflict over aliyah. Of course, a few such attempts will be made, but that part of the Jewish people (which for the sake of convenience we shall call Jewish People A) that accounts for three million out of the eleven million Jews in the *golah*, that nurses a very profound affinity to Israel and Judaism, and that supplies Jewish services to the other five million or six million (Jewish People B), can never sever its link. It is now in our power (Jewish People B), before it is too late, to cause group A a certain shock, and to demand that it make a choice to end the eternal schizophrenia from which it suffers. At present the *golah* and Israel tightly clasp each other's hands. But if we were to upset the inertia of this stability by quickly withdrawing our hands from group A's grasp, the resulting imbalance would pull them sharply toward us. A state of peace could free us from our dependence on the *golah*, and would restore our upright stance. But even before full peace comes, we must begin to develop a different attitude and posture with regard to the *golah*. Instead of engaging in Jewish education in the *golah*, we must engage exclusively in the promotion of aliyah. Too much Jewish education obscures the need to come to Israel. Instead of trying to tempt and induce Jews to come here, we must coldly expose the pathology, immorality, and hypocrisy of the *golah*. We must start a quarrel with the most warmhearted of Jews, the Jews who are most loyal to Israel, for they are our public. It is true that this will be a quarrel among brothers, but it seems to me that this would be preferable to the condition of peace that exists at present.

According to the most optimistic studies, in the year 2000 only about 50 percent of the population within the borders of greater Israel will be Jewish, and this assumes an aliyah of 25,000 a year, with only a small yeridah. There is the very real danger that in another fifty years we will lose our majority even inside the Green Line (pre-1967 Israel). With peace, of course, there will be the opportunity and the hope for large-scale aliyah. But let us not forget that there is also a possibility of emigration and the scattering of the Jews throughout the region. In conditions of economic prosperity, and in a world in which distances are becoming less significant, Jews could live in the *golah*—in Tunis, for example—and teach their children Judaism by means of Israeli television programs.

### Aliyah and Redemption

The virus of the *golah* is in our blood. Let us not forget that. We are descendants of those Jews of whom, at the time of the Second Temple, and in the difficult conditions of the ancient world, the famous Greek geographer Strabo wrote: "It is hard to find a place in the entire world in which this people does not live." Gershon Scholem once said that it is as if Israel, by its very existence, had absorbed the sparks of the redemption imprisoned in the *golah,* and as if it thereby freed the *golah* from the need for redemption and from the guilt of nonredemption. It is up to us to do everything in our power to avoid exculpating the *golah* from the guilt of nonredemption. (The absolute criterion in our relationships with the *golah* must be guided by what increases aliyah and what limits it.) It goes without saying that *yordim* are to be condemned and should on no account be given jobs in Israeli institutions abroad; however, there is no moral validity in condemning the *yordim* without condemning life in the *golah* in general.

Do we really need another internecine quarrel? Will it do any good? My answer is yes. The conflict with the *golah* will uncover what we in Israel have in common, as distinct from those living abroad. It will show once again what the cardinal things are, the things for which we are fighting: freedom and independence. Instead of fighting with each other tooth and nail over the issue of an acre more or an acre less territory, we shall see that the real issues lie elsewhere. The essence of our life in Israel is different from that of *golah* life, and the differences should not be obscured. Spiritual life in the *golah* is like that of a man who has built his house on the water's edge and, preoccupied with the question of whether the water will inundate his home, is engaged in endless efforts to keep it out. We in Israel, on the other hand, are like a man who has removed his house far from the erosive power of the waves. The problem of the water no longer preoccupies him. He is able to build his house, cultivate his land, and create something new.

I believe that deep inside every man lies a desire for redemption, and each man possesses a latent vitality. I shall never forget a wonderful story from the time of the "illegal" aliyah from Morocco. It happened early in the 1960s, when ships were collecting Jews from Morocco, which was already completely under Moslem control. One day a ship arrived in one of the ports to pick up some Jews from a remote village. For various reasons the expected emigrants did not arrive, and the ship could not wait. The Jewish agency representatives on the ship went to the nearest Jewish community, knocked on the doors, and said: "Are you prepared to leave for Israel, right now, without further ado? Take whatever you can. Take your chance." And, in fact, quite a number of Jews got up and left, then and there. This impulsive component can be found in every one of us.

I am always astounded to rediscover in conversations with Jews abroad—intellectuals and others well-established in their jobs and their businesses—that they do not rule out the possibility that one day they might come to Israel. It is not just talk aimed at making an impression on others; "the redemption gland" exists in every Jew. A thousand obstacles, personal and collective, lie in the path of anyone who wishes to make aliyah; yet the decisive fact is that there is a minority that has done so of its own free will.

One of the most compelling reasons for peace has not been heard: Peace is likely to increase aliyah and reallocate resources for aliyah. Peace is likely to release Soviet Jews from their prison. Our historical responsibility is not toward land. It lies first and foremost with people. History will never forgive us if, because of our attachments to the ideal of settlement in all parts of Eretz Yisrael, we abandon a huge Jewish community in the Soviet Union to anti-Semitism and assimilation.

For thousands of years the Jews have said: "Next year in Jerusalem," meaning it, yet not meaning it. The same is true today. However, in the past generation a new group has emerged that cannot say "next year in Jerusalem," because it is already living in the real, down-to-earth Jerusalem. This group will never again be satisfied with the abstract concept of "celestial Jerusalem." The great debate between Israel and the *golah* must be resumed at once, without hypocrisy, in all its fierceness and honesty.

# 18

# To Take Up the Gauntlet

## ELI EYAL

A new stage has arisen in relations between Israel and the diaspora: "the challenge of the diaspora," meaning that the diaspora is now challenging us. By this I do not allude to the fleshpots of the diaspora, to material temptations that entice our youth in a particular diaspora. I allude to the gauntlet so aggressively thrown down by George Steiner in England, Noam Chomsky in the United States, and others who negate the State of Israel, in a perversely brilliant exercise of intellectualism.

I have given the subject considerable thought and have spoken with outstanding personalities, authors, and thinkers, the dominant one being Amos Oz, the gifted writer. And I wonder whether we in Israel fully grasp the real meaning of the things they say, of their ideas, which seep through right down to the *yordim*.

Let's call a spade a spade. Today there is a tendency to have second thoughts about the very tenets of Zionism. If one were to summarize these "second thoughts" they would read as audacious questions: Do the Jews really need a state? Are the most fundamental diagnoses, and the resulting prognoses, of the Zionist founders still valid today, or has stark reality rebutted them? The conclusions: Hitler was a mere episode. We made a bad deal.

The Jews of the diaspora who say all these things are condescendingly prepared to promise us their continued support. You Israelis, say the new diasporists, have placed us in a complex situation by your doubtful venture. It is necessary for us to help you extricate yourselves from the muddle in order that you may continue to exist. But the price (as hinted), is that you Israelis should give up your pretension to being the solution to the problem of the Jews. Further still, that you give up your pretension to being the center of the Jewish people.

This challenge is garbed in intellectual phraseology. Chomsky, using the most extreme wording, says that the national state is a vain idea, an anachronism, murderous, childish, and superfluous. One must aspire to a world of a hundred civilizations rather than to one national state. During 2,000 years the Jewish people has, *nolens volens*, presented to the world a model of a civilization without a territory. What has happened to us, says Chomsky, is that we have gotten cold feet, and have joined the big regression, which started in the nineteenth century, the return to territory, to nationality, to all the primitive primordial features. Steiner calls it "an old man in a kindergarten." And a kindergarten whose toys are destructive and murderous.

To this there is added another argument, a very aggressive one: What have you done to the Jewish genius? Turned them into colonels and some tractor drivers. Look at what we have created in the diaspora and are still creating. What, by comparison, is the significance of the tidings of the Zionist enterprise? The answer is, of course, an ironical smile whose implication is that Israel is a semi-Levantine state constantly embroiled in quarrels with the Arabs.

Jews have a mission, say the new diasporists. They are the chosen people. The mission: to be the vitamin of Western civilization, or the salt of the earth for Western civilization. To be useful, a vitamin must be dispersed, not concentrated. Salt, too, if it is not to be harmful must be dispersed.

## *Fig Leaves*

This entire argument is draped in festive attire, with Spinoza, Freud, Einstein, Bashevis Singer, and various other Nobel Prize laureates festooned upon it like a row of medals. Very modestly, the new diasporists don't include themselves in this gallery. What has the Zionist enterprise to show opposite this array?

A methodological remark is in order. I am fully aware that the utterances of Noam Chomsky, George Steiner, and their like are extremely radical. I know that this is a small group of people, a mere handful. But I also know that they have their cronies, and that this coterie has individual sympathizers. And so their periphery becomes larger.

It is true that only a few Jews may openly identify themselves with the new diasporists. But more than a few find satisfaction at hearing this argumentation, and become followers.

Can one miss the thrust of the Report of the World Jewish Congress? It was drawn up by a panel of distinguished Jewish personalities, including a few Israelis, businessmen, and financiers, and was couched in terms and in wording somewhat similar to this rhetoric: "The classic Zionist ideology, which denigrates the prospects for a secure or meaningful Jewish existence in the diaspora and which conceives of diaspora existence as living in exile, is remote from the thinking of most Jews who live in full democratic societies."

And as with all intricate ideas, these, too, seep down to other strata to become platitudes, and are intoned as such by the former kibbutznik, now a garage attendant in Los Angeles, by a student in Buenos Aires, or an assistant lecturer in Berkeley. Arguments such as these are vulgarizations of the ideas of Chomsky, Steiner, and their like.

Today, much of this argumentation and reasoning serve as fig leaves for the *yored*. It reaches grotesque proportions. A young man, an accountant in Montevideo, or a radio salesman in Toronto, tells us that *he* is part of the true essence and culture of the Jewish people, a participant in the more creatively active of the two Jewish centers of the Jewish people; while "we" (meaning the Israelis) waste this energy on tanks and fighter planes. "We" (meaning the *yordim*) form part of the culture. You have abandoned it.

## *The Challenge*

I would not want our debate with the new diasporists to sink to the level of the cantankerous tit for tat to which we have become accustomed. Some of us, when under stress, wish the diaspora things that are quasi anti-Semitic: "And the day may come when you will regret you were not in Israel."

Some of the diaspora defenders, also with quasi-malicious joy, retort with outworn paradox: Zionism purported to provide safety and shelter for the Jews, yet the most unsafe place for Jews is Israel.

I want to start with this banal, though painful, argument of security.

There is no country on earth and no nation that enjoys absolute security. Even Belgium must have tanks and fighter planes. The basic difference between the Israeli situation and the Jewish situation abroad is the extent to which the Israelis can shape their own future. It does not depend on the Jew in Chicago, or whether he feels more secure than the Jew is Beersheba.

We Jews in Israel have what the Jews in the last 2,000 years never had: a correlation between what we do and what happens to us. It is not an absolute correlation. If, God forbid, a disaster should overtake us, it will not be one that the cossacks will have brought upon us, or the Polish nationalists, or the Nazis, or Czar Nicholas. It will be a disaster that we by our carelessness, arrogance, or anything else will have brought upon ourselves.

Freedom is a state in which there is a distinct correlation between conduct and results. In this respect the Jews or Israel enjoy freedom such as had never been possessed by the Jewish people in any diaspora, even the most serene and complacent, including the contemporaneous.

### Museum or Drama

Now, as to the Jewish genius and its creative force.

Culture can usually exist in one of two situations: either in a museum or as drama.

In the case of a museum, folklore, religion, values are all kept locked in glass showcases. And fathers come and explain these treasures to their sons, and teach them to feel pride in their great legacy. This is a cul-de-sac, because where there is no drama, but only a museum, the young will depart and search for drama in greener pastures: the New Left, Tupamarros, Jews for Jesus, and the like. Those, however, who are prepared to devote themselves to museum custodianship, keeping the showcases spotlessly clean, are few and far between.

Jewish culture in the diaspora today is a museum culture in which the only imperative, which informs fathers in the education of their sons, is to preserve, to avoid assimilation. "Behold what beautiful treasures are on show behind the polished glass" the fathers say. "They're yours."

The other alternative is drama. Drama is not a paradise. Drama means identity struggle, internal ideological tensions, and at times even civil wars. What we have had in the last eighty years in Israel is one long, cold, civil war. I say this with pride, because during these eight decades of Zionist enterprise I think that not more than twenty Jews have been killed by their brother Jews in ideological disputes.

No other nation has fought its identity battles with such deep respect for human life shown between opponents as we have.

Similar burning questions, such as religion and state, social class differences, the character of the ruling culture, have all been determined by bloodshed in civilized countries such as England, France, Germany, and America.

The Zionist drama is an enthralling drama because it has different interpretations. The only place where the Jewish people can offer the young generation not museum custodianship but active involvement in the drama is in the State of Israel.

Just as we distinguish between two cultural situations—the mummified museum and the vibrant drama—so must we distinguish between two kinds of national creation—individual creation and collective creation.

## Individual Creativity vs. Collective

If we assess the aggregate of the individual creations of diaspora Jewry for comparison with those of Israeli Jewry, there is no doubt that diaspora Jewry has more to show.

The diaspora has brought forth more brilliant Jews of world renown and more Nobel Prize laureates than we Israelis can boast of. But this is easily understood, because the numerical proportion between the *golah* and Israel is about 3 or 4 to 1. And the proportion is terms of years is 2,000 to 80.

But quite a different picture emerges when we look at the collective creations. There were at least three periods during which diaspora Jewry made outstanding collective creations: Babylon, Spain, and the most recent, Eastern Europe. And significantly, the most noteworthy collective creation of Eastern European Jewry before its destruction was the creation of political Zionism.

A collective creation is not one for which a Nobel Prize is awarded. By its very definition this is not a creation for which one person is granted the mark and distinction of celebrity.

In fact, since the tragic end of East European Jewry, the Jewish people in the diaspora has not made a single collective creation that can be compared to the hasidic movement; not a single social movement that can be compared to the Bund or to Jewish communism; not a single cultural creation that can be compared to Yiddish literature; and certainly not a single political creation that can be compared to the Zionist movement.

Since the destruction of East European Jewry, the diaspora possesses collective institutions that are but pale replicas of creations made in Eastern Europe

The impoverished *kehilla* has become the wealthy congregation. the *shul* has become the temple. The *rav* has become the rabbi, and the kopeck-pinched warden, the *gabai,* is now the president. *Heder* has become Sunday school. Nothing new. No innovation. All the diaspora has is merely a gilded replica of creations that existed in former centuries in Eastern Europe.

The only place where the Jewish people has come up with collective creations in recent decades is in Israel. Here are four examples:

1. The new Hebrew language. Contrary to the accepted myth, it is not the one-man creation of Eliezer Ben-Yehuda. It is a collective creation of the Jews of Israel. As a contribution to civilization, the revival of a dead language is, with due respect, more important than all the writings of Saul Bellow.

2. The cooperative agricultural settlements and at their core the kibbutz. The kibbutz has no peer. The kibbutz has no guru for whom a poster of sorts can be drawn to be hung up on a wall. No one ever received the Nobel Prize for having invented the conception and rudiments of the kibbutz. This is a collective creation of Jews that has deep Jewish roots. It is a revolutionary interpretation of the values of ancient civilization. There were extraneous influences, socialist promptings, but the kibbutz is not an imitation of an existing model of a way of life.

3. The Israel Defense Forces, which from its incipient nucleus of Hashomer up to the Palmah was never an imitation of any existing war machine. It was a new collective creation of the Jewish genius, again with deep roots in ancient civilizations.

4. The city of Jerusalem. Not necessarily the Old City, but indeed the new city. This is definitely a splended collective creation of the Jews of Israel. Nowhere throughout the *golah* is there anything comparable to the new city of Jerusalem.

I should in fact, also add that Israel is the haven for the survival of Jews. And this despite the physical dangers here. Seven hundred thousand Jews from Arab countries were brought to Israel, and today they number one and a half million, a symbol of pioneering and human creation. What would have happened to the 50,000 Jews from Yemen and the 100,000 Jews from Iraq if they had not come here? Can one ignore the messianic yearning of the tens of thousands of Moroccan Jews to come to Israel?

I do not want to wax idyllic about these four creations. All four are in danger of decline and degeneration. And therefore they are the reasons for our inner tension and turmoil, for our inner struggle to: maintain the resilience of our language and guard it from degenerative linguistic impurities; toil for the preservation of the soul and spirit of the cooperative agricultural settlements and prevent their decline; uphold the image of the Israel Defense Forces and avoid its taking on the pattern of a conventional war machine; making the new city of Jerusalem worthy of its illustrious Old City, of its holy name. It is a hard and constant struggle to preserve these four collective creations from the dangers of deterioration and decline—but this struggle is the essence of drama. It is not a museum.

### Critics, Audience, and Actors

If Chomsky and Steiner were to voice devastating criticism of these four creations, shrug their shoulders indifferently, and sneer ironically:

"Big deal. So what? You can't make the comparison with hasidism or with monotheism or with the Babylonian Talmud." I would say: "True, provided we agree to two modalities: that the theatrical critics living in the diaspora are brilliant professionals and criticize the performance of the Israeli actors, who are third-rate dilettantes; and that the critics nevertheless accept the fact that the theater is in Israel and that they are the audience in the diaspora (that the stage and setting are in Israel, and the stalls and balcony beyond the sea). What flows from all this is that we are the actors and they are the critics.

I feel it to be incumbent upon me to adduce a far-reaching argument against the assault by the diaspora.

All their magnificent individual creations, from Marx and Freud right up to Chomsky and Steiner themselves, all of them, have been breast-fed and nurtured by the treasure house that was Eastern Europe and that has been closed. Were it not for Eastern Europe there would not have been a Saul Bellow, a Bernard Malamud, a Bashevis Singer, or a Kafka. With the East European treasure house closed, the thriving individual creation of Jews in the diaspora is living on an overdraft on borrowed sustenance. And in years to come, not many years, ten or twenty, even diaspora Jewry's individual creation will wane, wither, and die unless it unites with us in Israel and obtains its nourishment from the thriving collective creation in Israel. Otherwise there will be no individual Jewish creators—there will be nothing Jewish in their creation. Let me set out the time-tested axiom: Any individual creation in whatever field—literature, music, or the exact sciences—is nurtured from the fertile soil of collective creation. Diaspora Jewry has its collective institutions. It has no collective creation, and shows no signs that it ever will.

It follows that in the context of Jewish culture, the affinity between Israel and the diaspora is just like the affinity that pertains between the stage and the hall. And only from those who agree with this premise will we accept the most severe criticism of what is being enacted on our Israeli stage—in culture, politics, way of life, army, rural settlement, language; in brief, everything.

Of course, we extend to them a standing invitation to come up onto the stage and participate in the play—even steal the show—and in fact help write the scenario while the drama is being acted.

I know that not all will or can come up onto the stage. I would propose that they learn Hebrew so that they may understand and follow the intensity of the drama without its being impaired by earphones. Try at least to move to the front rows, nearer to the footlights, to the very threshold of the stage, and get the feeling of the drama as it unfolds and of the message it conveys.

There is also a boastful argument vis-à-vis the Jews of the diaspora.

What can Steiner say to Mr. Levin, who has a corner drugstore in Brooklyn and who aspires to be like Steiner—an outstanding intellectual, the salt of the earth, one of the shapers of Western civilization.

But Mr. Levin just can't be Steiner. At most he can be a corner drugstore owner, or a building contractor, or a teacher of mathmatics, or a successful attorney, a merchant, an accountant or an industrialist. So what can one tell Mr. Levin? You are the chemical fertilizer spread over the fields of history so that from time to time the Jewish people (in the *golah*) may produce a genius!

Can one ask Mr. Levin to forgo the option of a free national life, knowing that to forgo a free national life means the growth of Jewish geniuses? This has a Nietzschean ring to it, a distant echo of worshipping the genius that was at the root of the German romantic movement. It implies that the teeming multitude is not important (it is only the chemical fertilizer on the fields of history), that the genes function in Darwinian manner to produce and bring forth the chosen few (the rest just don't count).

I am prepared to accept the argument that the national state is an anachronism. We would all be happy to live in a world that has a hundred civilizations and not a single state. What I am not prepared for is to be the universal pioneer. I have been playing this role for 2,000 years—and no one ever joined me. Here and there, there was faint applause. From my point of view the experience of being a civilization without a territory ended at Auschwitz.

Therefore, out of sheer Jewish prudence—call it neurotic prudence, if you like—I shall be number ten in my region and number twenty in the world to divest myself of all the markings and trappings of nationality. When all the others have divested themselves of their armies, of their national frontiers' barbed wire fences, of their national passports—then I, too, will be happy to follow suit and join the tea party. In this respect I am no longer the universal pioneer.

## Come Let Us Argue

I ask myself why the Israeli drama holds the neurotic attention of hundreds of millions of spellbound people. It is not because a world war may begin here. It also cannot be attributed solely to an anti-Semitic undercurrent. It is because the Zionist enterprise constitutes an onerous challenge that has been set before the cardinal schools of thought of our time.

The State of Israel stands opposed to Marxist dogma. It is equally a problem for those who believe in the historiosophy of Toynbee (on the biological cycle of civilization, their youth, maturity, old age, and death), according to which we Jews are fossils. We constitute the phenomenon that disproves this theory. The same applies to the down-to-earth pragmatist. The Zionist enterprise endangers the very fundamentals of pragmatic political philosophy. And so we have a multitude of countless millions all over the world who look at our stage, waiting for it to collapse.

The Israeli epic is the universal test of two questions: Can idealism shape the course of history? Is historical determinism absolute or does it also contain free will?

Every Jew who misses this experience and the drama of it, at least intellectually, has wasted the years of a lifetime. No material wealth will ever be able to procure such an experience for him. No Transcendental Meditation, no drugs, will ever give him the spiritual abundance that participation in the Zionist enterprise affords the person who understands its significance (and I do not say that everyone who lives in Israel does understand it).

For many years the diaspora was on the defensive and apologetic vis-à-vis Israel. But in recent years the diaspora has gone over to the offensive.

We shall not be able to remain on the defensive. If what I have said causes some slight tension and even antagonism, I can only express regret. It should not be so, although the very fact that there is a tension at all makes the Jews of the diaspora partners in the drama.

I do not want formulas of agreement with the diaspora so that the *golah* can live with Israel, and Israel with the *golah*.

I would rather have a fight (where there is no fight there is a museum). A fight such as we Israelis have among ourselves. I like Israeli pluralism, and I like Jewish pluralism. I want everybody to be on the stage taking part in the play, the drama.

I quote Einstein: "It is not enough for us to assume the role and serve as important people in the development of the culture of mankind. It behooves us to take upon ourselves assignments such as can only be fulfilled by a nation acting as a collective group of people. Only in this manner can the Jews acquire spirititual excellence."

And Einstein added: "Israel is not first and foremost a haven for the Jews of Eastern Europe, but rather the reawakening of the spirit of collectivity of the Jewish people as a whole."

As a Zionist, I know that my country belongs not only to the citizens who live in it, but to the entire Jewish people. My roots are not solely in the homeland but in the people. This discussion, therefore is a matter of life for me, for us all.

# PART VII

# We Are One: Israel and World Jewry

# 19

# Israel's Obligations to the Diaspora

## MOSHE SHARETT

The entire discussion of the relation of the State of Israel to the diaspora and vice versa is actually conducted within the limits of the geopolitical framework of the democratic regimes of the world. The discussion does not encompasss the problem of our relations, or lack of relations, with the Jews of the Soviet Union and with other Jewries in Eastern Europe—not because we have written them off completely and acquiesced in their loss to us, but because in our relations with them we find ourselves confronted with cruel facts that we have no control over and that make all discussion futile.

When does the discussion of a subject make sense? When the conclusions reached can influence events—wholly or in part; when those taking part in the discussion not only feel free to express their views but capable of adopting some line of action that can change conditions and bring about the desired results—in other words, when the course suggested by the discussion is both feasible and of practical value.

Such talks are worthwhile only within the scope of democracy, not because democracy automatically safeguards the preservation of the Jewish people, but merely because it makes its struggle for existence possible by enabling it to strive of its own free will for survival. What a democratic regime means, in effect, to the Jews in the diaspora is that if they seize the opportunities that it affords them and make the most of them, they stand to achieve something. This being so, the discussion of the subject makes sense, for its end result is pertinent to reality. But with regard to the Jews who dwell outside the free world—those who have been severed from Israel, torn away from the rest of the people and from one another—there is nothing to discuss. As far as these Jews are concerned, our only resorts left are those of presenting a claim, voicing a protest, offering prayer, expressing hope, perhaps launching a message of encouragement into space, and striving—wherever legitimately possible—to establish contact with them.

Democracy, however defective and inadequate, provides freedom for that priceless possession—the live connection between Israel and the diaspora—which is the subject of our discussion. Soviet totalitarianism, even when restrained, offers no such freedom. A society governed by the principle of freedom of association in different organizational frameworks (without such free association conflicting with anyone's loyalty to the state concerned) makes possible a harmonious threefold relationship between Israel and the foreign country, between Israel and the Jews of that country, and between those Jews and their government.

### The Problem of the Near Future

The problem, then, is this: Given the diaspora's continued existence, what must we do and what can we do, taking advantage of the opportunities provided by the democratic regime, to strengthen the ties between Israel and the diaspora so that Jews are induced to come and settle in Israel and the diaspora's existence is centered around Israel?

We use the term exile (golah) by force of habit (for this has been the compelling reality of generations), but now a controversy has arisen as to the historic significance of this concept. I do not side with those who see in the diaspora, as such, a positive value. At most, I am prepared to consider it as part of a historic destiny. There can be no absolute certainty that this worldwide scope of Jewish life will last forever. For we do not hold that history must necessarily repeat and perpetuate itself. Were this our view, we would have to bow to the edict of yet another destruction. Has there not been alternation of destruction and return in our history up to now? Yet we believe that we have returned to the land and retaken possession of it forever and ever, and we are determined to break the historic "routine." All our statesmanship and all our practical efforts should be directed to this end: that a third destruction shall never come to be. But if a "break in the continuity of history" is possible in this respect, then the exile, as a decree of fate hanging over the majority of our people, need not last for all eternity.

### Bringing Jews to Israel

The Jewish people throughout the world numbers slightly more than eleven and a half million today. Of this number, a little more than a million and a half live in Israel. That is, about ten million Jews now constitute the diaspora. Let us assume that it is our mission to bring all or most of them to Israel. How long would this take? Can it conceivably be accomplished within a few years? This would obviously be a task not for years, but for generations. Even those who cry out, "Wherefore the diaspora?" would have to accept this premise. The question then arises: What is to be done in the meantime? How will these multitudes of Jews live? Will they assimilate and dissolve, or will they retain their identity? And what can keep them from dissolving if not a strong, living bond with the State of Israel? And if so, will this bond endure or not, will it be strengthened or weakened, and what shall be its nature and substance? Will there operate within the diaspora gravitational pulls of a spiritual character toward Israel, trends of thought and education that might direct the hearts and minds of Jews to settlement in Israel? And short of migrating to Israel, will they develop and maintain enough national consciousness to live Jewish lives in the diaspora? And what shall we here do in the meantime to forge the link, to pour content into the vessel, to create a dwelling place for the spirit?

The question is not one of a short-term program of action designed to cover a span of a few years. It is a matter of working out a plan for at least a generation—that is, for that period of time in the life of human society that can serve as a subject of planning. For we must distinguish between vision, on the one hand, and policy and planning, on the other. Vision extends to the end of days and is not subject to limitations of time. Policy and planning, on the other hand, are concerned only with that fragment or installment of vision that can be realized in a given period—a period in which there is a practical possibility of envisaging what lies ahead and concerting action accordingly.

What, then, is the controversy about? None of us is a prophet and none can discern what is shrouded in the mists of the distant future. But insofar as we meet to discuss the problem and to take counsel together, the basic principle that confronts us is not what will ultimately happen, but what we are to do now and within the next twenty to thirty years. This being so, it behooves both sides, those who uphold the eternalness of the dispersion, as well as those who envisage the ingathering of the exiles in totality—and, perhaps, particularly the latter—to face the problem in all its urgency and gravity.

## Israel—Quintessence of Jewish Existence

In this matter, a decisive share of responsibility and initiative must be assumed by the State of Israel. The diaspora cannot be absolved from its obligations, but the brunt of the liability rests on the state. For the two parties are not really comparable. The diaspora is scattered, while the state is concentrated. Israel is the only concentrate of Jewish existence and consciousness in the world, the only crystallization of Jewish strength and Jewish creative ability. Moreover, the diaspora, whether consciously or unconsciously, is subordinated and shackled, while the State of Israel is emancipated and free. The complete liberation of Jewish consciousness, the concentration and free expression of Jewish responsibility, emerged and took on substance in this country even before the establishment of the state. While we were still called a *yishuv*, we were actually a Hebrew people dwelling in its own land. As our numbers increased and our national aspirations gathered momentum, we became the focal point of universal Jewish life. There was not a Jewish community in the world that reacted with such a storm of indignation and wrath to the European Holocaust as did our *yishuv*. Nor was there a Jewry in the world to which the opportunity was vouchsafed to join in the war against Hitler as we did, moved by the national will of our people alone. And, it goes without saying, no other group of Jews felt the same sense of responsibility and obligation to undertake efforts for the rescue of the surviving remnant. In all other lands, Jews are scattered and intermingled among the nations; their reactions are inhibited and cannot enjoy free play. Their opportunities for collective action are also considerably limited by the force of circumstances. This is not the case in Israel, nor was it the case even before independence. Jewish emotions could here vent themselves without let or hindrance, and waves of elemental Jewish feeling could surge up spontaneously, leading to mass action. This high privilege of freedom always imposes obligations.

But the State of Israel, as a center of Jewish life and the focus of Jewish honor and pride, is not in itself secure and impregnable. Its relationship with the Jews of the diaspora is not limited to an obligation toward them entailed by the higher measure of Jewish vigor and liberty with which Israel is blessed. For Israel, it is a vital question and a primary condition of self-preservation that the entire Jewish people should always be ready to come to its aid; that the sense of destiny that Israel and the Jewish people share should grow ever stronger; and that Israel should be able to draw upon the human and material resources and the political and spiritual strength of the Jewish people for its security and progress.

The first question is thus: "What must the State of Israel do?"

The education of the younger generation in Israel is an issue of foremost importance. We are all aware that loyalty to the Jewish people—not only to the State of Israel—is one of the fundamental principles upon which elementary education provided by the state rests.

We must not rely on the automatic perpetuity of Jewish feeling and expect that it will always assert itself in all its depth and intensity and stand us in good stead in any hour of trial. Nor should we lose sight of the changes in this respect that are taking place in our own lives. Not all of them are a blessing as far as the prospects for our distant future are concerned. Just as we do not hold that moral values of a broad human character are automatically safeguarded in our lives, but try to incorporate them as central themes into the programs of our systematic and consciously directed educational activity, so—and perhaps with yet greater emphasis—must we act in regard to Jewish values.

The future of our young is beset by a peculiar danger, which might perhaps be called "the illusion of normalcy." Our youth deludes itself into thinking that its life is perfectly normal, that the condition of its state is normal, that it belongs to a people whose status and destiny are normal. This is not so surprising. All our efforts are directed to the shaping, for the generation born or bred in Israel, of a social and family environment that will enable it to breathe the pure and healthy air of freedom, walk erect, and rid itself of the psychological strains and stresses so characteristic of Jewish life elsewhere.

But unless a corrective is applied to this healthy and well-balanced soul-structure—a corrective that would illuminate the realities of Israel's existence and the problems of the Jewish people's destiny in the world—and, particularly, unless the normal mentality of the young Israeli Jew is permeated with a sense of attachment to, and love for, the Jewish people as a whole, then there will be danger of an unconscious repudiation likely to jeopardize the younger generation's own national existence. This danger is two-dimensional: in space and in time. There is, first, the danger of the contraction of the national horizon in space—its confinement to the State of Israel. And second, there is the danger of a national consciousness that focuses on short-term issues growing shallow in time. In other words, the peril lies in the narrowing of our field of vision to Israel alone, in disregard of the diaspora with its worldwide perimeter. Within Israel, the peril lies in our focusing attention on her present alone—a present of vigor and glory—forgetting the dark memories of the past and ignoring the complex problems of the future.

### The Bible Is Not Enough

We deal here with a serious and complex issue that lends itself to distortions despite the loftiest and noblest of intentions.

There are values in spiritual life that in all their sublimity cannot in fairness be charged with the burden of solving all the problems of the contemporary generation. Such is our Bible. With all its transcendent and eternal value, its literary wealth and spiritual profoundity, the supreme power of its inspiration, the exalted beauty of its language and the magnificent expression that it gives to the spirit of our people, and, above all, the majestic sweep of its humanism and the boldness of its prophetic vision, it alone cannot serve as a bulwark against all the perils of moral decline and spiritual deterioration that must ever be the subjects of our anxiety. By placing an undue emphasis on the paramount and absolute authority of the Bible, by making it an infallible moral oracle, the alpha and omega, so to speak, of the code of Hebrew-Israel nationalism, and this at a time when the negation of other values is not in the least necessary in order to exalt the Bible—by so doing we run the risk of aggravating the dangers confronting us and of turning the Bible itself into an instrument of transgression.

But even as I warn my fellow Jews, so do I proudly tell non-Jews that our children in Israel are the only ones in the whole world who are privileged to read the Bible both in the language and in the country of its creation. And I do believe that the place of the Bible in education in Israel is firmly established.

Yet the outstanding place occupied by the Bible in our school curriculum offers in itself no guarantee of the translation of the vision of the prophets into a body of rules effectively governing our daily lives. But this is a very general problem—one affecting the highest reaches of human ethics. Every emphasis of the problem is of importance, but you do not solve a problem merely by emphasizing it.

### What the Bible Does Not Teach

There are two cardinal values in our lives and in the education of our children that cannot possibly be derived from the study of the Bible.

The first is the singular emotion that we call "love of Jewish people." It does not mean love of the Jewish people as a collective unit or historic concept, but love of physical Jews, as they are. It does not mean love of them as they appear in the biblical world—as heroes, prophets, judges, kings, and warriors, figures hewn of rock, standing on the pinnacles of history and enunciating eternal truths—but as perfectly ordinary Jews of everyday life. Such love encompasses Jews of all the exiles—utterly prosaic, real *golus* types, strange in their appearance; types such as the immigrants who step off the boat on arriving in Israel, completely bewildered, wondering what will happen to them next; or the tourists who travel around the country with a seemingly idle curiosity, sometimes offering criticisms that sound absurd or waxing enthusiastic for no valid reason; or the other Jews who are scattered all over the world, popping up in all sorts of unexpected corners, most of them never thinking of settling in Israel, yet always turning their eyes to Zion and rejoicing in its regained freedom. The problem is how to bring up the children of independent Israel, Israel free and proud and often drunk with victory, so that they love these Jews; how to get them to realize that they may occassionally get angry with these Jews and tell them off, but must first of all love them as dear brothers and be devoted to them with heart and soul. They cannot develop this kind of feeling simply by studying the Bible.

The other matter that cannot be learned from the Bible—and yet it is as vital to us as the air we breathe—is a vivid memory and a keen awareness of our distress in exile, the suffering and the torment, the affronts and the humiliation, the insecurity and the helplessness, the tears and the blood. And if the child himself has not imbibed these sensations with his mother's milk—if he himself has not been party to those tribulations and hardships, if he has no recollection of wandering in the Polish forests, of his parents being led away from him in the ghetto or the camp, of all the horrors that he saw or was told of at the time—then a way must be found of imparting something of these experiences to him, just as a conscious effort is made by positive education to bring home to him ideas and values even when they are not part of his personal experience.

Memories of the past should comprise not only the torments of exile but the birth pains of independence. Let me cite an example. A most remarkable book is now circulating in Israel—a collection of poems by Natan Alterman, entitled *Ir Hayona*. The subject of its first chapter is the epic of illegal aliyah—its heroism and martyrology, its psychological crises and inner conflicts, its setbacks and final triumphs, and the whole poignant substance of that historic drama. I believe this chapter to be of tremendous educative value. For days are coming—have indeed already come—when this soul-shaking saga will begin to grow dim in the memory of the generation. This is not merely a question of the loss of an emotional experience; it involves definite dangers to our future.

This state of ours will not in the long run prosper or dwell secure without additional, large-scale immigration. Yet it will not prove capable of absorbing such immigration if the flame of love for their fellow Jews departs from the hearts of its sons—love for the Jews who arrive from afar, those who are yet scattered and may someday come.

Nor will Israel fully develop or the aliyah be productively absorbed without a steady flux of funds from the free Jews of the world for a long time to come. That generous outpouring is sustained by deep emotion, and draws its inspiration from the consciousness that Israel is a common spiritual possession of all Jews. This life-giving process will not be assured unless it finds an emotional response on Israel's part based on the realization by every Jew in Israel of the historic partnership between him and his fellow Jews abroad.

Above all, the security of this state will ever depend on the bravery of its sons, bravery that can hardly be maintained at its highest peak if the epic of the struggle for independence and of all the adversities that preceded it and ushered it in fades from the memory of the coming generations. Those who are called upon in the future to risk their lives in defense of their state must know what disaster their people escaped by obtaining sovereign statehood and to what ruination it would be doomed if ever it lost its statehood.

Love of Jewish people and memories of the past are pivotal for this nation's future. Our educational work must deeply ingrain them both, with the sublime and eternal values of the Bible, in the minds of our young.

As for past memories, no arbitrary limit to them can be set. History is not a stage that you can illuminate one corner of at will, leaving the rest plunged in darkness. Our educational program must be based on the integral unity of Jewish history, for only in this unity lies the truth. The pupil need not memorize all the details of the architecture and furnishings of the great mansion, but he must be brought up to feel at home in all its rooms, both those flooded with light and those steeped in gloom.

### Educating the Diaspora

The other main subject is education in the diaspora. It is quite possible to give a powerful impetus to Hebrew education in all the Jewish communities of the free world. There is no escape from assigning to Hebrew education a place of honor in the Zionist budget of each country, either by local appropriations or by grants from the center. If the aggregate budget is inadequate because the diaspora does not contribute enough, then additional efforts are indicated to obtain its increase; but at the same time, larger sums must be allocated to education, both centrally and along the perimeter. The United States presents a more complicated problem, through there, too, much more can be done. But in countries such as England, France, Western Europe as a whole, Canada, Mexico, Brazil, Argentina, Chile Uruguay, South Africa, and Australia great results can be achieved by establishing Jewish day schools, if only the necessary means are forthcoming. And these can only be provided from a central source, namely the United Campaign. Such schools will not only produce better Jews and spread the knowledge of Hebrew, but will also serve as a breeding ground for a *halutz* aliyah in the future.

Even from the practical standpoint of the Zionist budget itself, devoted as it is for the most part to financing the absorption of immigrants, a long-term investment of this nature appears to be imperative. If we are serious in talking about the settlement in Israel of an additional two million or three million, then we must make sure that a generation of contributors will arise to shoulder the burden of providing for the absorption of these millions when their time comes—whether it be in ten or fifteen or twenty years from now, or more. The generation that brought with it to overseas countries and to Western Europe the heritage of Judaism from the townships of East European countries will by then have died out. The new generation may turn its back on the past if it is not educated. And here, too, the problem is not limited to the school but extends over the entire field of cultural life.

### Israeli Emissaries' Mission

The third subject is the mission that must be fulfilled by emissaries from Israel. Israel's diplomatic missions abroad have done a great deal to strengthen the connection with the Jewish communities and deepen their sense of attachment to this country. But they have not been given the proper tools with which to develop this activity to the fullest possible extent. It is vital that a system be established of sending out emissaries who would serve as instruments of the connection for its own sake— carry the message of Israel, spread information about its achievements and problems, study the needs of the various Jewish communities for Israel's orientation, and, by their very appearance, demonstrate the importance attached by Israel to her bonds with the diaspora.

If there are Jews in the diaspora claiming the title of "Zionist," we should first of all welcome the fact and then, on the strength of this title, make calls on them. We are all familiar with the position of American Jewry. We have here a community several million strong who have been shaped by compelling circumstances of historic evolution. Any attempt to make demands on it by virtue of an analogy with other Jewries, past or present, is doomed to futility. Only those claims on it that are based upon a realistic evaluation of its unique condition, capacity, and needs can be effective. With all the tremendous merits and precious qualities of Russian Jewry, it is a patent fact that the waves of aliyah from it were touched off by pogroms, a first and a second and a third time. Not that the pogroms in themselves necessarily drove Jews to seek salvation precisely in this country—on the contrary, during the periods of the first aliyah and the second aliyah the large masses of the fugitives turned to the United States and not to Palestine. Those who came to Palestine were single individuals and small groups, but they carried in their hearts the yearning of the whole people for complete redemption in its own land, and this was their outstanding historic merit. Yet were it not for the pogroms, even they would not have pulled themselves up by the roots to come and settle here. Such has not been the fate of our fellow Jews in America, and none of us wishes that it ever should be. At the same time, American Jewry as it is has played an enormous part in Israel's rebirth.

Thus, if there is in the United States a Zionism that does not conform to the pattern of prerevolutionary Russia, it behooves us to remember that even the Russian Zionist organization was never an association of immigrants. From this viewpoint, American Zionism does not differ from its Russian counterpart of years past. It is true that attachment and devotion to Israel have overflowed the confines of the various Zionist organizations and spread over the entire field of American Jewry, leaving practically no distinction between Zionists and the so-called non-Zionists. Nevertheless, if there are established organizations claiming the designation of "Zionist" and assigning a central place in their programs of action to Zionist education and the affairs of Israel, their right so to be called should not be disputed, however much dissatisfaction may be felt with the themes and the intensity of their work—all the more so since that right does not depend on outside approval.

American Jewry, with all its size and importance, by no means exhausts the picture. In the United States, the mainsprings of practical activity in support of the work of reconstruction in Israel are to be found outside the official Zionist frameworks. This is not the position in England, Canada, South Africa, Australia and New Zealand, France, and Latin American countries, as well as in some smaller Jewish communities. It is the Zionist organization that plays there the part of the central lever for the United Israel Campaigns, Zionist information and publicity, political action in support of Israel, Hebrew education, Jewish cultural activity in general, *halutz* training, and such immigration to Israel as is taking place. By dissolving the Zionist organization you bring about the collapse of all this widely ramified activity. Communal organizations would by no means fill the void thus created. They, too, are imbued with a spirit of devotion to Israel and ready to lend support and assistance to any action undertaken on its behalf; yet no benefit would accrue to the cause of Israel from dismantling the body of which this cause is the sole concern and transferring the cause to a respectable place on the agenda of a communal institution encumbered with such current items as the erection and maintenance of synagogues, the emoluments of the rabbi and the cantor, local Jewish charities, aid to Jewish refugees, and such like. I have seen Zionist organizations whose spiritual life was not particularly rich. Had there been more frequent visits and more purposefully directed guidance from Israel, there can be no doubt that their work would have gained in interest and intensity. But even so, these were circles of men and women whose spiritual focus was the cause of

Israel and nothing else. They served as a framework for Jewish concentration on that theme. To them this meant Zionism. What useful purpose is served by snubbing this title or disqualifying them from bearing it? Will such an attitude produce one additional immigrant to Israel?

There would appear to be still less logical merit in denying this title to ourselves merely because other Zionists do not fulfill their duty to our satisfaction. The escape of resting content with the definition that we are just Jews, is, to say the least, inconsistent. Are there no Jews who in our view are not up to the mark as Jews, and are we therefore to cease considering ourselves even Jews? But why should we be defining ourselves at all by reference to the construction placed upon the definition in question by others? And why should we be causing confusion and distress to our dear brothers in far-off lands by proclaiming from a high and exalted rostrum in Jerusalem that we are no longer Zionists? Is not the work we are trying to do here, and for which we are enlisting their dedicated assistance, Zionism pure and undiluted, creative and triumphant in their eyes, and, they know full well, also in ours? This sudden attempt to divest Israel of the halo of Zionism must appear to them as tantamount to taking the soul out of a body.

We all pray for aliyah from the Western countries, but we are not going to call it forth by rebuke and reprimand, still less by the imposition of moral "sanctions" on ourselves in an oblique attempt to mete them out to others. We have already learned to give up the futile attempt to stimulate aliyah by intimidating our fellow Jews with the danger of pogroms. We have yet to learn to abandon the equally ineffectual method of mobilizing immigrants by castigation. What will induce Jews from the countries of the West to migrate to Israel will be the fear of assimilation and submergence, on the one hand, and the spiritual attraction of life in Zion liberated and reconstructed, on the other. It is for us to generate and enhance this drawing force by raising the moral and spiritual quality of the new society that we are creating and by bringing home to our people in the lands of culture and freedom the high promise held out for them by the fullness of Jewish life in a country where the Jewish genius has such far-reaching opportunity for constructive fulfillment. The task calls for much labor, much understanding, much patience, and, above all, much love. It is in this spirit that the State of Israel must approach, and assign a high priority to, the problem of its obligations toward the Jew of the dispersion.

20

# Israel and American Jews

## YITZHAK RABIN

Having been born and reared in Israel, for many years my concept of the disapora was essentially of East European Jewry. It was based on what I learned in elementary school and high school, and from Hebrew literature. (I am afraid they still teach that way in Israeli schools.) But in my five years of working and living in the United States, I came to understand the diaspora.

In discussing the relations of Israel and American Jewry it is well to start with the numerical discrepancy. We are talking about the relations between approximately three million Jews who live in Israel and about six million Jews who live in the United States. And if we take into account the fact that there are also some three million Jews in the Soviet Union, then this triangle—Israel, American Jewry, Soviet Jewry—constitutes the great bulk of the Jewish people. These three Jewish axes reflect the independent Jewish people (the State of Israel), the distressed diaspora (the USSR), and the affluent diaspora (the United States).

The importance of the Jews of the United States in Jewish life is tremendous, in both Jewish thought and Jewish education. Academic Jewish research in the United States may be said to be holding its own vis à vis its counterpart in Israel. The economic and political power of the Jews in the United States enables them to exert considerable influence on American policy with respect to Israel and the Jews. American Jewry also plays the leading role in determining norms and standards of Jewish behavior in all the democratic countries. The nature of the relationship between Israel and American Jewry is therefore of unique importance.

### The Historical Perspective

The relations of Israel with world Jewry should be viewed in the perspective of Jewish history. I shall mention a few principles that serve me as a point of departure for an examination of Israel's relations with world Jewry, and particularly with American Jewry. Historically, the main goal of Judaism and the Jews has been to preserve the Jewishness of Judaism both as a value and as a physical entity. This has been the aim of the Jewish struggle throughout history.

Through nineteen centuries of exile there were three main forms of the struggle for the preservation of Judaism. The first was profound faith, the extraordinary attachment to religion, to tradition, and to Jewish values. Without this attachment it is difficult to understand the phenomenon, which has no parallel in human history, of a people that has succeeded in preserving its uniqueness, its character, its religion, and its values—despite persecution, cruel treatment, forced conversion, and inquisitions. The Jews achieved this by regarding themselves as a chosen people bearing values not just for themselves, but values that could guide mankind. On the other hand, the belief that "Thou hast chosen us" gave rise to the concept of the Jewish nation being "a people that dwells alone" (Num. 12:9).

A second expression of the urge for Jewish preservation was the yearning and the unrelenting faith that one day they would return and establish an independent Jewish state in their ancient homeland. How could a people—an ethnic group, a religion—preserve this yearning and eventually attain its desire? This, too, is one of the most astounding phenomena in history.

The third expression was the Jewish dispersion. This was a curse, but it was also a saving factor in ensuring the survival of the Jewish people. There was no situation in which, by destroying some part of the Jewish people in a particular place, it was possible to liquidate the entire Jewish people. In addition, the Jews were imbued with the sense of mutual responsibility toward their persecuted brothers. The principle that "all Israel are responsible for one another" was fostered as a value, and it became one of the unique assets of the Jewish people, enabling it to survive. When misfortune struck a Jewish community in one place, the other sections of the Jewish people did more than any other people in history ever did for its compatriots or coreligionists.

Toward the end of the nineteenth and in the beginning of the twentieth centuries, Jewish history (the religious would say "divine providence") created a new reality: the Zionist movement, which led to the establishment of the State of Israel. This enabled the Jews to achieve three things: First, it allowed them to build a Jewish national and spiritual center that serves as an antidote to the decline in religion as the main element in the preservation of Judaism; second, it is a physical solution for the rescue of Jews; and third, it is a central core around which Judaism can continue to foster Jewish values, in the context of a progressive twentieth century society.

### Today's Issues: Preservation of Values

In exploring the contemporary challenges to the Jew and to Judaism, it is necessary to emphasize both the struggle for the upbuilding of the Jewish state and the building of the Jewish people. I am stressing both—the state and the people. There can be no state without a people and no people without a state. We must, therefore, face both challenges, the upbuilding of the Jewish state and the preservation of the Jewishness of world Jewry. And we will be unable to achieve both aims unless the connection between them is fully understood. So long as we do not understand the connection between the realization of the Zionist vision and the preservation of the bond with world Jewry, with the aim of preserving its Jewishness, we shall endanger both.

I realize that in the foreseeable future the Jewish people will continue to be divided into Jews who live in the State of Israel and Jews who live in the diaspora. People who reject this approach and who interpret the goal of contemporary Zionism as the liquidation of the Jewish diaspora are on very slippery ground. Without a realistic appraisal of the contemporary Jewish situation it will be difficult for us to explore the methods of shaping the relations between the two portions of the Jewish nation.

American Jewry must be understood against the background of the United States and the American people. The American people is a nation of immigrants in which the process of the absorption of the immigrants is not yet complete. The fact that it is a nation of immigrants is a decisive element in its national consciousness. Moreover, in the past years the ethnic minorities and national groups have been striving to stress their origins and the attachment to their own past.

Anti-Semitism exists everywhere, but the American people lacks that tendency toward national uniformity that characterizes other nations. This enables the American Jew to be an American and a Jew at one and the same time, without becoming entangled in contradiction. Since American society was founded by refugees from religious persecution, there is in the United States an unprecedented degree of freedom, and Jews enjoy considerable opportunities to achieve social, economic, and political success. This determines a pattern of life for the Jewish community in the United States that differs from that of any other Jewish group in the world.

Once, I flew to the United States—it was before I was ambassador—in the company of an American officer, an air force colonel. He was sitting next to me, and we began to talk. He discovered that I was an army man from Israel. Toward the end of the flight he was in a good mood, and then he said to me: "You know, I was born in the South. I was not brought up to like Jews, for all sorts of reasons, but above all because they did not fit into my conception of 'American.' True, we are a land of immigrants, there's nothing wrong about being an American and retaining one's attachment to a country of origin. The trouble with the Jews was that they did not fit into my world of ideas as to the nature of Americans. The English did not regard him as an Englishman, the Russians did not regard him as a Russian, the Poles did not regard him as a Pole, and the Germans did not regard him as a German. But now you have solved the problem. You have established the State of Israel. Now I consider the American Jew an American in every respect, since he too now has a country of origin. He is now a normal American as far as I am concerned."

More than anything else perhaps, this story indicates what Israel contributes to the American Jew, and why Israel is important to him, not only in terms of Jewish sentiment, but also with respect to his status as an American. The existence of Israel constitutes a reference point that determines his position in American society.

American Jewry has its own particular textures and structures, and these must be understood when considering its relations with Israel. What is American Jewry? How does it act as a Jewry? To this day, American Jewry has been preserved, for the most part, by living a Jewish life around the synagogue. This is not a synagogue in the Israeli sense of the term. The American synagogue is really a community. In the United States there is no Jewish life on a countrywide scale. Jewish life is concentrated around the nucleus of the synagogue community and its social activities.

Of course, there are also national movements, political movements, and Zionist movements, but their influence is surprisingly small. The basis of Jewish life always was and has remained the synagogue, in the broader American sense of the term.

The national Jewish organizations are not as strong as the community organizations. And the State of Israel acted wisely when it founded the Israel Bond Drive—which, with the United Jewish Appeal, is one of the greatest instruments of practical activity on behalf of Israel—not as a national organization but on the community system. In fact, the two strongest Jewish national organizations in the United States today (and not only as financial instruments) are the UJA and the Bond Drive.

## Shaping Relations, Strengthening Bonds

How should we shape the relations between Israel and American Jewry? What do we want? And what can be expected? Most American Jews are not interested in aliyah. In the history of Zionism we never had large-scale aliyah from affluent counries. The large waves of immigration were always spurred by Jewish distress. At the same time, it seems to me that there is a danger of a drifting apart between Israel and American Jewry, which may be caused by an estrangement from Judaism. Our common denominator is the Jewish roots of American Jewry. And if I were asked what should be the focus of our main effort today, I would say: to develop ways and means to strengthen the Jewishness of the Jews of the United States. Aliyah will be a consequence of success in this area.

I see this as a vital matter for the continued existence of Israel. There is really no need for me to argue that Israel cannot be satisfied with the number of Jews now living within its borders. The Jewish ideal is the existence of a Jewish state that assumes a Jewish mission vis à vis the Jewish communities in the affluent countries, and a Jewish rescue mission to the Jews living in distress.

There are, to be sure, Jews such as George Steiner who see an essential conflict between the existence of Judaism and the existence of the State of Israel. Steiner is not the only one. There are extremist groups— *Neturei Karta* on the one hand and communists and other leftists on the other—who oppose Israel. But the great majority of the American Jewish community (as far as I am able to judge) regard themselves as closely linked with Israel.

This stems primarily from two positive factors. The majority of the Jewish public in the United States still wishes to preserve Judaism, as it understands it, and to preserve Jewish values, and identity, as well as the attachment to the Jewish heritage and religion. Second, there is the unassailable connection that the non-Jew sees between Jews and Israel. The status of the American Jew, even if he tries to repudiate his Judaism, has become inextricably linked with the State of Israel, in the eyes of his surrounding society. The Six Day War restored Jewishness to Jews who had sought to flee from it, because they came to realize that they could not escape from it. In the consciousness of most of the American people, the Jews diminished or grew commensurately with the status of the State of Israel. And that is why Steiner and his colleagues in their academic ivory towers are utterly wrong. The American Jewish community is firmly convinced today that it is inextricably connected with the State of Israel.

It therefore seems to me that the time has come for us to consider not only what Jews in the diaspora can do for Israel, but what the task of Israel is vis à vis the Jewish communities. There are a number of things that I today consider to be essential:

1. Give full recognition to the realistic aspects of the situation, be aware of our mutual dependence, and realize that unless we foster these ties we shall undermine the basis of our existence.

2. Develop the potential inherent in the concept of the centrality of Israel, which is today firmly rooted in the Jewish consciousness of most American Jews, as a complement to religion in the preservation of Judaism.
3. Seek ways to strengthen the Jewish educational network. If we do not deal urgently with Jewish education—and I refer to the preuniversity levels—we shall undermine the attachment of Jews to Judaism and the ties between Jewry and all Jewish affairs, including Israel.
4. Find methods in addition to aliyah to engage American Jewry in Israel and in Jewish activities that are economic, social, spiritual, and political.
5. Attempt to introduce political content into American Jewish activity on behalf of Israeli and Jewish issues. This is one of the important factors that maintain the Jewishness of the Jews of the United States. Whan a Jew or the Jewish community in the United States declares, for instance, "As Americans and as Jews we are fighting for Israel, as Americans and as Jews we are fighting for the Jackson Amendment, for that has to do with the persecution of Jews as Jews," this infuses a content without which Jewish life in the United States cannot survive. For without Jewish activism it is impossible to maintain Jewish frameworks, and without Jewish frameworks it is impossible to maintain Judaism. I have not been able to understand the difference between certain persons in the United States who are defined as Zionists and others who are not described as such. I have not discovered any difference between such groups with respect to their attachment to Israel, their readiness to work for Israel, their willingness to do everything on behalf of any Israeli or Jewish matter.

It appears to me that in the American situation there is a basis for a broad network of relationships, which is essential for both sides. Israel is vital for the American Jew, for his status as an American and a Jew. For Israel, the preservation of American Jewry is vital. Even the issue of Soviet Jewry would probably not have developed as it did were it not for the tremendous importance of American Jewry. It seems to me that it is possible—and essential—to reexamine the network of relations between Israel and American Jewry. I see this as a matter of the utmost importance, second only, perhaps, to the internal problems of Israeli society. In any case, it comes before many other subjects that are exercising the Israeli public.

I share the belief that the State of Israel is bound to preserve its Jewish character. What we mean by Jewish character is, of course, debatable. To engage today in an antireligious conflict seems misguided. It should not be forgotten that there is a difference between the importance of religion in the United States or anywhere else in the world in the preservation of the Jewishness of Jews, and the political bargaining that we are familiar with in Israel.

The religious leaders, too, must take into account that they ought to adapt substantial parts of the Jewish legal system that are, in my opinion, only incidentally concerned with religious values. The problem for the Jewish religion is that for nineteen centuries it was not a state religion. In ancient times there was a struggle between priest and king, a Sanhedrin, and a working system that enabled the adaptation of religion to reality. This adaptive ability has largely been lost, at least since the establishment of the State of Israel. If religious Jews evince the need to adapt religion to changing realities, I believe that a broad basis for understanding can be found. If not, then in five or fifteen years the clash will come—a clash from which no one will emerge victorious. The Jewish people will be the loser.

## Conclusion

The framework of Jewish life in the diaspora will continue to be religious. I have not discovered any concrete suggestion as to how to preserve the Jewishness of the Jews by other means, and that is why I do not propose that we now destroy frameworks, patterns of life, or values, before we find substitutes that will better answer the overall Jewish problem. It is not just that we have no choice. I think that every framework that serves to maintain Jews ought to be strengthened and developed.

I believe that we have been granted the opportunity to concentrate on two issues: building a society (in addition to building a state) in Israel, and strengthening the ties between Israel and world Jewry. If we do not accomplish this, we will miss a historic opportunity, which is of vital and lasting importance for the future of the Jewish nation.

# 21

# The Vital Partnership

## NAHUM GOLDMANN

My fundamental position is that Israel has been, is now, and will have to be, the joint venture, the greatest common enterprise of the Jewish people outside of it, which I shall deliberately call diaspora. The relation between the *yishuv* living here and the part of the people not living in Israel has to be one of the fullest cooperation and partnership, not one of builders who are citizens of Israel and helpers who are friends of Israel. On this partnership, on this greatest common effort of our and future Jewish generations, will depend, in my judgment, both the destiny of Israel and the destiny of the Jewish people as a whole. Failure to bring about this partnership, which is a unique task in history, will be disastrous to Israel and catastrophic to the Jewish people, and will, in the final analysis, distort and destroy the uniqueness of our history and the specific character of the great epic—at once heroic and tragic—of our destiny. A creative solution to this problem, however, will normalize our life and enable Israel and the Jewish people to realize the innermost sense of our past and of our destiny.

In trying to prove this thesis, I shall discuss it first from the point of view of the present situation and then in the context of Jewish history as a whole.

From the point of view of the actual situation of Israel, it is obvious that the state will need the closest cooperation of the diaspora for many decades to come. Economically, it is impossible for the *yishuv* to build a highly civilized country in a tiny territory, for the time being poor in natural resources, while at the same time discharging its main historical task, one of its basic raisons d'etre: namely, the absorption of all the Jews who must come to Israel or want to settle here. The best Israel could hope to achieve by its own efforts would be to provide for normal functions and to take care of the elementary needs of its population and its security; but all the rest, raising the standard of living, taking in tens of thousands of immigrants, can naturally be accomplished only with the full cooperation of the diaspora, be it in the form of donations, of investments, or of manpower. If I wanted to formulate the task of the Jewish people in this respect, and the division of functions between the *yishuv* and the diaspora, I would say that the *yishuv* has to provide the bread, the diaspora the butter, and although the people could live on bread alone in times of emergency and austerity, it would be more than a calamity if Israel were condemned to live in such conditions forever.

More important even than economic aid is the full cooperation of the Jewish people on the political scene. I am not referring only to the present situation, in which the Arab world refuses to accept and recognize Israel and to normalize its relations with her. That in such a situation the fullest political cooperation of the Jewish communities of the world is necessary in order to overcome the daily dangers of Israel's isolation in the Middle East is too obvious to be elaborated. It has often been said that of all the allies Israel may have from time to time, the only reliable political ally is the Jewish people.

## When Peace Comes

Even when the present situation changes, peace is established, and Isreal becomes integrated into the family of nations of the Middle East, the absolute necessity of Israel's being backed by the Jewish people in the world will continue. I do not want to discuss foreign policy problems here, even from a historic point of view; my opinion is that there cannot be security and stability for Israel unless it is fully integrated into the Middle East, this great area that is much in the ascendancy and will turn,—in my judgment, sooner than we think—into one of the important centers of the world, both for economic and geopolitical reasons. Yet if Israel is to be at peace in the Middle East it will need the continued backing of the Jews in the world, in order to escape coercion to become, against its will and its destiny, a satellite of the Arab world.

I have no doubt that in the long run the Middle East will consolidate itself and form some larger bloc or some political and economic unit. Israel will have to be part of this. Left alone, Israel would be in danger of being dominated by the Arab world, because of the sheer weight of its numbers and area. However, backed by the Jewish people of the world, Israel will no longer be merely a tiny part of the Middle East, but will represent forces and influences spread all over the world that will make it, as was once said, a small great country.

From the point of view of Israel, full partnership with the Jews of the world is no less important in the cultural sense. I will not discuss here at length the cultural and spiritual problems of Israel's development, nor am I competent to do so. But as one who watches the development of Israel's new civilization with one foot in it and one foot outside of it, being close enough to know what is going on and distant enough to approach it more objectively, I feel that there are inherent dangers in Israel's cultural development that should be understood and remedied from the beginning.

There is the danger of Israel's forgetting the past of our people, becoming alien to the values of the past at least in its *galut* part, losing sight of the great problems of the world and the issues of Jewish life outside of Israel. Briefly, there is the danger of becoming provincial and narrow-minded. I do not want to create the impression that all this has already taken place, but dangers should be recognized before they translate themselves into facts that are difficult to change.

Partnership with the Jewish people could be of decisive importance to Israel's creativeness. It would bring into Israel's art and literature, into its social and philosophical thinking, the ideas and tendencies that influence Jewish communities that are part of other civilizations. It could make the civilization of this small country a world civilization in the best sense of the word, contributing to world developments. To be sure, partnership between Israel and the diaspora in this field is even more complicated and difficult than in others. It will take a long time till methods of mutual influence can be worked out, but the more difficult this is, the greater the effort must be.

In sum, without the fullest cooperation of the diaspora in the upbuilding of Israel economically, politically, and culturally, Israel will not be able to achieve even a part of what the dreamers and thinkers of Zionism have always envisaged. Zionism has never wanted just a state that would be of a few million Jews on the Mediterranean. It wanted a state that would be commensurate with the uniqueness and greatness of Jewish history; a state that would play quite a different role from that which a normal state of a few million people ordinarily plays.

This ambition can only be fulfilled if Israel is the joint creative effort of the whole Jewish people. In the absence of this, Israel may be able to exist—but it would be something quite different from what we hoped and prayed for.

### The Diaspora's Need for Partnership

Now let us discuss this problem from the point of view of the situation prevailing in the diaspora. I have tried to prove that lack of partnership would be calamitous for Israel; for the diaspora it would certainly be catastrophic. Israel may possibly be able to exist in the future without the diaspora; the diaspora, in my opinion, will not be able to exist, in the long run, without Israel. There are two main reasons for this: first, the destruction of the largest part of European Jewry, and second, the disappearance of brutal anti-Semitism as a threat to the physical existence of the Jewish people.

What the Nazi Holocaust, resulting in the destruction of six million European Jews, means to our existence as a people is often discussed and needs no elaboration. We have, I feel, not yet begun to realize the extent of the catastrophe. It is not only that we lost a third of our people, something without parallel, at least in modern history, but we lost that part of the people which was the main center of our cultural and spiritual existence, the chief heirs and bearers of the inheritance of thousands of years of our civilization.

This Central and Eastern European Jewry, the greatest part of which was annihilated, created nearly all the values and ideas on which our generation lives: Zionism and Jewish socialism, Hebraism and Yiddishism, Orthodoxy in its modern form and Reform Judaism, hasidism, and Mitnagdism. To expect that any other part of the diaspora—which means primarily American Jewry—will take the place of Eastern European Jewry is naive and illusory. America has not and cannot have the objective conditions of life that enabled Eastern European Jewry to live its autochthonous life. The Jewish shtetl cannot be reconstructed in the United States and, as I once said, a yeshiva in New York with a movie to its right and a drugstore to its left cannot replace the atmosphere and cultural climate of Tels or Volozin.

The kind of creative center that Eastern European Jewry constituted for centuries cannot be recreated in the diaspora. Even if the surviving remnant of Eastern Jewry were free to live its own life, it could not realistically be expected to continue the tradition that existed before Hitler and the communist regimes.

The second grave peril to Jewish continuity in the diaspora is the absence of brutal anti-Semitism. Both economically and politically, Jews now live better in most parts of the world than they lived during any period of our diaspora history. In most parts of the world neither their physical existence nor their civic equality is endangered. There is, naturally, discrimination here and there, but compared with what anti-Semitism was in tsarist Russia, not to speak of the Nazi period, this is insignificant. The result, to use Toynbee's formula, is that there is no challenge to the Jewish diaspora. It no longer has to fight against brutal, visible, and immediate enemies. All the techniques and the genius of resistance that we developed in centuries of persecution have no object any more.

Because of the character of our history, we have learned how to be great in times of danger but not in times of comfort. The moment there is no challenge, our mechanism of resistance and self-preservation collapses. Being a people blessed or cursed by too much optimism and wishful thinking, we tend to believe that everything is perfect and do not worry about visible, anonymous dangers that threaten us more today than brutal anti-Semitism ever threatened us.

What is going on in large sectors of Jewish life, both in the free world and in the Communist world, is a process of indefinable assimilation. Assimilation is not an ideology as it was in German Jewry; it is not an ideal or a program that you can fight. It goes on, but those who are its victims do not even know that it is going on. A German Jew who wanted to assimilate could be influenced not to do it, and many of the best German Zionists were so-called postassimilationists who switched from the ideal of assimilation to the ideal of Zionism. A young Jew in America or Argentina who assimilates does not even know that he is being assimilated, and therefore cannot be reached by education and propaganda. You do not see him, you cannot get hold of him, and therefore it is so difficult to combat this anonymous, silent, and unconscious form of assimilation.

### Israel and Assimilation

For all these reasons, I have grave doubts about the possibility of Jewish continuity in the diaspora unless Israel steps in, plays the central role that used to be played by Eastern European Jewry, and by its existence counteracts the silent process of assimilation. A young Jew in the diaspora who lives in comfort and well-being, who is rarely reminded by anti-Semitism that he is a Jew, and who if reminded reacts by trying to make his Jewish identity disappear, who finds no great slogans or ideas, visible and dramatic, to remind him of his Jewishness and to give meaning to his being a Jew—such a young man can find in Israel what he lacks. Once he has learned Hebrew and is able to be in touch with Israel's civilization, a new source of real values will be opened, not just books and sermons, resolutions and programs. Ideas are essential to the life of a people, but only if they are implemented in life and reality.

A philosopher can live on purely abstract ideas, a people cannot. What made Eastern European Jewry so powerful and creative was not its theoretical adherence to Jewish religion and Jewish culture but the fact that it implemented the Talmud and the Shulchan Aruch in its daily life. Such realization of ideas can be provided for diaspora Jewry only by Israel. Here one does not have to learn what Judaism is; here one sees it. It is manifest in a hundred and one daily aspects of normal, real life, and participation in this reality alone can serve as the primary source of Jewish continuity in the diaspora.

## The New Jewish Pride

One more aspect should be mentioned. Like individuals, peoples and collective groups cannot exist normally and creatively without a certain measure of self-belief, pride, and self-respect. An individual, and even more a group, has to have some raison d'etre. It cannot live only because it lives and vegetates. It must have meaning in its life.

The Jew in the centuries of the ghetto had this in very large measure. It may seem paradoxical to say so, when one considers the misery, persecution, and abject humiliation that characterized Jewish life in the ghetto, but those who think that the Jew in the ghetto accepted humiliation have not begun to understand the psychology of ghetto Jewry. Had it given in psychologically, the Jewish people would have collapsed and disintegrated morally long ago. What saved the Jewish people, and what, in a certain sense, may have been the most paradoxical and creative act of Jewish psychological self-defense, was not only the refusal to accept psychologically the status of inferiority, but also the tendency to overcompensate by a feeling of superiority, which was sometimes even highly exaggerated.

The notion of the chosen people, which in the Bible was a great metaphysical and ethical concept, had a day-to-day psychological significant for the Jew in the ghetto. He reacted to persecution, attack, and humiliation as to the barking of a dog; one protects oneself against a mad dog or runs away, but one does not feel humiliated because one is threatened by a dog. The ghetto Jew regarded his persecutors as barbarians, idolators; they could make him suffer physically, but never morally. He was persecuted in this world but conscious of being the chosen servant of his God in the future world, a slave of barbarians but a protégé of God Almighty. Persecution simply increased his pride. It had meaning for him; it was part of his historic destiny. He lacked neither self-respect nor a consciousness of the meaning of his existence.

All this the emancipated or assimilated Jew has lost. Rabbis may preach the theory of the chosen people and believe in it, but the Jewish member of an American golf club does not believe in it. If anything, he regards his non-Jewish colleagues as superior, and his desire is to be equal to them. If the Jewish people in the diaspora does not find a new source of pride and self-respect, it will collapse psychologically.

And this is precisely where Israel comes in. From the first hour of its emergence, the greatest benefit the Jewish people have had from Israel is its new pride in a people fighting, daring, creating. This is a more normal pride than the paradoxical overcompensation of the ghetto Jew. Have we forgotten how virtually every Jew in the world walked around in the days of the War of Liberation when the papers reported Jewish victories? Every Jew suddenly grew in stature, certainly in his own estimation. Without this source of a new collective pride, diaspora Jewry is psychologically doomed.

This, together with the spiritual and cultural values that diaspora Jewry will take from Israel, explains my conviction that without Israel there is no real future for the Jewish people in the diaspora. But this relationship to Israel, which can enable Israel to flourish, and diaspora Jewry to exist, is dependent upon a genuine partnership, upon shared responsibility and a common destiny. Friendliness, help, donations, and deep interest constitute philanthropy, which is indeed a very noble attitude; but no philanthropic attitude, no philanthropic enterprise, has ever molded the destinies of a people. Philanthropy can help suffering friends, it can alleviate misery, and it can give a certain satisfaction to the philanthropist and and a little material help to the object of his philanthropy; but it cannot be regarded as a historical force, as a tendency that shapes the development of a people. To make the Jews outside Israel mere friends of Israel relegates them to a philanthropic position. This denies them the psychological and cultural benefits Israel could shower on them.

The diaspora can naturally be only a junior partner, but a partner it must be; otherwise there is no historical basis for its permanent tie with Israel, and even its philanthropical help will not last forever. The diaspora, to formulate it differently, must not react to Israel in terms of "you" and "we," which is the normal relationship even in the closest friendship. Its feeling about Israel must be summed up by "we"; it must feel that somehow it has a share in this great enterprise, which represents the main meaning of Jewish existence today.

### The Uniqueness of the Partnership Concept

Now let me discuss the difficulties in implementing the concept of moral and psychological partnership between a people's center and the majority of that people living outside the center. It would be naive and quixotic not to see the difficulties. What I have in mind is something unique. There are, except for the Jewish past, no parallels or examples in history. Many people have had and continue to have diasporas. For a few generations they remain attached to their country of origin, but then they disintegrate and dissolve into the life of their new fatherlands.

Furthermore, Germany, Ireland, Italy, even Great Britain could live very well without any help from their respective diasporas. Therefore, they provide us with no pattern and no indication of how to solve any problem.

I can easily understand the contention that what I envisage is against the laws of history. History generally dictates that diasporas disintegrate and disappear. In the many discussions I had with my friend Jacob Klatzkin, the most consistent, brilliant, and logical exponent of the theory that there cannot be a permanent diaspora once a Jewish homeland is created, he used to argue in this way. My reply to him throughout the years was that the so-called laws of history—if they exist at all, which is very doubtful—do not always apply to Jewish history and Jewish destiny. I once said to him that had there been a Jacob Klatzkin alive at the time of the destruction of the Temple by the Romans, he would have proved with the same logical consistency and brilliance that there was no chance whatsoever for the dispersed Jewish people to survive without its center. But logic is one thing, and the genius of the people another.

The most extraordinary achievement of our people was its creation, in seemingly impossible diaspora conditions, of forms of life that, against all historical laws and all "normal" patterns, secured our national survival. This is not the place to discuss the methods by which it was done, methods that utilized all the values of Jewish culture, religion and philosophy, ethics and literature, social life and communal organization. These methods succeeded. Why, then, should it be impossible to expect that, with the center now recreated, the genius of our people will find new methods and forms of life to secure its attachment to Israel and its continuity?

I know that with the collapse of the ghetto and the diminished influence of Jewish religion this is much more difficult, but, on the other hand, we have the tremendous advantage today of having the State of Israel, which for 2,000 years the Jews in the diaspora did not possess. It would be ludicrous for me to try to indicate the forms of life and methods that our national genius, if it is strong and creative enough, will now have to develop. No blueprints can elaborate them. It will take decades and perhaps generations to crystallize them. They will be various and manifold, different for different Jewish communities, and different in the various spheres of diaspora-Israel partnership.

What our generation can do is, first of all, see the problem. Nothing would be more catastrophic then to rely on our people's instinct. If we do that, the tragic prophecy of Jacob Klatzkin will be realized sooner than we think. The partnership we hope for has to be accomplished in the teeth of the normal tendencies of life. It is an uphill effort. It will require tremendous wisdom, statesmanship in the best sense of the word, ingenuity, and resourcefulness to work out something for which there is no real pattern, at least in the history of other peoples, and for which we can get only some briefing and guidance from our own past.

## Both Diaspora and Israel Must Change

What this first generation after the emergence of the state must do is to create the necessary psychological conditions that will enable us and future generations to solve the problem. Both Israel and the diaspora must be convinced—this is the sine qua non—that without a true partnership there is a dim future for Israel, and no future at all for the Jewish people outside Israel. To concretize this consciousness, both the diaspora and Israel have to readjust their attitudes.

Diaspora Jewry must have the courage to proclaim and defend its relationship or partnership and responsibility vis-à-vis Israel. It has to overcome the conscious or subconscious fear of so-called double loyalty. It has to be convined that it is fully justified in tying up its destiny with Israel's. It has to have the courage to reject the idea that Jewish communities owe loyalty only to the states in which they live.

This is not specifically a Jewish question, although no people has such a vital interest in it as we do. The claim of states that their citizens owe them exclusive loyalty is the most immoral notion in human history. It is the result of a trend in nineteenth-century philosophy that culminated in what I consider the insanity of Hegel's philosophy, making the state the climax of human history and the sacrosanct, supreme value in human development. From Hegel to Hitler there is a straight line of logical development, just as from Hegel to the Communist form of Marxism, which makes the same claim of exclusive loyalty to the Communist state. There is no more dangerous cul-de-sac in political philosophy than this glorification of the state. Every human being possesses many loyalties, and the more manifold the loyalties, the richer the personality. A modern human being owes loyalty to his state, to his family, to his friends, to his class, to his church, to his religion, to great social movements, etc. Naturally, there may be conflicts, but there is no reason to assume that in such cases the state can claim the supreme loyalty. There are certainly more sacred loyalties, such as religious loyalties.

For our period, which has paid with two world wars and with the lives of dozens of millions for this barbaric, immoral, and perverse deification of the state, be it in the form of fascism, Nazism, or communism, it is imperative to do away once and for all with the absurdity of modern Hegelianism. Fortunately, the notion of the sovereign state, which is the basis of this deification, is beginning to come to an end. Today no state is really sovereign any more. Each is dependent on many others, and, if not our generation, then certainly the next will see units larger than sovereign states, with their prestige, their petty vested interests, their antiquated forms of diplomatic relationships. In Europe and in Asia, in Africa and in South America, larger blocs are in formation, economically and politically.

This should make it easier for the Jewish people in the world to reject the notion that something reprehensible is involved in partnership between them and Israel. There is certainly the same dignity in the demand of Jews to be allowed to develop forms of life that will secure their people's survival as there is in their natural loyalty to the states of which they are citizens.

There are no fundamental conflicts between the two loyalties, and in case a conflict develops here and there, everyone has the right to choose and determine his position. Pride in having a share in Israel's destiny, rather than fear, is the one indispensable psychological and spiritual condition for the development of true partnership with Israel in diaspora Jewry.

As for Israel, a similar although not exactly identical attitude is necessary. Israel, too, has to avoid overglorification of the state. I have been a political Zionist from my youth, and I fought for the unpopular slogan of partition with the main argument that statehood is so important as to warrant giving up part of the territory of Israel. Nobody has to tell me what the State of Israel means for our life and our future. But the State of Israel, just like other states, is no aim, but an instrument.

As long as peoples live in the form of organized national states, which is certainly not an external form, as history proves, the Jewish people, to secure its survival, needs a state and has the same right to do as do other peoples. But the aim is the *people,* not the state. Whatever Israel does and becomes, it has to be conscious of being the servant of the people, of the whole people, those who live within the boundaries and those who are outside of them.

The State of Israel is the climax of Jewish history in its development till now. It is certainly not a substitute for our history, nor the beginning of a new history, of a new Jewish people. The people living in Israel must feel that they are the heirs and the successors of thousands of years of the Jewish past, of those parts of our history that took place in Israel and those that took place outside of it. A people cannot select and choose those parts of its history that it likes and discard those it may dislike, just as a balanced, normal human being has to absorb into his mental and psychological structure all of his experiences, and cannot pick out those experiences that are pleasant and gratifying. Many try to do so. It is the type of process that usually ends with neuroses and frustration, and can be cured only by bringing back into the consciousness of the neurotic those parts that he tries to eliminate or forget.

The same process applies more strongly to peoples. Jews in Israel cannot start a new history of an Israelite people: That would be meaningless and ridiculous. It would, at best, lead to the creation of another little Levantine people without dignity and record, without the pride and the glory of a great past. Morever, Jews in Israel cannot leap over centuries of the diaspora and try to continue only those chapters that ended in ancient Palestine, forgetting and eliminating centuries of heroic suffering in the diaspora. This, too, would end in frustration and collective neurosis. What Nietzsche once called *amor fati* (the affirmation and love of the whole destiny, its heroic parts and its tragic ones, its glorious chapters and its humiliating chapters) applies to peoples even more than to individuals, and applies to a people in our revolutionary position, after the creation of the state, even more than to other peoples living in normal continuity.

Only if both the diaspora and Israel understand that they depend on one another as two parts of the same people, as two bearers of the same responsibility, as two fulfillers of the same destiny, will this partnership, this vision of one people rebuilding its center and securing its survival everywhere, become a reality.

## In the Light of Jewish History

Put into the context of our history, the problem is not new. It has recurred several times in different forms, but as substantially the same problem. *Galut* is not a one-time phenomenon in our history. It did not start with the destruction of the Second Temple. Our history started with *galut*, with the exile in Egypt. The migration of the Jewish people from Egypt to Palestine was not, if I may make this observation, one of the normal migrations with which the history of so many peoples begins. The migrations of the Hellenes and the Romans, of the Germans and the Slavs, were never originally directed toward one country; the tribes began to be on the move, then, after a conquest somewhere, they settled down. In our history, Eretz Isrel was the immediate goal when Moses led the Jews out of Egypt. Theirs was not a migration that would stop in the most fertile lands or where the easiest conditions for settlement could be obtained. It was directed on the basis of a religious concept to the one country promised to Abraham, to Eretz Israel. After centuries of statehood come the second *galut*, the Babylonian, and again statehood and again *galut*, which lasted till the emergence of the new State of Israel. Can this be an accident, this repetition, this unique phenomenon of the polarity of our history developing between these two terms and realities of statehood and diaspora? If these are accidents, then no history of a people has meaning.

Can one do away with the part of our history and destiny called *galut* which has lasted longer even than the periods of statehood and has created some of the greatest and most eternal values of our civilization? I agree that what we created in Israel was more monumental than what we produced in the diaspora, but can one overlook our wide influence on world civilization, our tremendous contribution to the social, philosophical, political, and artistic development of humanity through our *galut* creativeness? I know that the Bible and Isaiah are unique, but Philo and Maimonides, Spinoza and Bergson, Einstein and Mahler, Marx and Lasalle—can they be eliminated from the balance of our creative contribution to humanity?

If there is meaning in history at all—and why continue it if there is no meaning—then there is meaning in this unique phenomenon of our destiny, for which there is no parallel in the history of other peoples. I am convinced that there is a deep sense in this phenomenon. It is more than a certain globalization in our genius, an unwillingess to be limited forever to one country, our deep urge to cover the world and take it in— it is deeper even than all this. The explanation for the *galut* phenomenon in our history seems to me to be rooted in our supreme characteristic, in our will to live in order to realize the ideas of our civilization in the reality of life.

Other peoples had ideas that were holier to them than the will to survive—glory and honor, the lust for power. Once they could not realize these ideas, they gave in and disintegrated. For us the supreme aim was to live, because Judaism, if I may try to define it in one phrase, means realizing ideas in this real world. I remember, to quote an unforgettable experience, a discussion I had as a young student with a great German historian, not too great a friend of the Jews. He argued with me that the fact that after the collapse of the Jewish state—or even the feeling of its coming collaspe—the Jewish people ran away into the diaspora, as he put it, in order to save their lives as a people is a proof of the proletarian and mean character of our people. An aristocratic people is proud of itself, remains loyal to its land when its state collapses, and collapses with it, he argued.

With regard to the facts, this German historian was right. There is no doubt that if the Jews had stuck to Palestine when their state collapsed and when the whole Middle East entered into a period of decay, there would have been no Jewish people today, just as the other peoples of the Middle East of that period did not maintain their national identity. What was wrong in the position of the German historian was his lack of understanding of the motives of people.

We did not run away, to use his expression, out of cowardice. If the individual Jew had wanted to save his life, he could have become a Roman, or a Christian, or a Moslem, and solved his individual problem very easily. We "ran away" because we felt the sacred duty to maintain ourselves as an instrument for the realization of the ideas that make the raison d'etre of our history. This is what this German scholar could not understand. His idea of *Ritterlichkeit* and *Treue* made him blind to the attitude that gives out *galut* history its great dignity and historical uniqueness. The Jew in the ghetto was not as spectacular and fascinating and dramatic a hero as the Israeli boy on the battlefield, but I doubt if his life, as a whole, very often did not require and display as much heroism as does courage in a war. In dignity and silence he suffered misery, persecution, and humiliation day in, day out, without any accompanying glory, without any drama, although he could have escaped it all very easily by one act of baptism and assimilation. He did it to maintain the identity of his people till that better time when the Messiah would come, and the people would again have the opportunity of creating its own reality and implementing its eternal ideals within this country.

That is why our people never put its destiny on the one card of the state. It always maintained reserve positions. It felt that it could not risk its survival, and had to do everything to remain alive.

The time has come, fortunately, when the last *galut* has come to an end. Once there is the national center and our own state, our position is, in principle, normalized. Naturally, a much larger percentage of the people will have to live in Israel than does so today. A center cannot continue forever with only one-sixth of the people living in it. But once there is the state where every Jew can go and live a full life, the tragedy of the diaspora has ended.

Yet with all gratitude to our destiny, which allowed us to bring this about and to create the new national center of our existence, we should not wipe out the part of our fate that is called *galut*. In it, however paradoxical this may sound, the unique character of our history expresses itself. Hundreds of peoples have had their states, but no people has had a history like ours, with its mixture of statehood and diaspora, with its tendencies of territorial concentration and worldwide decentralization, with this unique rhythm, this unique greatness, this unique tragedy, and this unique heroism. Have we not the right and duty to take all this into consciousness and be resolved to build a future commensurate with, and worthy of, this past?